NAMES AND HISTORY

Names and History

People, Places and Things

George Redmonds

Hambledon and London

London and New York

Hambledon and London

102 Gloucester Avenue
London, NW1 8HX

175 Fifth Avenue
New York, NY 10010
USA

First Published 2004

ISBN 1 85285 426 X

A description of this book is available from the
British Library and from the Library of Congress.

Typeset by Carnegie Publishing, Lancaster,
and printed in Great Britain by Cambridge University Press.

Distributed in the United States and Canada
exclusively by Palgrave Macmillan,
A division of St Martin's Press.

Contents

Illustrations

Text Illustrations

Illustration Acknowledgements

The author and publisher are grateful to the Huddersfield Examiner for
plates 5, 6, 7, and 10; and to the National Portrait Gallery for plate 1.

Introduction

First, it is important to stress that a concern with language when writing history is much more than just a formal philological exercise. Words express ideas, emotions, attitudes, beliefs and aspirations; as well as describing material objects. If a material object falls into disuse, so in time does the word which describes it, so that eventually both are lost. A spoken word, therefore, may itself be an historical fact, just as valid a fragment of evidence as, say a shard from a Roman pot or a word in a printed document.

Peter Frank, *Yorkshire Fisherfolk* (2002).

Names are words; special words that we use to identify a person, an animal, a place or a thing, and they all have a meaning. In many cases that meaning will lie concealed in the name's history, but in others it will still be transparent. These special words surround us almost from birth, for we automatically inherit a surname, are soon given a first name, and names of different kinds help to make up the address that we are taught as soon as we can repeat what we are told. I was called George by my parents partly because my father wished to remember his brother George, who had died in the Great War, and he taught me at an early age that it had once been a Greek word for 'farmer', a sort of compound of elements that meant 'earth' and 'worker'. I was hooked.

I lived near Bradford and wanted to know if this name also had a meaning but had to wait for the answer until we went into the town to do some shopping. I remember walking along a street and being told that under my feet Bradford Beck ran through a culvert, on its way to the River Aire three miles away. Bridge Street marked the crossing, on or close to the site of the original 'broad ford'. Here was a name that needed to be explained and yet as soon as I had the explanation it made immediate sense. In the address I had learnt as a child West View seemed obvious because the terrace faced west but Westgate Hill made only partial sense since it was clearly to the east of Bradford. Only much later would I find it on a map of Christopher Saxton's as Wiscard Hill and realise that we must be careful not to take names at their face value.

I was given no explanation of my unusual surname, although other family names were dealt with quickly. The names of grandparents included Ackroyd and Rushworth. Although my father had no ready etymology for these he was at least able to take me to the places locally from which they derived – the farm called Akroyd near Heptonstall and the hamlet of Rishworth near Sowerby Bridge – pronounced 'Rusherth' by dialect speakers. Nicknames proved equally fascinating, for my grandfather Redmonds was known as 'Old Plym', having arrived in Yorkshire from Plymouth as a young man. I would later discover that his grandfather was from Dublin. My grandfather Rushworth was the village barber in Northowram and my mother, as a child, had been called 'latherpot', a name she hated. It had been her Saturday job to lather the quarrymen who came to her father for their weekly shave. I was soon persuaded that words of this kind were an essential part of my family and local history.

The study of names has many branches, but these overlap at key points and have direct connections with numerous less obviously related subjects. The best-known fields of study are those which deal with place-names, surnames and first names, but each of these has several significant sub-divisions. Place-names, for example, has been tradition-ally concerned with the names laid down during the early waves of invasion, up to and including the Norman Conquest, and scholars have used this material to throw light on the ancient landscape and on a wide range of related topics such as clearance, settlement and husbandry. This aspect of the subject requires special skills in one or more ancient languages, Celtic, Old English and Old Norse, for example, and the non-specialist cannot therefore hope to make a significant contribution where matters of etymology are concerned.

That is not to say that he can make no contribution at all, for a thorough knowledge of archaeology or botany, allied to an intimate knowledge of the local landscape, might well qualify a person to com-ment on suggested etymologies, and even more on their interpretation.

There is a grey area where the evidence for major place-names is concerned, even for specialists: the earliest spellings, and these are the ones on which the etymology must be based, are likely to have been recorded several hundred years after the name was coined. They are seldom found in contexts that make the meaning clear, unless they are specifically topographic in origin. The temptation for the scholars who specialise in this field may be to over-analyse the material. Oliver Rackham, in particular, has accused the experts of 'clutching at straws and reading into place-names more than they can say', and it is difficult to rebut that criticism.

Of course the majority of our place-names were coined in the post-Conquest period, that is to say in the last nine hundred years or so, as Old English gave way to Middle and Modern English. This opens up the subject of place-names to many more researchers. It is a vast field: few people realise how intensively the English landscape is named, although any series of parish or township maps will reveal how many lexical items the local historian might be concerned with. Some years ago I entered the names from a survey of 1838 onto a blank map of Honley township. There were over one thousand named places at that time, including fields, woods, lanes, hamlets and wells, and these are just one part of the township's name history. This number has increased as I have accumulated information about earlier names that did not survive and others that have been coined since 1838.

Honley is not unusual in this respect: each township is certain to have hundreds of names that can be used to throw light on its history, and many of these will have developed in later centuries, either in contexts where the meaning is apparent or where contemporary references make speculation less of a lottery. It is names of this kind that will be looked at in the present book, and a variety of sources and techniques will be used to demonstrate exactly what each element means and how this relates to its etymology. If we remember that each of the words used by our ancestors in the naming process might be applied to different landscapes, at different periods, we shall understand how easy it was for the 'meaning' to differ from one locality to another. The approach is one that requires a thorough knowledge of a region's landscape, customs and dialect, and this should be allied to abundant and precise evidence. There will be advice on the ways in which this information should be located and marshalled, and the techniques will hopefully be implicit in the text.

There are also chapters on less well-known areas of place-name study. These include field names, the names of houses, streets and inns, and what I have chosen to call 'unofficial names', that is those names that are used locally by people but seldom appear on a map or in official sources. Each of these categories has attracted some interest in the past and, in particular, there has been excellent research carried out into the names of fields and public houses. The emphasis in this case, however, will be on the use that can be made by local historians of groups of such names, or of single names that are repeated over a wide area. It is less the etymology that counts in such cases than the social and economic implications of the names within their local communities.

The study of christian or first names was until recently the almost exclusive preserve of the etymologist, but ground-breaking research has been carried out recently into historic naming practices and the regional and chronological popularity of first names, and this is leading to a reappraisal of the subject. Those advances can now be illustrated through individual name histories and there are fascinating implications here for genealogists and historians. It is clear, for example, how fundamental it is to discover when and where a name was first used or revived, who the name-givers were and what their motives may have been. The popularity of names in the Tudor period, and as late as the early 1700s, was still hugely influenced by the godparents, and through christian names we are offered an insight into the very different communities of the past and the spiritual affinities of our ancestors. It is no exaggeration to say that some first names were once so distinctive that they were peculiar to one social group, even to one family.

The third of the major fields is 'surnames'. Until 1999 I would have hesitated to write anything more about this subject, for I have spent a lifetime working on it and felt that, with the publication of *Surnames and Genealogy: A New Approach* (1997), I had exhausted what I could usefully say. It was then that biologist Bryan Sykes published his findings on the Sykes Y chromosome and opened up exciting new avenues of research: suddenly surnames were in the news, and experiments along similar lines, both in this country and abroad, assumed renewed significance. My part in the BBC Radio 4 series of 2002 persuaded me that the most productive research in this field will now be carried out by surname specialists working in cooperation with genealogists, biologists and social scientists, and I welcome this opportunity to comment on those experiments and explore some of the future possibilities. Great advances have been made in surname studies over the last forty years, but these have been along more or less traditional lines; new mapping techniques and DNA now promise to revolutionise our approach to the subject.

There are also sections introducing less traditional 'name' topics, one or two of which have been neglected in the past. The chapter which deals with the names of different groups of animals, including oxen, stots, horses and hounds, will examine the different ways in which each of these throws new light on ancient institutions, some of them long forgotten, and on certain developments in language, whereas a section on plant names will look first of all at their close links with places and people, and then at the contribution they make to our understanding of former farming practices and health care. Ships' names help to identify some of the earliest craft on our rivers and sea coast. Their names are further evidence of the importance of Christian saints in the middle ages, although here there are interesting contrasts with first name practices. The names also remind us of the international trade links of English seamen, links reflected in the names of fabrics which tell their own fascinating story of textile manufacture throughout the ancient world.

When we talk of nicknames we usually mean those alternative names that were once such a common feature of the playground and work place. They expressed affection or ridicule, unerringly identified physical and moral characteristics, or commemorated a sublime moment of folly or achievement. Now they seem to be on the decline, replaced at best by a colourless diminutive: our sportsmen, for example, are content to press this into service whenever they mention their colleagues. In recent accounts of local football and cricket teams I have noted Booth, Gough and Vaughan become simply Boothie, Goughie and Vaughnie – names that lack the individuality and quirkiness of our ancestors' choices. For example, in a recent letter I was told that James Beaumont of Golcar was known to his contemporaries as 'Tinlocks'. It seems that he lived in a hillside cottage and nailed a piece of tin over the keyhole in an attempt to keep the draught out. It worked well enough, but then he found that he couldn't use his key. The nickname Lizzie Plushcock never allowed its bearer to forget the careless confession she made after her first intimate sexual encounter.[1] In fact nicknaming was not confined to personal names; it was so much part of our ancestors' lives that its influence is apparent also on place-names of every kind.

I have always felt that local studies should properly be the basis for any national survey in name research. There has been some appreciation of that more recently by surname and place-name scholars, who have understandably used the counties as the regions. This has worked reasonably well, although such boundaries are to some extent artificial. The fact is that many of the counties are made up of several distinct regions, and these can be linked to marked differences in their topography, history and language. It may be impractical to hope that we can complete such regional studies before discussing the picture nationally, but we can at least be aware that regional studies will require us to modify some earlier conclusions and we can encourage researchers to concentrate their efforts on one area. Local history should not be seen as inferior to national history but as its foundation.

An attempt will be made here to demonstrate the value of such local studies, within the national context. In one or two cases the subject matter may tentatively open up new topics, but mostly the aim will be to show how a more thorough use of the local material can cause us to look again at some of the received ideas in standard reference works. The key to that is the accumulation of as much relevant information as possible. With that in mind I shall begin with a short piece on sources.

Source Detective

In recent years a number of publications have concentrated on the vast range of sources that are available to researchers in local and family history. David Hey's *The Oxford Companion to Local and Family History* (1998) was conceived as a reference book for those who are working in these fields. It provides A to Z information on the terms researchers need, followed by a list of our national archive offices. A work more directly aimed at genealogists is *Ancestral Trails*, written by Mark Herber and published by Sutton in 1997, in association with the Society of Genealogists. All the sources are dealt with there, clearly and in depth, with excellent illustrative material and an eye to method. Of course neither of the books will be the last word on these subjects, which have developed such momentum of late that new material is constantly being brought to light: new discoveries open up fresh areas of research from one month to another. Anybody who doubts that need only consider the most recent advances made in surname studies linked with genetics. These are exciting times.

In an appendix to *Ancestral Trails* there is a very full list of the county record offices and other archives which house the sources used by genealogists: it is both inspiring and daunting. It is inspiring because it demonstrates the richness of our British records, and daunting because that very richness warns us of the endless searches that can lie ahead. Even so Mark Herber's list could be accused, in some cases, of over-simplifying the picture. For my own county of Yorkshire, frustratingly subdivided because of its sheer size, we are given details of Record Offices in North and West Yorkshire, Cleveland and Sheffield; the diocesan records are kept at the Borthwick Institute and that too is listed – five localities in all. A more careful look lists 'branches' of the West Yorkshire Office in Bradford, Halifax, Huddersfield and Leeds, another four places that the researcher needs to know about.

These are not 'branches' in the sense that word is sometimes used, that is convenient sub-offices which hold copies of the major records, but genuine district archives in possession of extensive major collections. It is in such places that we should be looking for bundles of title deeds, estate records, court rolls, maps and many other categories of material. I know these offices well and can testify to the wealth of deposits there. But Herber appears to have omitted some major Yorkshire archives, notably those for Humberside, which includes the former East Riding, and the treasure house in Leeds we know as Claremont, the former headquarters of the Yorkshire Archaeological Society, holding perhaps the finest collection of books and original records in the county. David Hey has information very similar to Mark Herber's but lists over twenty record offices that hold archive material for the county.

The lesson for those of us who undertake local and family history research is that we should not be satisfied with any one guide, no matter how excellent it might be in general terms, for there is always another perspective. Nor should we imagine that we have discovered the whereabouts of all the possible record locations that might concern us simply by identifying those in the county. In addition to the vast amount of relevant material in the major national repositories, there are quite often important collections in the record offices of other counties, especially the muniments of a major landowning family that had estates over a wide area. For my research in Yorkshire, for example, I would need to know that relevant material can be found in Nottingham, in the extensive Savile MSS, or in Lancashire in the Townley Papers: the Savile collection in particular relates to scores of townships in south and west Yorkshire. In fact, my experience has taught me that the search for relevant sources is virtually endless. Although that is daunting as I said earlier, it is also encouraging, for it means that just around the corner we may come across the vital reference that helps everything fall into place.

The Landlords

I shall now take up in more detail the point raised by the Savile MSS. Most of our ancestors, at least into the nineteenth century, were tenants of one landlord or another, and information about that relationship can be vital to us, not just when we are looking for specific genealogical evidence, but in the more general search for local history material and information about the historic landscape or the communities in which our ancestors lived. We can find out who the landlord was in a variety of sources, including land tax returns and the surveys and maps which relate to the Tithe Commutation Act of 1836. These records are particularly useful when studied in conjunction with the census returns of 1841 and 1851, for they tell us exactly where our ancestors lived, the names of their fields, and how they cultivated the land. Once we have identified the landlord we can then hope to find the surviving estate papers of the landowning family. These are likely to contain numerous useful items, from rentals and surveys to leases, court rolls, estate maps, correspondence and legal papers. And there is usually that unpredictable but potentially exciting section labelled 'Miscellaneous'.

On the other hand, such material may still be in a working estate office or in the hands of a family solicitor, in which case we at least know where to direct our enquiries. In my own area I have often located vital material in the Slaithwaite office of the Dartmouth estate and been given excellent advice about the Thornhills' documents by their land agent. For example, the so-called Dartmouth Terrier of 1805 is kept in the safe of the room in Slaithwaite where the rents are still collected and, on request, it can be consulted. It holds the names of the tenants, a full description of their properties with the name of each field, its acreage and cultivation, and details of the old and 'improved' rents. The estate consisted of properties in more than a dozen villages, and it is annotated and indexed. The entry for Joseph Haigh is typical: it names his property as Brockholes Colliery, which can be identified on the accompanying map, and notes that the rent in 1799 had been £20. That was raised to £120 in 1805, on the advice of the estate surveyors, and it gave Haigh 'the Privelege of digging Coal under His Lordship's Land by Grincars Wood, etc'. A memorandum follows:

> This Colliery has been worked for many years by the present Tenant's Family, but on a very small scale. The present Occupier is however an industrious, speculating man and has increased his workmen and consequently the sale of the Coal. The present Rent is fixed for working the Upper Seam of Coal which is Eighteen Inches thick and the Tenant is to get at least an acre a Year and if he gets more to be paid for at the Rate of £120 per acre.

An Institutional Landlord

Even less predictable are the locations of records belonging to land-owners which were not individuals or families but institutions. We can easily forget that manors and estates could be held by schools, hospitals or colleges, and it is often in the nature of such an estate for the properties to have been acquired piecemeal and to lie in widely-dispersed locations. An estate of the Knights Hospitaller will serve as an example, in this case a collection of properties that had originally belonged in part to the Templars. It consisted of lands right across west Yorkshire that had initially been granted to the orders by grateful or apprehensive landlords in the twelfth and thirteenth centuries. These lands had been administered from an office or 'preceptory' in Normanton; manorial courts had been held and leases drawn up and, over the centuries, the scattered community had developed its own customs and practices. Of course at the Dissolution such estates fell under the control of the king and were subsequently sold. We might expect therefore that the lands would have passed to private owners and that all memory of the former estate and its customs would have disappeared. That is not quite what happened, as a succession of lay landlords clung to the prestige and status inherent in the former estate. In 1634, for example, almost a century after the Dissolution, we find the following memorandum in the estate accounts of the Beaumonts of Whitley:

> I, Henry Beaumont of Whitley, have Constituted and appointed my tenant Christopher Syke my true and lawefull atturnay in this behalfe to doe suite and servies for me and in my place att the Courte of Seinte John's holden att Kirkeheaton for those my landes in Lepton now in the tenure of him the saied Chrisofer Sykes.[1]

This tells us not only that the court of the Knights Hospitaller was still meeting but that the customary obligations and services were still due. In fact the manorial court rolls of this estate have survived and, thanks to the above reference to Kirkheaton, I was able to discover them among the Dartmouth Papers in Sheepscar Library in Leeds, classified under Kirkheaton court rolls.[2] These rolls contain information about families and farms in a number of scattered parishes, many of them some miles from Kirkheaton. These include Barkisland, Elland, Emley, Kirkburton,

Rastrick, Thurstonland and Wakefield and, once we realise that the families were meeting on a regular basis, it makes sense of migrations and family connections that would otherwise remain a mystery. Just the list of tenants at the head of the earliest surviving roll (1615) provides us with a clue to that information.

Alerted to the fact that the estate had been kept together, and that these tenants still lived 'under the cross', I was able to find rentals and leases in various record offices, houses in the neighbourhood that still bore the cross, and the inn where the meetings had taken place.[3] Moreover, since the court was classed as a 'peculiar', there was testamentary material in the rolls, which explained why I had previously been unable to find certain wills. The rental guided me to other important tenants whose family papers contained Hospitaller material. These included those of the Green-Armytages and Ferrands. I later noted, in an article written by William Cudworth in 1879, that 'Mr William Ferrand of St Ives ... still exacts a small yearly tax as a Knight of Jerusalem, by which appellation he sometimes designates himself'. The Hospitallers' estate had in theory ceased to exist after the break with Rome but local conceit had kept many of its customs alive and the relationships forged in earlier centuries endured well into the nineteenth century.[4]

Collections Overseas

It has been my good fortune to travel widely and one of the unexpected pleasures that has come my way has been the discovery that there are important collections of archive material abroad that relate specifically to the areas in which I have a research interest. The first discovery of this kind that I had was in Kenya, where I lived for a time in the mid-1960s. A weekend visit to a friend of a friend in the Aberdares saw us introduced to a gentleman called Henry Horsfall Turner who was operating a processed cheese factory in that remote spot. It took only a couple of minutes to establish that he was a relation of the J. Horsfall Turner whose earlier research into Yorkshire archive material had fuelled my interest in local history, and not much longer to discover that many of his relative's papers and original documents were upstairs in the attic. Game-viewing that weekend had to take its place in a revised timetable as I pored over early Halifax wills and deeds.

In 1988 I was in Wellington, New Zealand, lecturing at the Turnbull Library at the invitation of Bruce Ralston. He had advised me that the library held a collection of early documents that had never been properly catalogued. He knew, however, that it was mostly from north-west England and wondered if I might find time to look through it. In the event I spent several days going through the documents in detail and discovered numerous fascinating items. Some old deeds related to the Knowles family of Arncliffe in Littondale, naming their farms and fields and giving explicit relationships, one of which linked them to a haberdasher in London. There was a will of Miles Smithson of Horton in Ribblesdale, with bequests to his son Lancelot and several under-age daughters. Other families documented were the Bucks, Silsons, Sedgwicks and Taylors, and there were items that had to do with the land tax, enclosures, sales, surveys and correspondence, not to mention several early charters for Sawley Abbey and a family tree going back to 1514 for the Johnsons of Whittington in Lancashire.[5]

A major deposit that tantalised me for years lies in the Kenneth Spencer Research Library in Lawrence, Kansas. It contains more than 700 items, mostly for the period from *c.* 1200 to *c.* 1700, and it represents a major part of the early muniments of the Kayes of Woodsome. There is already a substantial amount of archive material for this family in Yorkshire record offices and libraries and more is preserved in the estate office. Other significant items have found their way into Liverpool University Library and the Folgar Shakespeare Memorial Library in Washington, so this is a widely dispersed collection. The Kansas deeds, as I have called them, help to pull these separate strands together. They throw new light on the pedigree of the Kayes, many of their tenant families and several important properties. The index I was able to compile contains over 800 surnames and includes numerous references to the family of Sir Richard Saltonstall shortly before he emigrated to Watertown, Massachusetts, in 1630.[6] Elsewhere in this library are 10,000 British deeds.

Private Collections

We do not need reminding that vast amounts of archive material were formerly kept in the offices of solicitors who represented both private individuals and important gentry families, for much of that has now found its way into the county archives. The wealth of documentation in such cases can be overwhelming. I think, for example, of several hundred boxes relating to my home town of Huddersfield that were formerly in the safekeeping of Eaton, Smith and Downey. They are now available to researchers in the Wakefield Record Office. Unfortunately, not all solicitors have been so careful with their 'unwanted' collections; and some of these have been quietly disposed of or sold off. There are various places where we can see such material up for sale, much of it in shops that sell antiques or rare books and some in flea markets and stamp auctions, and the suspicion is that in many cases these collections have never been offered to a local repository. Sometimes of course they have been offered, but with strings attached, and an unrealistic asking price is one reason they have not been accepted. In the past dozen or so years I have been able to 'collect' hundreds of items in this way. Eventually all these will be deposited in the appropriate offices. I mention this to emphasise how slowly vital documents can find their way into the system and become generally available.

Few people realise also how much of our heritage is still legitimately in private hands or how worthwhile it might be to follow up clues as to the whereabouts of key items. Some years ago I was reading a parish history by Legh Tolson which quoted extensively from the manorial court rolls and even had a fine old photograph of one membrane dated 1483. These rolls were in none of the local record offices and enquiries further afield proved fruitless, but they had been in the private possession of the book's writer and it was inconceivable that he would have destroyed them. The problem was to find where he might have deposited them, for none of the learned societies to which he had belonged could help and the National Register of Archives had no record of them. I enlisted the help of Janet Burhouse, who was then the archivist at Huddersfield, and her location of Legh Tolson's will pointed us in the right direction: the rolls had gone to a great-nephew who was also difficult to trace initially but who was finally located by Janet in Hampshire, aged eighty. The rolls were on the top of his wardrobe, along with some important title deeds, and he readily agreed to put all these at the library's disposal.

Probably the most exciting experience I have had in this respect took

place four or five years ago. It developed out of a telephone call to the
county record office by a gentleman who had inherited his family papers.
He was willing to deposit them, he said, if something could be done
with them straight away. By that he meant that he wanted an archivist
to produce a catalogue of the material, which he felt might be important
but was difficult to read. Record offices may not be able to respond
directly to such requests, as they have an enormous backlog of manu-
scripts all equally deserving of their attention, so it was suggested that
he try contacting me. When we spoke on the phone it was clear that
he had experienced a good deal of frustration in his attempts to have
somebody deal immediately with the collection. For example, it had
been turned down by one major repository because the man's family
was 'only minor gentry'. As nobody had yet seen the documents, it was
not clear how significant the collection might be, but it is easy to
understand his disappointment at the cautious reactions to his offer.

Long stories have to be cut short in a brief account such as this but
I can confirm that the family papers concerned were a major 'find',
consisting of several thousand items of all types, the most valuable from
my point of view being several medieval court rolls, some very early
legal documents and scores of thirteenth- and fourteenth- century title
deeds. I used them subsequently to solve several outstanding genealogical
problems and a number of issues relating to the boundaries of territories
in the district. It is no exaggeration to say that if the papers had
disappeared those problems would never have been solved.

John Swift

Diaries and commonplace books were common enough in the nineteenth century and many have survived in private hands, passed down
through the family. Some of them have found their way into record
offices and others have been transcribed and published by their owners,
but many more must have been discarded over the years, especially
during the annual spring cleaning that was once a regular feature of
people's lives. Such items are inevitably of varying quality. It is rare to
come across one that presents us with a unique insight into the past,
but it can happen, and it did, some thirty or so years ago, when a most
unusual notebook fell into exactly the right hands.

Jennifer Stead is a local historian with a special interest in matters such as food, health, dialect, customs and all aspects of local life in the West Riding. It was in August 1970, while she was browsing round a second-hand furniture store in Huddersfield, that she spotted among the bric-à-brac a small leather-bound book with a strong brass clasp. It had presumably been in the drawer of an old item of furniture bought at a sale and she was able to purchase it for five shillings. Inside the front cover was the date 1850 and the name of the writer, a man called John Swift who ironically came from Newsome, the village where Jennifer also lived. Folded inside the book were five letters to the writer's daughter, a bill of sale relating to property at Newsome and an agreement to buy 100 shares in local railway property. Intriguingly John Swift described himself in the notebook as an 'aurist', or ear specialist, and inside the back cover was an old-fashioned engraving of a deaf-and-dumb alphabet.

It was easy enough for Jennifer to discover more information about the diarist's family in the census returns and the registers of local chapels and churches, and there were entries in the diary that guided her to revealing advertisements in the *Leeds Mercury and Times*. These were all headed 'Deafness Positively Cured' and they quoted from the letters of grateful patients. These helped her to build up a picture of John Swift's travels round the north of England as an itinerant 'aurist', journeys made possible by the new railway system. It was, however, a visit to an old lady in Newsome, on quite a different matter, that threw new light on John Swift, for she was able to produce copies of the parish magazine of 1882–86, in which there were biographical notes about local personalities, written by the vicar.

The notes revealed that the vicar had John Swift's diaries and account books in front of him as he wrote, and these showed that he had formerly been a successful cloth manufacturer, producing shawls and other fancy goods. Unfortunately, the business had collapsed in January 1838, and he had been forced to look for alternative employment in what was a difficult period. However, he had long had an interest in disease, and particularly in afflictions of the ear, and this prompted him to take the unusual step of setting himself up as a travelling doctor. Knowing now that there had been other diaries, as recently as the 1880s, Jennifer put a query in one edition of *The Dalesman,* a popular magazine, and she was amazed to receive an answer almost immediately, from a Mr Alton Swift Crosley.

Mr Crosley was eighty-six years old and had just returned to the north of England after forty years in the south. He was not a reader of the *The Dalesman* but his sister had bought this single copy for him on impulse, unaware of its contents. Amazingly John Swift was their great-grandfather and, although they knew nothing of his other diaries, they did have his commonplace book of 1816, a scrapbook and the family Bible, sources that would provide more details of John Swift's life. Moreover, they could remember childhood visits to their grandmother's house in Newsome in the 1890s, and she was the lady who had loaned the various books to the vicar. Above their fireplace were gilt-framed portraits of John Swift and one of his wives.

There were other minor finds after this and fellow local historians provided information about John Swift's involvement in early trade union activity and the school at Hall Bower, all contributing to the story and making it possible eventually for Jennifer Stead to publish a re-markable book on a remarkable man. A chance find, followed up with skill and determination, finally produced a fascinating insight into the life and background of a quack doctor, a man we might now describe as an alternative practitioner. As such it is a unique contribution to the history of unorthodox medicine.[7]

David Bower of Port Adelaide

Not unnaturally the emphasis so far has been on English sources in unusual locations, at home or overseas, but sometimes it is possible to discover material from overseas that throws new light on England. I have come across two such items in recent years, the first a journal that relates principally to Port Adelaide and the second a bundle of corre-spondence written from Melbourne and the gold fields.

The Port Adelaide item consisted of some ninety or so pages of handwriting in an exercise book that had come into the possession of Mr Percy Bramald of Huddersfield. I did not know the gentleman particularly well but, one evening, after he had been on a local history tour under my direction, he mentioned the book to me and asked if I would be interested to read it. Of course I said yes and, once it was in my hands, I found it hard to put down. It turned out to be a fascinating story of a young lad from Saddleworth called David Bower whose uncles, William and Eli, had left for America in the early 1800s. He had a spirit of adventure and, since he was determined to follow them, he left home as soon as he was twenty-one to try his luck in the wider world. The hand-written book was the story of his adventures, initially in Britain, as he tramped round the country trying to find work, and then in different parts of New Zealand and Australia, where he became a very successful colonist.

The scribbled cover note is enough to whet the reader's appetite. It says: 'A short account of the Life and Rambles of Mr David Bower MP for Port Adelaide South Australia and a native of Dobcross in Saddleworth England'. Among the highlights in this account of an apprentice machine maker who rose to be the Minister of Public Works in Adelaide are his building of a boat to sail from New Zealand to Australia in 1846, his journeys on horseback through Queensland's outback, his time in the gold diggings in Victoria, and the three world tours that he completed once he had made his way. He even returned to Saddleworth for a year, where he set up a successful textile business with a cousin that brought him £1000 profit. It is a remarkable story by any standards and it really came alive for me after I had contacted the Mortlock Library of South Australiana. With their help I was able to supplement the story with contemporary pictures and newspaper articles, finding details of the ship on which he sailed in the *Liverpool Advertiser* of 18 March 1841. Finally, in 1988, I felt that I was in a position to publish the text and take copies with me to Port Adelaide, where I met local historians who took me on a tour of all the places with 'Bower' connections. It was a memorable visit and before I left I had the pleasure of handing David Bower's original account over to the library, restoring it to the local archives.[8]

William Norton of Melbourne

The second story that I came across by chance concerned a young man called William Norton who was also from the south Pennines, this time from near Buxton. I was at a stamp sale, looking for examples of old correspondence, when I noticed one letter bearing an early stamp for the state of Victoria. The asking price was based on the value of this stamp, not on the contents of the envelope, and it was beyond what I was prepared to pay. However, I discussed the letter with the stall holder and was allowed to read it. It was written by William Norton and the content and style were fascinating: as we talked about it I discovered that he had other letters available that were 'not particularly valuable', that is to say there were no stamps on the envelopes. I purchased the one or two that he had with him and arranged to visit him again once he had been able to look through all the items that had turned up in a house clearance.

Over a period of several weeks I purchased more than twenty letters, and numerous other documents that had all come from the same source. These included detailed business accounts, wills, deeds and receipts, even some churchwardens' records. We were both delighted with the deal, each of us no doubt convinced he had had the better of the bargain. Unfortunately, one or two letters had been sold previously, and I have been unable to trace those, but I was able to get photo-copies of the ones that were still for sale in 'valuable' envelopes. It was another intriguing story and it really began to hold my attention once I had visited the old farm called Plex that was mentioned in many of the letters, and the Cat and Fiddle, a public house up on the moors which young William had remembered with some nostalgia.

It is of course a one-sided story, for we have no record of the letters written to William by his parents or siblings. Nevertheless it is possible to fill in some of the gaps from the answers given by William. What emerges is a personal tragedy that could be the plot of a novel. It seems that the young man had left home under a cloud, perhaps badly in debt, since he was repeatedly reassuring his relatives that he would make enough money to repay his father and regain his self-respect. At first he worked in a variety of jobs, even as a butcher, but when news came through of gold being dug out of the ground in Victoria, and fortunes being made, he simply had to go and try his luck.

As we read his letters we sense at times that his optimism is a little forced and smile to ourselves as he confidently talks of making money quickly and returning on a visit home. He expresses his affection for the friends he has left behind and his nostalgia for the moors and hills, even for the duck pond in the farmyard; he recalls memories of rare days out and of happier times with his brothers, and we read on, hoping to learn that his luck has changed. Instead we discover that he has been obliged to leave the diggings because of a slight injury that he has sustained, one that makes heavy work impossible. He assures us though that he will be all right, for he is going to Tasmania on the doctor's advice and should make a full recovery there.

The final brief letter is not in his handwriting but that of a friend, who sends his condolences to Mr and Mrs Norton on William's death. The brief lines that have to do with William's final few days are heart-rending in their simplicity. In truth this is exactly how many emigrants must have ended their days, but it is in such contrast to the brash success of David Bower, and William's own expectations, that it seems unusually poignant. His parents had obviously kept all the letters in a bundle and they were preserved by their descendants until the last Norton left the farm, over 150 years later. Although the 'story' may be the main attraction of the letters, they are full of incidental details that are of use to local historians in both Derbyshire and Victoria; hamlets, farms, fields and family matters, on the one hand, life in the outback and on the gold diggings, on the other. In one sense, of course, no surviving documents are really 'discovered', for there is usually somebody somewhere who knows of their existence, but as I progressively salvaged the Norton letters I truly felt that I had discovered something.

The Three Greenhorns

Not all discoveries consist of substantial amounts of archive material, at least not initially. For example in Canada, in 1972, it was a visit to a Calgary restaurant called 'The Three Greenhorns' that provided the clue to a fascinating story. A brief note on the back of the menu said that the name commemorated the 'folly' of three young Yorkshiremen who had left England in 1862 to join the Cariboo gold rush. They were called John Morton, Samuel Brighouse and William Hailstone and when they arrived in New Westminster, then the capital of British Columbia, young Morton bought a tract of wild and almost inaccessible land in the area around Burrard's Inlet. It was this that earned the three their nickname, for locals thought that a dollar an acre for swamp and forest was indeed folly. In fact the three bought 540 acres in all and raised the money by taking whatever work was available, peddling milk, and digging ditches on Lulu Island.

One of the terms of their agreement was that they would build a log cabin on the land and that one of them would live there. It was Morton who had taken the initiative and he was the one willing to stay there, so not surprisingly it came to be known in time as Morton's Place. The three friends jokingly registered their claim under the name 'The City of Liverpool' but they could never have anticipated that an even greater city would one day occupy the site. As Vancouver grew up around it, Morton's Place went through several different phases, first of all being transformed into the city's most fashionable residential area, and then becoming a commercial centre, with apartment blocks, offices and industrial premises. Today it is worth millions of dollars.

The city archives in Vancouver tell us that Morton was prompted to take the risk after meeting an Indian who had brought a lump of coal into the town. His experience told him that where there was coal there might also be clay, suitable for making bricks, so he had the Indian take him to where he had made his find, following him twelve miles through forests of cedar, fir and hemlock. They clambered over fallen logs and slashed their way through the undergrowth before arriving at the inlet, and it was there that Morton decided he would buy the land. It had been discovered seventy years earlier by Captain Vancouver and was a natural harbour. Morton is said to have realised its potential immediately. Whether or not that is the case, he certainly persuaded his friends to support him in the land-buying venture. The result of that was that the 'greenhorns' later became three of the city's wealthiest and most prominent citizens.

What caught my attention in the menu's advertising feature were the surnames of the three young men, the mention of clay and the Yorkshire connection, for I already knew of a family called Morton who were pot-makers, in a tiny place called Salendine Nook, just outside Huddersfield. Once I had returned home, I was able to locate John Morton in the census return of 1851 as a youth of sixteen. He lived in Salendine Nook with eight brothers and sisters. Almost next door, at an inn called the Spotted Cow, lived a farmer called Samuel Brighouse. Samuel was too old to be the emigrant but he had a son of fifteen whose name was also Samuel, and living with them was the innkeeper's grandson Edmond Morton. The two young emigrants were therefore relatives as well as neighbours and they would have been in their twenties when they left for British Columbia. They met Hailstone on the Atlantic crossing and forged a friendship that lasted fifty years. John Morton died on 18 April 1912.[9]

Novia Scotia

During the last seventeen years I have spent a good deal of time in North America, working with genealogists and historians there and coming to understand something of the successive phases of settlement that have shaped the continent's history. It was a while though before I realised how little common understanding we have of the individuals and families who crossed the Atlantic to make those settlements. Of course the Americans know a great deal about the migrants from the time of their arrival, and they have been very successful in reconstructing their family trees, some of them back to the early 1600s. They are less successful though in finding out where their ancestors lived before that, and which parish or even county they were born in. Few English family historians are in a position to help, because their energy is spent on the families who stayed behind. There are occasional references in English sources to relatives 'beyond sea', but, in general, we know very little here about the people who chose to emigrate. Indeed we can be completely in the dark about individuals who merely moved into the next county, never mind overseas: the name simply disappears from the records and its absence can go unnoticed.

Although I have long been aware of this problem I was astonished two or three years ago to be invited to Novia Scotia to take part in a conference at Mount Allison University that had as its theme the region's Yorkshire settlers. I knew nothing about such a movement and yet, in the four years from 1772 to 1775, over a thousand people left the county for Nova Scotia, drawn there by the prospect of land and independence, their hopes fuelled by speculators and agents.[10] It was the only substantial eighteenth-century movement of English people to the North American colonies that would survive the Revolution intact, and it has come to be seen by some historians as a defining moment in Canada's history, having a profound effect on settlement, politics and religion in the Maritime Provinces.

I was even more astonished to discover that a man from my home town figured prominently in the lectures and discussions, for his name was not known over here. Just how significant the Yorkshire settlement in Nova Scotia was in the long term may be open to debate. What cannot be denied is its influence on religious life in the growing community, for many of the emigrants were staunch Wesleyan Methodists, and they were responsible eventually for establishing the first Methodist chapels in Canada. A key figure in that group was Willam Black, whose family sailed from Hull in April 1775. He was just a fourteen-year-old boy at the time, but he was destined to play a major role in Nova Scotia's history and would be known by his contemporaries as Bishop Black.

In many ways William Black was not typical of the group, since most of the emigrants were farmers, who claimed that they had been driven from the land by high rents and rising prices. William, on the other hand, was the son of a tradesman, a grocer and linen draper who had moved south from Paisley some years earlier. William Black senior had travelled alone to Nova Scotia in 1774, where he had purchased land near to the present town of Amherst, returning to the colony the following year with his wife and five children. His appointment as a JP at the time of the Revolution is claimed by some to have helped to shift the balance of power away from the New Englanders.

Young William's parents were both devout, his mother in particular 'redeemed' after years of soul searching. He is said to have felt an awareness of his own sinfulness when he was only five years old, and he became a convert to Methodism after the family arrived in Nova Scotia, where he shared the prayer sessions and love feasts of the other Yorkshire settlers. He made friends with an elderly Methodist and together they prayed and sang almost every night, each striving to give meaning to his existence, until at last William felt that he had been 'saved' and could move on to the next phase of his life. He was still not twenty years old.

Almost immediately he took to preaching publicly, concentrating initially on his own kith and kin and on the Yorkshire families on the Chignecto Isthmus. Soon, however, he felt obliged to spread the word further afield and became an itinerant preacher, 'a heroic itinerant' in the words of one historian. He travelled great distances in the still untamed wilderness, along ill-defined trails and over dangerous waters, south to the farmers in the neighbourhood of Nappan and Maccan, west to the Peticodiac river, and even as far as Annapolis and Halifax. It is not difficult to imagine the hardships he suffered nor the importance of his visits to these isolated families, for he helped them to sustain their devotion and to feel part of the settlers' wider community. Their faith and courage is apparent in a letter home by Nathaniel Smith, who wrote 'how the poor people at a great distance row against both wind and tide, in small canous up and down the rivers, often at the risk of life, rather than miss a Meeting'.[11] It would be years before the settlers had their own place of worship.

William Black's sense of purpose and his evangelical zeal brought him rewards over and above the spiritual solace that he sought. He became Canada's first ordained Methodist minister in 1786 and subscribed to the building of what claims to be the country's first Methodist chapel at Point de Bute in 1788. His successful mission also made him a confidant of John Wesley, who eventually came to address him as 'Dear Billy'. His skill as an organiser was recognised in 1789 when he was made superintendent of the Methodist societies in Nova Scotia, New Brunswick and Newfoundland; he was still only twenty-nine. Long before his death, which occurred in 1834, he was commonly referred to throughout the region as the Father of Methodism and his exploits were remembered in the year 2000 in picturesque re-enactments of those stirring years.

At Mount Allison University and in Halifax there are archives relating to this group which contain numerous items of real interest to English historians. There are town books, correspondence, wills, inventories, land records and family papers which bridge the years of departure and settlement, revealing how the settlers relied on the customs and practices they had brought with them and how they adapted to those of their non-Yorkshire neighbours. There are details of marriages, births and deaths, everyday entries about farming, road mending and the making of fences and pounds, and, not surprisingly, brave and moving letters that bring home to us the realities of emigration over two hundred years ago. A letter to William Trueman in 1776 contained interested enquiries about his health, the condition of his cattle and grain, and the productivity of the soil – one farmer to another – but the writer also said 'I think we shall never have the opportunity to see each others' face any more here below'.[12]

2

The Surname Revolution

There has been a revolution in our approach to surname origins in the last thirty or so years that did not seem possible when Dr P. H. Reaney published his two ground-breaking books on the subject. The first of these, *A Dictionary of British Surnames*, was published in 1958, and it was followed in 1967 by *The Origin of English Surnames*. His great contribution to surname studies was the early evidence that he accumulated on names of all kinds but especially on personal names of both Old English and Norman origin. He also made perceptive connections between words in the Middle English vocabulary and by-names denoting moral and physical characteristics, status, trades and occupations. We were made aware that these had their roots in the everyday language of the household and market place, with its stimulating mix of English and French. His aim was to emphasise that the meaning of surnames must be looked for in the language that our ancestors were using as hereditary names stabilised, essentially that is from the Norman Conquest until the mid 1400s.

There can be no argument with that, of course, but we know more now about other matters that must be taken into account if we are to be sure of a surname's meaning. Each surname is unique and we need to find out when and where it became hereditary and how many other names there might be with similar origins, contrasting Smith and Robinson, which are likely to have had a great many, with the much rarer Arkwright and Auty, where single origins seem possible. We have learnt also how important it is to have information about the frequency and distribution of names at different times, so that we can discover which of them declined or became extinct and which of them expanded successfully. We must also recognise the changes that affected some surnames throughout much of their history, both predictable linguistic changes and those resulting from social pressure, illegitimacy perhaps, or local nicknaming practices. All these have a bearing on how distinctive

each name might be, with implications for both genealogists and geneticists, two groups of researchers who are making an increasingly
significant contribution to the subject. The first intimations of this
fundamentally changed approach were there even as Dr Reaney's work
was being published.

The New Approach

> If a Suffolk parish is thick with Kerriches or a Lancashire one with Entwisles
> the difficulty of sorting out lines and individuals may be very great. With
> some such names, it seems likely that all the bearers are, however remotely,
> of one kindred. Of others, on the contrary, there are certainly many distinct
> families.

These lines were written in 1960 by Sir Anthony Wagner, a genealogist
with a keen and vested interest in surnames, who later became Garter
Principal King of Arms. His views marked a significant move away from
the linguists' preoccupation with etymology, inviting us to concern
ourselves with the nature of surname origins, and related matters of
expansion and distribution. His enormous influence on the English
Surnames Survey, which has seen seven county volumes published since
1973, helps to explain the emphasis in those volumes on the major topic
of heredity, and the new role assigned in that period to the historian.
As the survey was based in the English Local History Department at
Leicester University, it is scarcely surprising that surnames would be
seen as a field of research that might throw new light on England's
economic and social development. Regional studies were seen as an
essential foundation for the project but the ultimate aim was undoubtedly an investigation at the national level that would lead
ultimately to a complete dictionary of English surnames.

Distribution

Another great step forward in the subject has to do with the new role
given to the study of surname distribution, and here we must acknow-
ledge our debt to the much maligned H. B. Guppy, author of *The Homes
of English Family Names* (1890). With the help of Post Office directories,
he was able to show that many of our English surnames have meaningful

patterns of distribution, some of them confined to a single area. His work was one of the influences that ultimately led me to plead the case in the late 1960s for the single origin theory, and at the heart of that argument were the statistics I had drawn from telephone directories. There is no news more exciting to a genealogist than the suggestion that all those who bear the same name may share a common ancestor, and the key to that is often distribution.

Colin Rogers, in *The Surname Detective* (1995), chose to investigate the distribution of less distinctive surnames, mapping many which are most unlikely to have a single origin. He again used telephone directories but observed that for small areas the computerised electoral register can also be useful. Despite the apparently unpromising subject matter, his maps raise many interesting points, not least the fact that numerous surnames of all types still appear to be concentrated in areas where they occurred six and seven hundred years ago. He found that even a name like Smith has a pattern of distribution that raises interesting questions.

The topics of distribution and origin were skilfully linked by David Hey recently in *Family Names and Family History* (2000), with numerous maps illustrating surname concentrations in different parts of the country. These were based on registered deaths for a five-year period from 1 January 1842 to 31 December 1846. The single origin theory was supported by data for every class of name: Arkwright (occupational), Auty (personal name), Bunyan (nickname) and Akehurst (locative). Informative distribution maps have also been produced by Kevin Schürer, who recently prepared a display at the Science Museum in London. Using the information from the census returns of 1881, and comparing this with modern data, he was able to show that there is a remarkable correlation between the two, confirming what others have said – that the modern distribution of a surname can be very revealing about its earlier history and even its origin.

The topic is one that has benefited enormously from the increased use of computers, both in the technical possibilities and the dissemination of the information. The advances are clear to see in Stephen Archer's new CD-Rom *The British 19th Century Surname Atlas*: it includes maps for all the more than 400,000 surnames that are recorded in the 1881 census and, for good measure, all the first names too! It offers researchers the opportunity to enter any surname and see immediately what its distribution was in Great Britain in 1881, the regional and local patterns enhanced by data for either the counties or the Poor Law unions and statistics that compare the actual totals with the density per 100,000. The CD offers other facilities, but its success lies in the visual impact of the maps, the accessibility of the accompanying data and the user-friendly instructions.

Of course all these aids to research are at best diagnostic, and conclusions about origin and meaning should not be drawn from maps alone. They have the potential to alert us to significant aspects of surname development, and they certainly point us in the right direction, but distribution is only part of the story. We may have come a long way from the hand-drawn maps of the 1960s, and statistics laboriously extracted from telephone directories, but we are still faced by the changes that affected surnames during the course of their history. In this respect, and long before we concern ourselves with meaning, there is important work for the linguist. We are all familiar with the genealogists' complaint, when they have reached an impasse in their research, that a particular ancestor, despite their most disciplined search of the records, is somehow 'not there'. The truth often is that he or she is there, but concealed behind a nickname or an unusual variation of the surname. Identifying that variant demands additional skills and dedication.

I attempted to establish some ground rules for a changed approach to surname identification in *Surnames and Genealogy* (Boston, 1997), a book reprinted in 2003 by the Federation of Family History Societies. It stresses the important role of our ancestors' aliases, explicit or implicit, and I am pleased to say that research in the last few years, by both amateur and professional genealogists, has reinforced the points I was making.

At the professional level this has been demonstrated by John Titford, with work on the variants of his own name Titford and research to show that Vavasour, Vawser and Bavister share a common origin.[1] He was also able to prove that the London name Stonhold derives from the Dutch Van Steenholen, and warned genealogists about the dangers of some dictionaries and databases. One of the examples he quoted was the discovery by Cecil Humphery-Smith, a professional genealogist, that the surname Sunley could derive from the place-name Sunley or, more perplexingly, from Somers and Summers via Sumner.[2]

Amateur genealogists are increasingly aware of such possibilities and I have received numerous letters detailing successful solutions to similar problems. Enid Tittensor, for example, has proved that her own name Tittensor, which derives from a Staffordshire place-name, formerly alternated in some cases with the Derbyshire Tidswell. This confusion between two quite distinct names occurred because of their similar pronunciation in north midlands dialect, and the solution depended on her ability to identify an implicit alias. That is to say she was able to prove that a man who appeared in one document as Tittensor was called Tidswell in another. The alias was occasionally explicit in the register of Bradley in the Moors.[3]

Similarly David Austerberry found clear evidence in the Frickley register of a connection between his unusual name and the Scandinavian Austerby, a development that I had suspected but could not prove. An equally strange variant was Oxtoby.[4] John Lindley has been able to show that the surname of his ancestor John Marlbrough had nothing to do with Marlborough in Wiltshire or one of several Malboroughs, but was a variant of Malburn. The family lived in Guisborough and, as Malburn has no obvious place-name origin, he is now considering a possible connection with Milburn, a common name in north-east England. It is not out of the question as the variation between Rispin and Raspin demonstrates.

Such developments are not as unusual as genealogists might suspect: migration and linguistic change often went hand in hand, and the secret is to identify the aliases, especially if they are rarely explicit. It is particularly gratifying therefore when an explicit alias is discovered after the link has been inferred. For example I had deduced from the Almondbury registers that Penny was an abbreviated variant of Wimpenny, and I went to great lengths to prove it.[5] No sooner had I published the findings than I came across a title deed of 1591 signed by Gilbert Penye alias Winpenye. The family's use of the christian name Gilbert had been one of the pieces of circumstantial evidence that first alerted me to the abbreviation. I suspect that abbreviations and contractions will turn out to be a more important aspect of surname development than I once thought, for, in the last couple of years, I have

come across scores of cases in my own immediate area, including the
following explicit examples:

> 1598   William Manglinge alias Man of Leeds
> 1607   James Kilton alias Kilvington of Thornbrough
> 1611   John Lockey alias Lockwood of Scorton
> 1611   John Chester alias Lanchester of Greystoke
> 1616   Roger Lecke alias Leckby of Stearsby
> 1640   William Barrowe alias Lickbarrowe of Doncaster

Many of these aliases persisted well into the 1800s: the editor of the
North Riding quarter sessions rolls noted an entry in 1776 for two felons
described as John Ridsdale alias Rudsdale and Thomas Tyerman alias
Tyres. In his footnote he wrote 'These aliases for the same names occur
still, or, at least, are of very recent as well as customary existence, in
this immediate district. The same may be said of Bell for Balfour, and
others like'. He was writing in 1892.[6] Where the abbreviation is not
explicit the genealogist's task is particularly difficult: Mrs Parry of Doncaster had experienced difficulty for several years with a family called
McLoughlin, but eventually found them in the census of 1891 as Mack,
a development that she 'blamed' on one of the sons who had moved
only a few streets away. His sister gave her name as McGloughlin. It
should not be presumed though that Mack is always a short form of
some longer Scottish name. Dr Reaney believed that it could be an Old
Irish personal name, a form of Magnus, whilst a Beverley family called
Mack descended from James Macke 'dutchman' (1576).[7]

There is further evidence also for some of the more unusual developments that I commented on in 1997. I had noticed the strange
inversion of Bywater to Waterby, where a surname that derived from
one type of place-name had been assimilated to another. I can now add
to that the explicit Sussex example of Richard Woodburne alias Burn-
wood (1584).[8] Here a place-name has been converted into an apparent
nickname. In the same source we find John Sparkes alias Parkes (1582),
William Harmer/Harman (1578) and Robert Olliffe/Colliffe (1592),
examples which show that practices were much the same in Sussex as
in Yorkshire. In fact there were scores of aliases in these Sussex records,
and many of the non-explicit ones were successfully identified by an
editor who was clearly alert to such developments. One of the problems

for genealogists is that many editors do not bother to index both the names, even in explicit aliases.

The difficulty that some genealogists have with variations of this type was forcibly brought home to me recently when I read an account of some English settlers in North America.[9] In one case the family being researched had the surname Beasley. The author wrote 'oddly enough the 1704 Virginia Rent Rolls ... do not reveal the names of any Beasleys owning land ... but a Robert Eseley died ... in 1711. One might almost suspect that the Easleys and Beasleys were one and the same family'. They almost certainly were. We need to remember that clerks were often given a person's full name and they had to decide where the break came. If we remember that initial 'H' was often not pronounced we are prompted to think that Christopher Rumfrey (1615) was probably Christopher Humphrey, and that James Scaverley (1623) was almost certainly James Caverley. Given that Robert would readily have been called Rob or Bob, it seems almost certain that Robert Beasley was indeed Robert Eseley.

Genetics

The significance of surname distribution had already attracted the attention of geneticists.[10] In 1985 G. W. Lasker made the point, in *Surnames and Genetic Structure*, that inherited surnames serve as models of the genetic structure of populations, providing readily available data about both the past and present. His work involved some of our commonest surnames and is of limited value at the moment to genealogists, but it was symptomatic of the growing interest that experts in other disciplines had in the subject and heralded their deeper and more productive involvement. Some examples of surname frequency were plotted in the *Atlas of British Surnames* which Lasker edited in 1990 in conjunction with C. G. N. Mascie-Taylor.

The interest of geneticists in surnames and genealogy actually goes back well over a century, for George Darwin, the son of Charles Darwin, used surname frequencies in his research into first cousin marriages, a subject in which he had a direct interest. In the 1960s Crow and Mange also carried out research into inbreeding, looking at marriages between individuals in close-knit communities who shared the same surname. Some of their results were considered controversial.

If we are to profit from the most recent progress made in this field by geneticists, however, we have to read carefully what they say about the male Y chromosome. We should not be put off by the complexities of advanced genetic research and need only seek to follow their arguments. For example, Mark Jobling stated that 'one part of our genome, the Y chromosome, is passed down in the same way as a surname; the distinction is that although all of the children get the *name* only the sons get the Y chromosome' – not the daughters. Bryan Sykes spelt out the implications of this for genealogists when he said 'all the males have inherited their Y chromosome from their father, who got it from their father and so on ... in societies where surnames also follow a patrilineal inheritance the Y chromosome offers the possibility of comparing *the true genealogy* with written records'. The italics in this case are mine but the implication that genetic evidence can confirm or disprove the links in the genealogist's family tree is Bryan Sykes's.

As early as the 1950s it was thought by some medical men that certain kinds of abnormalities, a particular kind of scaly skin for example, were associated with the Y chromosome inheritance. One result of that was research published in *Annals of Human Genetics*, in which the pedigree of a family in Suffolk called Lambert was subjected to reappraisement, using traditional genealogical sources such as parish registers. The authors were able to show that the skin of the so-called Porcupine Man of 1755 was not Y chromosome linked.

In the last thirty or so years the Y chromosome itself has played a more direct role in the research, with studies in various countries demonstrating the general validity of the principle of associating surnames and the Y chromosome. In Ireland it was possible to make a distinction between Irishmen who had Gaelic surnames and those who had Norman or English surnames. In other words it demonstrated the broad connections between names such as Harrison with 'Englishness' and Fitzgerald and Burke with the Normans. Other sub-groups were the Scots (Boyd) and Norse (Doyle). In the United States it has been used successfully in research into immigrant sub-populations of Chinese and Hispanics.

Some legends have been tested in the process. The Jewish priesthood is supposed to come down from Aaron via patrilineal descent, over a period of three thousand years. The link here is with the surname Cohen and related variants such as Kahn and Kane, said to mean 'priest'. Y chromosome analysis has shown that there is some support for this story. On the other hand, the Korean legend which claims that the country's entire population descends from a single man cannot be true, and Y chromosome research there points rather to multiple lineages, as one might have expected.

Far more interesting genealogically speaking were the experiments carried out using certain distinctive Y chromosomes – distinctive because they were larger or smaller than usual, or because they had an untypical shape. The 'Y' in Y chromosome is descriptive of its characteristic shape, but there are cases where a small piece of another chromosome attaches itself to the long arm of the Y, resulting in what might be called a distortion. Using this so-called satellited Y chromosome, one researcher was able to show the descent of eleven generations of French Canadians from an immigrant who crossed the Atlantic about 1665. The same misshapen Y chromosome occurred in another family. The conclusion there was that it provided evidence of an illegitimacy in the family over one hundred years earlier. Genealogists have to decide whether or not they want what Sykes called the true genealogy!

Other studies have linked three families in Colombia who shared the same surname but had no genealogical evidence to demonstrate a connection. Another family with the same Y chromosome had a quite different surname, a result on similar lines to the experiment in Canada. Small Y chromosomes were used positively in 1972, again in French Canada, to confirm the descent of seventeen people from a settler called René Brisson, and also to link René with a Pierre Brisson when no genealogical proof was available. However, experiments with an exceptionally large Y chromosome were much less satisfactory, in that they pointed to a connection between several families with different surnames. This actually raises a very important point, for it shows the potential that genetic research has to take our ancestry back beyond the period when surnames stabilised.

Some very exciting research in America has demonstrated how it is possible to link families across the oceans. Ten males of the Amish family called Beiler were initially able to trace themselves back to a Jacob Beiler, who left Switzerland for the United States in 1737. The Y chromosome in this case also demonstrated a link between the Amish families and a non-Amish man called Beyeler who emigrated as recently as 1900. The potential the Y chromosome has to identify relationships in this way, confirming or disproving linguistic theories, should not be under-estimated. In a similar case it had proved impossible, using traditional genealogical methods, to prove a connection between families in Virgi-nia, Pennsylvania and Bavaria. In the year 2000, however, Frederick Haury and Justin Howery had their DNA tested and they matched at twelve sites on their Y chromosomes. The Mennonite Jakob Haury had moved to Bavaria from Switzerland in 1711 and his descendants emigrated to the United States in the 1800s.

Bryan Sykes and the Sykes Family

Just three years ago Bryan Sykes and Catherine Irven published their article entitled 'Surnames and the Y Chromosome', attracting unpre-cedented media coverage for genetic and genealogical research. The key to that heightened interest was Bryan Sykes's conclusion that his experi-ment demonstrated that the surname had a single origin, that is to say that every male person called Sykes owed his name to one progenitor, and that the DNA was distinctive enough to prove or disprove blood relationship. If the surname had been something as distinctive as Haw-thornthwaite or Swinglehurst there would probably have been less interest, for in these cases there are several indications of a shared history – the numbers involved, the distribution, and the 'unusual' nature of the surnames. In the case of Sykes, which is numerous in some regions, the claim by Bryan Sykes was guaranteed to excite discussion, even disbelief, for the name has one naming element only and is well known to us through a variety of personalities world wide. The conclusions he arrived at with regard to its origins placed genetic research at the heart of genealogy and surname studies.

It is important therefore that the claim should be examined rigorously, both by other geneticists and by specialists in genealogy and related fields of study. The first stage in that process is a close examination of the circumstances in which the experiment was carried out. These are explained by Bryan Sykes in the first part of his article. A sample of males named Sykes was compiled from electoral rolls and other pub-lished sources. There were at that time 9885 registered UK voters with the surname and it was clear even at that stage that the highest concentration was in the counties of West Yorkshire, Lancashire and Cheshire, notably in that area of the south Pennines where the three have common boundaries. A postal request for a cheek-cell sample was then sent to 269 male Sykeses 'chosen at random from the three counties'. The replies numbered sixty-one, and DNA was successfully extracted and genotyped from forty-eight of these. As a safeguard there were two 'control' groups, one made up of 139 native English males from different parts of the country, and the second made up of twenty-one males, neighbours of the Sykeses, who had responded to the request for a sample but were unrelated to them.

For those of us who are not geneticists it is here that the difficulties are likely to start, if only in understanding what Bryan Sykes means when he says that all three sample groups were genotyped 'at four microsatellite loci in common use'. That is to say that four characteristics of the Y chromosome were available for comparison, creating a profile called a 'haplotype', a rather small number according to some experts, for whom twelve or more is now usual. These four characteristics were typed as 15–23–11–14 and the table of results shows that twenty-one of the forty-eight who had been tested successfully shared this pattern. In several other cases there was a direct parallel except for a single digit, e.g. 14–23–11–14 (1) and 15–23–10–14 (3). These four persons had what have been called 'one-step derivatives' and were seen as acceptable mutations. The total of blood related descendants was therefore said to be just in excess of 50 per cent of the sample.

The fact that the remaining haplotypes exhibited nothing in common was also of fundamental importance, for it suggested that there were no other significant clusters among those successfully tested. If a small group of two or three had shared their own identical characteristics that would have been evidence of an alternative origin; more than one such small cluster would have pointed to multiple origins. For Bryan Sykes this was further evidence that the surname could have only a single progenitor and he explained the remaining, more than 40 per cent as 'non paternity' events, that is the result of illegitimacies or adoption. Historians would say that statistically this was a perfectly legitimate conclusion.

Faced with criticism of the numbers sampled and the small number of 'loci' used, Bryan Sykes carried out further tests, this time on a group

of Sykeses who were thought likely by genealogists to have a separate
origin. Although these results have not been published, they were quoted
on a BBC Radio 4 programme which devoted itself to the topic, and the
percentage of positive results on this occasion was rather higher, somewhere in the region of 70 per cent. Identification using four 'sites' only
was possible, according to Sykes, because the Sykes profile is so very
distinctive, more typical of somebody from the Baltic than from the
north of England. He was himself astonished at the results, for he had
no knowledge of any connections with the south Pennines and was
informed in reference works that Sykes was a surname with multiple
origins.

At the time when surnames were stabilising the word 'syke' was
commonly used of hillside streams that defined boundaries, or of water
channels between holdings in the open arable fields of the community.
In either case it was a very common place-name element, if only in
the northern hill country, and early records show that in the thirteenth
and fourteenth centuries numerous families were described as 'atte
Syke' or 'del Syke', although both versions could be in the plural right
from the beginning. No doubt some of these were by-names, each with
the potential in the dynamic society of the time to become a hereditary
surname. They would normally be compared with names such as
'Brook', 'Shaw' and 'Wood', which are thought to have had multiple
origins, rather than with the more distinctive 'Holbrook', 'Grimshaw'
and 'Eastwood'. It is the number of potential origins that explains the
reluctance of some surname experts to think of Sykes as a possible
single origin surname, and the results were bound to lead to debate.

On the positive side, the evidence clearly demonstrated a relationship
between significant numbers of people bearing the name. It was also
clear that much of the name's expansion took place in the Slaithwaite
Hall area from about 1450. More significantly a link was shown between
the Slaithwaite area families and those in Flockton, Holmfirth and
Derbyshire, where the earliest examples of the name occurred from 1270.
Armed with the DNA evidence, family historians can now confidently
trace the migration routes pursued by the early generations of Sykeses
from one valley to another in the southern Pennines.

If there is a disappointment it is that genealogists still have to be
convinced that one family alone is responsible for all those who now

bear the name. Had the sample been larger, and deliberately targeted to take account of Sykes families away from the 'heartland', the conclusions would be on a firmer footing. One reason why family historians are reluctant to embrace Sykes's conclusions wholeheartedly is that research has shown how some families expand prolifically in the course of their history, whereas others scarcely ramify at all but survive perilously from one generation to another. It is difficult therefore to suppress the suspicion that one or two such survivors might be amongst the over 40 per cent who did not share the 15–23–11–14 haplotype.

Moreover the reservations we have about all kinds of documentary evidence are still there with DNA evidence. Bryan Sykes himself anticipated this, saying 'of course non-paternity events involving other males with the core Sykes haplotype would not be detected'. Another reservation that has received little attention is the probability that families now with different surnames will prove to have the same haplotype. When the first Sykes adopted that name he already had relations who chose or were given other names. If there should be any in the case of Sykes they are possibly somewhere in the Baltic but there will be other cases surely where the descendants live much closer together.

In the last two years there have been numerous other important tests carried out into surnames using the Y chromosome. Together they are beginning to define the possible contribution that it can make to genealogical research. In the case of very distinctive surnames the geneticist can confirm whether or not the genealogist is dealing with a single, plural or multiple origin. Dyson, with an 85 per cent positive result is the most spectacular success, and Blencoe, with evidence of three origins, is the one that runs closest to the genealogical findings. Pomeroy was disappointing for some, because it showed that the surname may belong to as many as seven different families, but it was positive for others, either because it confirmed a link with the aristocratic family of that name or because it linked families who had been unable to prove their kinship. Increasingly there will be situations in which DNA is used to check the facts in established pedigrees and it will prove decisive in some legal cases. For my part the most satisfactory test was the one carried out into the names Reddiough, Ridehalgh and Ridgwick, for it demonstrated that all three could share the same origin. Until then my conviction that they had a common source had relied solely on a mix of linguistic and genealogical probabilities.[11]

If they have not done so already, genealogists will soon come to see that DNA is an excellent tool, flexible enough to provide solutions to all sorts of previously intractable problems, but it is only a tool and not a magic wand. The highs and lows of the traditional approach are still there and a family history will still require far more than proof of a blood connection. It will require us, as always, to keep on digging in the records for all those wonderful items of information that reward the researcher and ensure the continuing attraction of the subject.

3

Surname Excursions

The individual study of any English surname is usually linked to genealogy but it can be more rewarding to put the family history into the much fuller picture of the surname's development, taking into account spelling variations, aliases, and such matters as expansion and distribution. A successful search ideally provides information about why, when and where the name became hereditary and details of the progenitor. This should help to determine what kind of name it is, the nature of its origin, whether multiple or single, and finally its meaning or etymology. These points are all touched on in this chapter, although it will not be possible to deal with them separately.

Ambler and the Language of Chaucer

In 1881 there were 2647 people called Ambler in Great Britain and more than two thirds of them lived in Yorkshire, mostly in the West Riding. Yorkshire accounted also for more than 80 per cent of people called Ombler, but this variant was more common in the East Riding.[1] The historical evidence suggests that the two names probably had the same origin and that the progenitor may have been Nicholas le Aumbleour, who was a tenant of Wakefield manor in the early 1300s, holding land in Halifax parish. It was there that much of the name's expansion eventually took place, in and around Northowram, and the variant Ombler has been noted there from the sixteenth century. The will of Richard Ambler, who died in 1526, indicates how the surname may by then have started to spread further afield, for he had property interests at that time in York and several other west Yorkshire parishes.[2]

There has been much speculation about the possible meaning of the surname and one suggestion is that it was an occupational term, either for an enameller or for somebody in charge of a stable. An alternative theory is that it was a nickname, describing a person with an ambling

gait, or used as a facetious alternative to 'walker', the northern word
for a fulling miller. However, none of these takes full account of how
'ambler' was commonly used in the late middle ages. To amble now is
usually to walk or take a gentle stroll, but it formerly meant to move
at a smooth and even gait and was applied especially to horses, particularly those that were suitable mounts for ladies.

For example we are told in Chaucer's *Canterbury Tales* that the Wife
of Bath had made numerous pilgrimages on horseback and that she
rode 'esily' or comfortably on 'an amblere'. It was a word used frequently
in early wills for fillies, mares and geldings, especially those that were
expressly bequeathed to widows: in 1556, for example, John Smythe left
his wife an 'amblinge gray mare called Throstell', and here the animal's
name contributes to the idea that it had a sweet temperament.[3] It would
not be surprising therefore if Ambler was a nickname given to somebody
who was very easy-going or, since many nicknames were given ironically,
to somebody who was anything but easy-going.

In fact horses were so important in medieval society, and there was
such a large vocabulary devoted to them, that nickname analogies seem
almost unavoidable. Other 'horse' names used by Chaucer's characters
include Hakeney, Rouncy and Capel, all of which are also found as
medieval by-names. If my theory about Ambler is right it may throw
new light on the Border surname Trotter, since 'amblers' were often
linked in medieval wills with 'trotters'. The surname is usually said to
mean 'messenger', but it also described a horse that trotted, moving
rather more briskly than an ambler. In 1423, for instance, the archbishop
of York had a bay horse in his stables described as an 'ambeler', and a
grey described as a 'trottar'.[4] The two terms are often found side by
side in wills and they would have come readily to mind as nicknames
in an age when it was commonplace to liken humans to birds and
animals. Also in Chaucer's vocabulary were 'stot' (heifer or bullock),
'naddre' (adder), 'laverokke' (lark), 'ruddok' (robin) and 'papejay'
(parrot or green woodpecker) and all these gave rise to by-names.

Chaucer's English

If we need confirmation that there are clues to medieval by-names in
Chaucer's English we can find it in the vocabulary associated with love.

In *The Romaunt of the Rose* there is an attractive portrait of the allegorical figure *Mirthe*, whose lady-love had made a wreath of roses and set it on his head. She was said to have done this 'by druerye', an Old French expression for a love-token. The by-name is recorded in Suffolk and Lancashire from about 1200 and there was actually a Joanna Drewerye living in Southwark in 1381, where the *Canterbury Tales* had their beginning. However, the word had a variety of associated meanings which ranged from courtship and sweetheart to illicit love and we should have to take these into account in any attempt to interpret the name's meaning. Illicit love seems more likely if we consider the by-name 'Dernelof', since this derived from the Middle English word for hidden love. In *The Miller's Tale* the clerk was said to be a secretive, sly man who knew all about 'derne love', so the inference may be that it was a nickname for a philanderer. Not surprisingly it later became Dearlove, which some writers have mistakenly accepted at face-value as a term of endearment. Lemmon or Loveman was also used by Chaucer and signified a sweetheart.

There is an old saying which suggests that in England we measure a man's worth by his 'manners', whereas in Germany a person can be judged by his *Kleider* or clothes. Actually there is a long tradition in this country also of linking clothes to character and Shakespeare's 'hempen home-spuns' come immediately to mind. It would not be surprising therefore if Chaucer's 'burnet' and 'burel' gave rise to nick-names. This seems to be almost explicit in the Prologue to *The Franklin's Tale*: 'I am a burel man ... have me excused of my rude speche', since 'burel' was a term for coarse woollen cloth of a reddish-brown colour. The material known as 'burnet' was dark-brown in colour and said to be of better quality than burel, although Chaucer portrays *Avarice* as wearing very poor clothes, including 'a burnet cote ... furred with no menivere'. Miniver was a very fine fur, sometimes used in ceremonial costumes.

In fact there are words right through Chaucer's verse that link with medieval by-names. These include such characteristic French phrases as 'beausire', 'pardee', 'par amour' and 'bel amy', recognisable in the names Richard Beusir (1297), Henry Pardeu (1332), Roger Paramurs (1301) and Peter Belamy (1379). There is French influence also in 'parfit', 'pert' and 'gaylard', although here the connection with the names may be less immediately obvious. William Perfyt seems straightforward enough, as an early form of 'perfect', but the others require a little explanation. Henry Perte (1324) had a name derived from 'apert', an Old French word for 'skilful', whilst the equally positive 'gaylard' meant 'high spirited' or 'lively', and is found in the name of Robert Gaylard (1225). There has been some change in meaning in words like 'deyntee' (handsome) and 'jolif' (gay), but these were certainly used as by-names and Alice Jolyf was another resident of Southwark in 1381.

There were other by-names in Southwark, linked to occupations or status, that have direct parallels in Chaucer, such as Thomas Bachilor, John Botiller, Matilda Lavender and John Pardoner, and once again we need to note possible fourteenth-century meanings and interpretations. The 'bachilor' was a young knight as well as an unmarried man, the 'botiller' a servant with responsibility for the bottles, and the 'lavender' a laundress, whilst the 'pardoner', a central character in the *Canterbury Tales*, sold indulgences under licence. Other Southwark by-names in this category which had a Chaucerian ring to them were Robert Ostyler, John Pegrome (pilgrim), John Pyebaker and Thomas Poyntelmaker (a 'poyntel' was a style or instrument for writing).[5]

Modern Surnames

The following modern surnames are linked to the by-names discussed above, often correctly I feel sure, but alternative explanations have been offered for some of them and others would need genealogical evidence to prove the connections: Ambler, Bachelor, Bellamy, Bowser, Burnett, Burrell, Butler, Capel, Dainty, Dearlove, Drury, Gaylord, Hackney, Jolliff, Lavender, Laverack, Lemmon, Nadder, Ostler, Paramore, Pardew, Pardner, Parfitt, Peagram, Peart, Pobjoy, Pointel, Pyeman, Ruddock, Runcie, Stott and Trotter.

Gaukroger and its Aliases

A close examination of the early history of Gaukroger will serve to illustrate some of the problems that can complicate the explanation of less ordinary surnames. Many of these are simply not dealt with in the standard reference works, partly because they have no obvious origin and partly because they are not numerous enough to have captured people's attention. On the other hand, writers may be attracted to them because they seem to have a bizarre or amusing origin. Gaukroger fits the bill exactly, so it is often omitted from sources where it might be expected to feature. Guppy, for example, makes no mention of it, even though it can be traced throughout its history to the Sowerby district of Halifax. Others are likely to be attracted to it because it seems idiosyncratic.

Initially I accepted the explanation offered by other writers that it was a nickname meaning 'clumsy Roger', an interpretation based on the colloquial word 'gawk'. This was usually a noun, not an adjective, but it was widely used on its own to describe an awkward or a clumsy person and it is recorded in compounds such as 'gawk-handed'. It is tempting therefore to assume a connection with French *gauche*, which is the word for 'left' as opposed to 'right' and can also mean 'clumsy'. The surname evidence put forward previously took the name no further back than Gawkeroger in 1539, and this spelling appeared to support the 'clumsy Roger' theory.

In fact the surname almost certainly had a single origin, and it was initially very uncommon, but I have been able to find examples as far back as 1402 and these are early enough for us to dismiss the possibility that Gaukroger was a nickname. In that year John del Gaukerogg(er) was fined at the manor court for trivial woodland offences and the 'del' clearly points to a place-name origin. He was referred to again that year but on this occasion as John de Gawkerocher.[6] The two alternative spellings are found side by side in other fifteenth-century references to the family, but later those with 'rocher' as a suffix became uncommon, suggesting that scribes were already interpreting it as 'Roger', whether deliberately or by accident.

The place-name which gave rise to the surname is not well documented but it is in Smith's *Place-Names of the West Riding of Yorkshire* (1961), recorded in Sowerby from 1624. This late reference convinced Smith that it had been named after the local family, and he too thought that the surname suffix was 'Roger'. More recently though a published volume of the court rolls, for 1351, mentioned '1½ acres in Sourby called Gaukrocher', a piece of land formerly held by Margery del Lane that had fallen into decay. The date suggests that this may have been because of the so-called Black Death, but the tenancy was taken up by a man named Hugh Otesson and it is reasonable to suppose that the settlement and surname came later, possibly as late as the last quarter of the century.

What these examples prove is that the suffix was 'rocher', a common enough word in the Pennines for an exposed rock or crag, and one that has given us several local place-names: Rocher in Slaithwaite and Rocher in Thurlstone are well-known localities. Compounds also occur and there is 'a close called Jackrocher' in Holmfirth, a territory in the same manor as Sowerby (1585). The word 'rocher' actually remained in every-day use for centuries, as we see in a petition at the quarter sessions, in 1675, in which Ann Wood claimed that she was lame 'by reason of a fall she had from a rotcher'. It seems likely therefore that the prefix 'gawk' is the dialect word for the 'cuckoo', an element found in several other place-names and particularly in the common Gawthorpe. Perhaps the crag had been one of the bird's favourite perches.

Linguistic and Social Development

Although Gaukroger remained uncommon well into the 1500s there was some expansion in Sowerby itself and at least one family had already migrated further down the Calder Valley. In a roll of 1545, for example, six individuals were taxed in Sowerby and two more in Hartshead and Liversedge.[7] It was not a prolific surname but probably more numerous than these figures suggest, for there would be some families who were not sufficiently well off to be included. Moreover, the true extent of its ramification in Sowerby was masked until recently by its instability, for this came to light only when the aliases used by different branches of the family were looked at more closely.

Three of these have been identified, that is Platts, Barker and Brigg, and the first can be seen to derive from a property named Platts which had been in the family's possession from the 1460s at least. For well over one hundred years they were said to be 'of Platts', as when Richard Gawkeroger of Platts 'surrendered half a messuage called le Platts ... to the use of Abraham Bates' in 1585.[8] It was in the same period, however, that the alternative 'alias Platts' came into use, implying that the name of the farm had begun to develop as a by-name which served to identify this particular branch of the family. For example, the parish register records the death in 1569 of John Gawkroger of Sowerby; yet in his will, proved in the same year, he was named as John Gaukeroger alias Plates. After that it was not unusual for Platts to be entered into the records instead of Gaukroger. In 1672, for example, John and Joseph Platts were listed alongside John and Jonas Gawkeroger in the Sowerby hearth tax returns. Another Sowerby man, called either Jonathan Platts or Jonathan Gawkroger alias Plattes, was a prominent local attorney in the 1650s.[9] A less successful alias was that of his contemporary, John Gawkroger alias Brigge, a butcher, who probably lived down at the 'brigg', now more usually called Sowerby Bridge.

The 'Barker' alias is recorded from 1538 when John Gawkeroger alias Barker of Sowerby was fined 12*d.* at the manor court, for lodging 'divers vagabonds within his house by night',[10] and other examples occur after that in a variety of records, well into the 1600s. For example Joseph Gawkroger alias Barker of Halifax, another butcher, made his will in 1610. It is likely therefore that the Thomas Barker taxed in Sowerby in 1672 was also a Gaukroger, although I cannot yet confirm that. In this case the alias appears to have had its origin in the 1490s, when a William Gawkrogger of Sowerby was described in the rolls as a 'barker': this is the north country word for a tanner, an occupation that was common then in the West Riding but distinctive enough as a nickname in Sowerby to identify yet another branch of the family.

For information about a later development in the Gaukroger story I am indebted to local historian Walter Rodgers, who has been able to establish that he bears an abbreviated form of the surname. There are many aliases which demonstrate how common it once was for surnames to be shortened and it is not surprising to find that it happened in this case. If there was already a perception locally that Gaukroger was somehow uncomplimentary then, no doubt, some bearers of the name would have preferred Roger(s) to Gaukroger. Walter Rodgers found confirmation of this in the registers of St John the Baptist, in Skircoat near Halifax, when he came across John Gawkroger alias Rogers, buried in 1782. Of course it may be that the suffix too was occasionally dropped, as when Janet Gauke was buried in Rothwell in 1554 – her surname otherwise unknown in the parish. It was certainly not unusual for the two elements in the name to be deliberately separated; for example Martin Gauck-Roger was buried at Heptonstall in 1627.

In fact all these developments are typical of what happened to a
number of surnames in the sixteenth and seventeenth centuries and
these Gaukroger aliases might be said to have followed certain rules or
practices. Much less predictable are those changes which came about
through genuine misunderstanding – so-called popular etymology – or
the intervention of a mischievous individual, two types of development
that require some explanation. Popular etymology describes the conver-
sion of the unknown into the more familiar, as for example when
Birtwhistle and Pitchford became Birdwhistle and Pitchfork, transform-
ations that we assume were innocently made when the names were
misheard or misinterpreted. On the other hand, they may have been
the deliberate work of a scribe or clerk with a sense of humour, fully
aware that the illiterate informant would have no idea what was being
recorded. I first began to suspect 'mischief' of this kind when I identified
Smoothways, Gravestone and Shipyard as versions of Smirthwaite, Gray-
son and Shepherd, but I could not be certain.

Gaukroger certainly lent itself to such changes, especially when
Sowerby families moved to areas where their surname was not known.
We assume that popular etymology was responsible for the spellings
Cockrogers, Corkroger and Choak-Rogers, all found in York in the late
1600s, even though we might suspect that the clerks had allowed themselves a quiet smile at the informant's expense. Confirmation that some
spellings of this kind were deliberately humorous is found in two entries
in the registers of St Mary's, Hull, in the 1650s. On this occasion a child
baptised as Daniel Cockroger was buried a few months later as Daniel
Cockrobin. The lesson for genealogists is clear, for while they would
probably accept that Gaukroger might have variants such as Gawkroger
and Gaukrodger, or even Corkroger and Cockroger, they would find it
more difficult to come to terms with aliases such as Barker, Platts, Brigg,
Ro(d)gers, Gawke and even Cockrobin.

Rare and Extinct Surnames

Surnames that are extinct or exceptionally uncommon seldom find their
way into our national dictionaries. No doubt part of the reason for that
is economic: the number of pages available to a writer, and the pub-
lishers' need to target potential customers, mean that such surnames

are of low priority and have to be omitted, even though they may have intriguing etymologies and important histories. Their lack of numbers is usually enough to condemn them to obscurity.

It is essentially a dilemma that faces the person who is compiling a dictionary of surnames. There is no similar problem for place-name scholars, who derive a positive advantage from studying names that have long since disappeared, showing us how we can use them to throw light on forgotten aspects of husbandry or vanished landscapes. For those who study personal names, especially those of pre-Conquest England, it is their almost total extinction that excites our interest, obliging us to ask how the language could survive Norman dominance but the names could not.

Perhaps the dilemma arises partly from the wide interest there is in the subject. The popular appeal of surnames is not difficult to understand, for they can have such fascinating meanings and are steeped in tradition and history. Their practical value is that they identify us in the community and can be used to trace our ancestry, so it is hardly surprising that many of us want to know more about them. The problem is that the surnames we bear are the successful ones, successful in the sense that they have survived, and there are enough of them to fill the dictionaries.

There are very good reasons though for looking much more closely at the less successful surnames. Certainly genealogists cannot afford to ignore them, since there can be few of us today who do not have extinct names in our ancestry. Moreover, our local histories would be very lopsided if we concerned ourselves only with families that have expanded successfully. Sometimes, of course, we may think that a name has died out and then find that it survives in some other part of the country. I had an intriguing letter some years ago from a Mr Horlington of Walton on the Naze, who had been able to trace his descent from a John Horlington of Holborn in the seventeenth century, and before that to the Hartlingtons of Slaidburn. This family had a long and distinguished history in that part of the Pennines, but I had no entries in my own files after 1600 and I doubt if I would ever have considered Horlington as a possible variant. The name derives from the hamlet of Hartlington, in Wharfedale, and Hugh Hartlington or Hurlenton was living in Slaidburn parish in the mid 1500s. There must be many similar cases.

In fact there can be a very fine line between expansion and extinction, especially from 1340 to 1540 when the population was at a really low ebb. Because of the Black Death and recurrent bouts of plague, one generation of daughters could be enough in those centuries for a name to disappear for ever from the records, and the court rolls of the 1400s bear witness to that. Even later, when the population was rising, we find evidence of families failing to produce male heirs, a situation that caused particular consternation in the ranks of the gentry, for whom continuity in the male line was a key matter of status. One way of securing continuity was for the owner of an estate to insist that a prospective son-in-law should take the surname of the heiress. That happened often enough for us to see how close to extinction many prestigious names once were.

Expansion Overseas

Indeed, there are some quite startling statistics that demonstrate how often the survival and expansion of a surname can be traced to a single individual. In the Radio 4 series *Surnames, Genes and Genealogy* Peter Addyman claimed that all the Yorkshire Addymans descend from an orphan who was moved into Nidderdale from the Pontefract area less than three hundred years ago, and similar stories are told by other genealogists. The phenomenon is even more obvious in America, where there are prolific surnames of English origin that are now either extremely rare in this country or have disappeared completely. I was surprised, for example, to discover several years ago that Longstreth is quite a popular name in some parts of America. It was once popular enough too in the northern dales, notably in and around Langstrothdale where it originated, but it is rare now to find it in any English record, and only a handful of families survive in the Pennine towns, mostly in Lancashire. Many of the American families claim descent from a Quaker called Bartholomew Longstreth whose departure from this country is referred to in a document known as the Settle Certificate. He emigrated to Pennsylvania in 1699, followed shortly afterwards by his brother Martin, and their descendants are described by one American writer as 'a numerous and scattered clan'.

There is no hint in earlier population lists for that part of the Dales of a decline in the name's fortunes. William Langstroth was listed in a muster roll for Langstrothdale in 1511; Thomas and William were taxed in Buckden in 1522, and there were other branches of the family at that time lower down Wharfedale and in neighbouring Littondale.[11] In the hearth tax returns of 1672, shortly before Bartholomew's birth, the surname was established in Bentham, Buckden, Horton in Ribblesdale, Ingleton, Rathmell and Hartlington, a less concentrated distribution pattern than in the early 1500s but still in that part of the northern Pennines. There is evidence in the parish registers to suggest that the name was sometimes confused with both Longstaff and Langster, and that may have played a part in its decline, but even so we know that there were still Langstroths in Langstrothdale in 1708 and others later in different parts of Airedale. One of those families is known to have moved then over the Pennines to Nelson in Lancashire.

This pattern of decline in England and expansion in America is by no means uncommon. That is apparent if we consider for a moment the English surnames Sanborne, Crandall and Dearborn, which belong to three of the longest-serving staff members of the world's oldest genealogical society, based in Boston, New England. Both Sanborne and Dearborn appear to be extinct now in this country and Crandall is rare, found in just a few south-eastern localities. In America, on the other hand, all three have expanded successfully and Dearborn in particular is prolific. Not surprisingly our standard dictionaries have no entries for such surnames and the explanations found in American sources about their origins and meanings are quite often speculative.

One very fortunate survivor is Askern, which derives from a place-name near Doncaster. It features consistently in English records from the twelfth century, and references occur in south Yorkshire into the late nineteenth century, but it appears to be missing from modern sources. It may not be extinct in this country, for there are several Yorkshire families called Askin and this was one of the late spelling variations, but the original version of the name is certainly more familiar in America. In fact an American correspondent claimed descent from Thomas Askern of Burghwallis in south Yorkshire, a man who was convicted at York assizes as a highwayman in or around 1714, having carried out an attack on a traveller at Saltergate in the North Riding. The intriguing part of the story is that he was sentenced to death but then reprieved and transported, ending up eventually in New England where he founded the American branch of the family. It is hard to avoid a pun when commenting on the miraculous survival of this name.

There are parallels in the case of the surname Blechenden or Blechynden, which has a long history in Kent but is of disputed origin. I recently had a letter which claims that there are several hundred families with that surname in Australia, and that they share a common ancestor called Harrison Blechynden. He arrived in Australia as an indentured servant in the early 1800s and the successful expansion of the surname is attributed to his seven sons and twenty-six grandsons. Other branches of the family in New Zealand, India, Jamaica and America have almost died out, and just a few individuals in this country still bear the name – none of them in Kent. One married New Zealand lady called Blechynden is said to have retained her maiden name simply because it is so rare.[12]

When a surname is missing from present-day English sources it is easy to presume that it has died out, but that may not always be the case. From what has been said above, it is clear that it might survive away from where it originated, in some other part of Great Britain or elsewhere in the world. Sometimes its survival is masked behind a variant spelling, even close to where it originated. One of the problems where surname studies are concerned is that our ancestors have been so mobile, especially since the first landfall in North America, and they are difficult to trace. Researchers in this country have rarely shown any curiosity about the fate of families that dropped out of the local community, and we can hardly be surprised at that, for we have no ready access to the vital information. On the other hand, researchers overseas who are keen to discover more about their English ancestors are seldom clear where to look and they find very little in English sources that is of direct help.

Campinot

The story of Campinot will serve as an example of a surname that has survived for over seven hundred years but is now on the verge of extinction, certainly in this country. Most of its history can be traced to localities in the Colne Valley or to neighbouring areas, and it is there that the variant Campnett can still be found. In fact, it occurs just once

eless it was frequent enough in
nches of the family have been
Colne Valley, including Slaith-
ltham and Stainland. Further
t times in Halifax, York and
have survived.

s are fairly routine but at least
isted. From the court rolls we
he by-laws: in 1434 an insigni-
aks and holly trees, failing to
he 1630s digging peat illegally
quarter sessions records there
ft of a pig in 1638, and beef,
nce brought John Campinett
long list of things that he had
ther breeches, an ivory comb
one of several local men who
from the low gaol in Halifax.
Slaithwaite in the 1500s and
pieces of cloth they took to
arms called Netherend and
minor localities were named
ary name of a dwelling that
ot Wood in Slaithwaite has
a butcher in Elland in 1793
alehouse in Meltham in the
ving at Badgergate in Mars-
oseph and Hannah, James
ill there at the time of the
d farmers, an integral part
unt all the variants of the
with the name in England

unusual origin. We know
Woodsome Hall that John
in the late 1300s and that
in south Yorkshire. An

earlier John Campiun or Campinot had been taxed there in 1297. The probability is that John was the family's preferred first name and that the diminutive served over several generations to distinguish the son from the father. Just why it became hereditary in Slaithwaite is not clear but the migration northwards may have played a part in that.[15]

There is an important postscript that relates to several of the points already made. It concerns the name Campey, which may not be particularly common but is well established in both east and west Yorkshire. In 1881 there were 154 Campeys in England and 136 of them lived in Yorkshire, others in Lincolnshire. I find no reference to this surname in our dictionaries but it is almost certainly an abbreviated form of Campinot. There was a Thomas Campinett alias Campie in Stillingfleet in 1611 and this village is at the centre of today's distribution of the surname.

Topographic Surnames

It is usual for writers to say that our surnames can be divided into four main classes. These were defined by Dr Reaney as: 1. Local surnames; 2. Surnames of Relationship; 3. Surnames of occupation or office; 4. Nicknames. Basil Cottle went so far as to say that this is 'a simple and undeniable statement',[16] but not all scholars are happy with that classification. It is certainly convenient for writers, since it allows books on the subject to be divided neatly into different sections, but each of the so-called classes of name has important sub-divisions, and some names sit very uncomfortably on the barriers between the classes.

We need only look at local surnames as a category to understand the problem. A dozen examples will illustrate how diverse such names can be. Stafford, Holdsworth, Kent, France, Hemingway, Beaumont, East, Sotheby, Atwell, Nash, Bridger and Churchman are all said to be local, because they tell us where a person lived, or had lived, but they are clearly of different types. The first four relate to obvious place-names, a town, a hamlet, a county and a country. Hemingway was also a place-name, for the first bearers of the name were always 'de Hemingway', but nobody has yet been able to say where that place was; Beaumont looks like a French place-name but could actually be from Beaumont in Lancashire. East now sounds a very vague name but it must once have had a reasonably precise local meaning, akin to Sotheby which meant something like 'south in the village'. Of course neither of these was actually a place-name. Atwell seems straightforward, a similar formation to Nash which was originally 'atten ashe', and both could have referred to minor place-names or, alternatively, to local landmarks. Bridger and Churchman have been said to indicate residence at the bridge and the church, but in each case an occupational meaning is also a possibility.

It is disquieting, when we are discussing matters such as this, to find ourselves saying of a surname that 'it meant either this or that', when it clearly meant one or the other. It has not been a problem for most compilers of dictionaries, who like to present alternative meanings and to include several names under one heading, but these practices confuse the non-expert and sometimes reflect the experts' own confused thinking. That confusion is understandable once we examine certain 'local names' which are said to be topographic in origin. These were defined by Richard McKinley as names deriving 'from a feature of the landscape, whether natural or man-made' and he contrasted them with 'locative' surnames which 'derived from the names of specific localities'. Amongst the 'topographical' names he then went on to discuss were many with one syllable, such as Brook, Field, Green and Wood, and a few compounds, such as Barkhouse, Broadhead, Cockshoot, Crabtree and Waterhouse. In fact it is not an easy classification to justify, for many of these so-called topographical surnames can be shown on closer examination to derive from identifiable localities.[17]

We can take Wood as an example. A man called John Wood was taxed in a township called Fixby in 1545; he was the owner of a house called the Wood that his family had already lived in for more than two hundred years. The title deeds for the property take its documented history back into the 1300s; the bundle is endorsed 'Wood Farm'. In fact, John Wood's ancestors may have been there even earlier, for there are references in Fixby to individuals called 'del Wode', or the equivalent 'de Bosco', from the mid thirteenth century. John died in 1570 without a male heir. When his daughter Agnes married Edward Saltonstall, 'her house called Wodd in Fixby' passed into that family's possession. It is just possible that we can say with reasonable accuracy when the place-name came into being, for a charter written just prior to 1202 refers to a grant of 'thirteen acres of land of the assart in the wood of Fekesbi'. A key reference in a separate charter suggests that this assart or clearance may have been the site of the farm that was later called Wood. There can be very few cases where the transition from clearance to settlement, place-name and family name is so explicit.[18]

We cannot presume that other families called Wood acquired their name in a similar way. The surname Brook, for example, has a long history in the same area as Wood and seems to be of the same type, but its origin may be genuinely 'topographical'. Examples occur from before 1300 and in the poll tax of 1379 four families called 'bythebroke' were taxed under Huddersfield, the only ones in the immediate area. The evidence suggests that they did not live in the town itself but beyond the stream or brook that runs between Huddersfield and Fixby, in a part of the manor that was the subject of continuing boundary disputes and where much of the woodland had still not been cleared. The stream was known at that time as the 'town brook' and is likely to be the source of the surname.

There is no evidence, though, of a settlement called Brook or Brook-house and, as the spelling 'bythebroke' survived much later locally than was usual for such names, it is far from clear whether it was hereditary in some cases. In 1434, for example, two Fixby tenants were named as William Diconson bythebroke, and John Maykinsone bythebroke. Dicon and Maykin were diminutives of Richard and Matthew, so we can interpret these names as William, the son of Richard, and John the son of Matthew – both living 'bythebroke' in a topographic sense. It was only after 1490 that the preposition 'by' was finally dropped and Brook(e) became the usual spelling.[19]

The impression is therefore that 'bythebroke' was a kind of place-name, referring to territory on the north or Fixby side of the town brook that was still common or waste for much of the 1400s. It was being progressively 'colonised' and, by the early 1500s, numerous settlements had been established and given place-names. These included Barkhouse, Blackhouse, Fieldhouse, Flashhouse, Greenhouse, Hillhouse, Newhouse, Woodhouse and Yatehouse. There were families called Brook in every one of these hamlets in the fifteenth and sixteenth centuries and the popularity of 'house' as a suffix seems unlikely to have been accidental. Finally, from the 1530s, the territory started to be called Fartown, the name it now bears: it was literally the 'far town' of Huddersfield, beyond the town brook, and seems to have replaced 'bythebroke' as a place-name.

The poll tax records of 1377–81 prove that 'Brook' occurred in many parts of England as a by-name and no doubt a good proportion of these became hereditary surnames. However, its distribution in 1881, with or without the final 'e', is evidence of its overwhelming expansion in and around Huddersfield. The total for Brook in Great Britain was 11,574, but of these 7613, or 66 per cent, lived in the West Riding. In Huddersfield alone there were 2387. The next highest totals were Middlesex 621, Lancashire 537 and Devon 420. Migration to the neighbouring county and to the London area might explain the first two of these, but Brook in Devon seems likely to derive from a place-name in that county, possibly Brook near Tavistock. The counties with fewest Brooks were Dorset (1) and Buckinghamshire (2). The picture for Brooke is very similar, although the overall total was only 4471 and the West Riding percentage was rather lower, only just over fifty. Again, the next highest totals were for Middlesex and Lancashire.[20]

When I suggested in 1973 that Brook was principally a Huddersfield surname, with a very restricted number of family origins, it was not a popular view, but the recent research into the Sykes Y chromosome has made the idea far more acceptable. However, if Brook was 'topographical', in the way that I suggest here, the families taxed in Huddersfield in 1379 need not have been related, so there would be added interest in a Y chromosome test. Whatever the results might be, the important points remain the same: we should not seek to classify a name until we are certain about its origin and meaning, and the terminology we use ought to be clear.

Place-Name Origins

Many surnames derive from place-names which appear to be unique. Typically distinctive examples are Pugsley (Devon), Edsall (Surrey), Greatorex (Derbyshire) and Fazackerley (Lancashire). From the point of view of those interested in surnames, the main problem in these cases is to discover whether more than one family took their name from the place. What we also need to remember, however, is that many place-names are not unique, which means that some surnames with identical spellings have origins that are totally unrelated. Sutton and Bradley are obvious examples.

Moreover, even apparently distinctive place-names can occur more than once. There are two Ringsteads, for example, one in Dorset and one in Norfolk: there is a Torrington in Devonshire and another in Lincolnshire; a Dorchester in Dorset and a Dorchester south east of Oxford; and there are Broughtons, Farleighs and Draytons in several counties. Few of us are familiar with every part of the country and we can be completely unaware that a place-name we know well has its counterpart elsewhere: for my part, when I first became interested in place-names, I was surprised to find that there is a Sheffield in Sussex, an Otley in Suffolk, a Whitby in Cheshire and a Wakefield near Stony Stratford. Occasionally, of course, the duplicated names are found not all that far apart and I remember how strange it once seemed to come across a Skipton in Swaledale, when the Skipton I knew was in Craven. It would be all too easy to jump to wrong conclusions about the origins of surnames derived from such place-names.

In the case of the surname Fenwick, for example, we need to take into consideration the fact that there are three major places in England so named, two of them in Northumberland. According to Godfrey Watson, *Northumberland Place Names* (1995), the innumerable Fenwick families along the border 'took their name from Fenwick near Stamfordham', not from Fenwick near Belford. Be that as it may, there were Fenwicks from the early 1300s in south Yorkshire, and others in Ayrshire, each family taking its by-name from a neighbouring village of Fenwick. It is slightly surprising therefore to read that Black, the authority on Scottish surnames, believed that 'the Border clan of Fenwicks were most probably kin to the Fenwicks ... of Northumberland'. If the earliest history of this surname is to be unravelled, it is clear that sources in all those places need to be studied.

It is also possible that place-names with the same spelling can have developed in quite different ways. Terrington in Norfolk, for example, has a different etymology from Terrington in North Yorkshire, but it seems to be identical in meaning with the Torrington in Lincolnshire already referred to, one case among many where the modern spellings mask a shared etymology. In fact the identification of a surname's origin is likely to prove difficult whenever a place-name occurs more than once, and further problems arise if it is spelt differently from the place-name it derives from. Dictionary entries for such names, especially for those which derive from a place-name that is widely distributed and has more than one meaning, can be very unreliable. The early history of the surnames Brearley and Brierley will illustrate some of these points.

A Linguistic Variation

The first thing that can be established here is that Brierley and Brearley are alternative forms of the same surname, a variation that reflects the history of 'brier' itself. This spelling dates only from the sixteenth century, or perhaps a little earlier, but the change from the earlier 'brere' remains a mystery and the word's etymology is unknown. There has also been a semantic change, for it formerly referred to any bush or shrub that was prickly and is now more usually associated with the wild rose. The change is reflected in the spelling of two major place-names, Brierley in Staffordshire and Brierley in Yorkshire, but it is less clear-cut in the development of the surname. That may be because some people feel very strongly about the spelling and pronunciation of their surname and have refused to break with tradition, but even so the two variants are found side by side in the parish registers, for instance 1583–85 James Brearley or Brierley of Elland. Just occasionally the alias is explicit, as in the following reference from the quarter sessions, i.e. 1764 Moses Brearley otherwise Brierley of Halifax.

The modern spelling of the place-names has probably helped Brierley to be more popular than Brearley but, even if they are counted together, they are far from being common generally. Lancashire is the 'home' of most Brierleys, accounting for 75 per cent of the national total in 1881, with Rochdale at the heart of its distribution, whereas most Brearleys are found in west Yorkshire. There Halifax is the major home of the name. Of course Rochdale and Halifax share a common boundary and this distribution certainly points to a northern origin, although it does not point to Brierley in Staffordshire as the likely source. Nor does it initially point to the Brierley which lies just to the north east of Barnsley. Because the surname is now so prolific in Rochdale, I had imagined that it might have a Lancashire origin, but Richard McKinley discounted this possibility and decided that it must derive from Brearley, a tiny place near Midgley in Halifax, just a few miles away.

He was mistaken, I feel sure, for this is a late place-name, not recorded before 1536. Brearley at that time was just a single dwelling, the home of a gentry family named Lacy whose main seat was a few miles away at Cromwellbottom. However, the family had property interests in Rochdale and also in Brierley near Barnsley, so they may have chosen the name to commemorate that connection. Transferred manorial names of this kind were not uncommon and there are places called Trimmingham and Dersingham in Halifax that appear to derive from Trimingham and Dersingham in Norfolk. If Brearley is such a name it could explain why the spelling did not change and that in turn may have influenced the spelling of the surname.

Of course that does not explain the massive expansion of the surname in east Lancashire, but the key to that may be a man called Thomas de Brerlay, who was taxed in 1379 in Saddleworth, a township on the Lancashire side of the Pennine watershed. It is a place with a curious history, for it was originally in Rochdale parish and yet formed part of Agbrigg wapentake in Yorkshire. The key to Thomas de Brerlay's presence there in 1379 may be that Brierley near Barnsley and Saddleworth in Rochdale had both been part of the Duchy of Lancaster.

4

The Local History of Place-Names

Books on place-names all agree that the subject goes far beyond etymology and that it can appeal to a wide variety of readers. Indeed it
has long been recognised that our place-names are interesting not only
as lexical items but also because they throw light on the topography of
the English landscape and on its historic development: they tell us about
settlement and clearance, highways and river crossings, husbandry, dialects, social customs and religious practices, and they reveal much about
our predecessors, both as groups and as individuals. Not surprisingly
non-linguists can be tempted to become more involved in the subject,
even to offer their own explanations of names, but that is not as easy
as some people imagine.

Indeed it is usual for books on place-names to begin with a warning
about the difficulties of place-name research and then to advise the
interested reader to consult two major sources: the appropriate county
volume of the English Place-Name Society series, where that is possible,
and, for more wide-ranging reference, Ekwall's *Oxford Dictionary of
English Place-Names* (1960). I am quite happy to endorse those recom-
mendations and to add to the list the names of scholars such as Margaret
Gelling and Gillian Fellows-Jensen, whose fascinating books on the
subject are models of accuracy. Although I am an admirer of all the
above works, however, I do not feel that they have said the last word
on the subject and I am confident that there are ways in which the local
historian can help the experts to find solutions to some of the problems
which place-names present.

Those who seek to be more involved are not immediately encouraged
by what they read. Kenneth Cameron's *English Place-Names* (1961) begins
with a useful chapter on the techniques which the researcher requires,
and which makes it clear how fundamental it is to record the name at
each stage in its history, right back to the very earliest spellings. More
dauntingly, as far as the amateur is concerned, he emphasises how

necessary it is, for those who seek to analyse the spellings, to understand the historical development of English sounds. Margaret Gelling's experience with enthusiastic amateurs has made her unashamedly impatient with all those who fail to understand that place-name study is an exacting philological discipline. She fully realises the value of the material to historians and archaeologists, but does not really want them to get involved in the linguistic arguments.

Nonetheless the informed and interested non-expert also has a point of view. Oliver Rackham, in *The History of the Countryside* (1986), was critical of philologists on three counts, accusing them of refusing to admit to ignorance, of sometimes clutching at straws, and, more seriously, of reading into place-names far more than they tell us. It was his opinion that the explanation of a place-name such as 'Staveley', for example, should not go beyond the identification of the two Old English elements involved, that is 'stave' and 'clearing'. He was scornful of interpretations such as 'clearing whence staves were cut', claiming that both 'whence' and 'were cut' are unwarrantable inferences. It is difficult to disagree with him when he says that we shall never know what the relation was between the stave and the clearing.

Clearly the study of place-names is a subject with many pitfalls for the unwary, and yet most place-name scholars concede that local historians have a part to play, not in the 'etymologies and identifications', it is true, but in the non-philological aspects of the subject. In other words, there is a role for the person who has a detailed knowledge of the topography and history of the local landscape, and this extends even to the so-called major place-names. It is these 'major' place-names which are the experts' priority, however much they express an interest in more recent material; but the study of names is not confined to those that evolved in the Old English period, and the interests of the experts and so-called amateurs are not incompatible when it comes to the interpretation of later names.

The earliest place-names derive from ancient languages which are completely unfamiliar to the average person, and even the experts are not familiar with them all. They can derive from a Celtic language, from Latin, Old English, Old Norse or Norman French, even from an obscure pre-Celtic language which may have left traces in the names of some rivers. Such a list is enough on its own to warn most people off. So, where the oldest place-names are concerned, much has to be taken on trust and that trust is readily given; such etymologies must be left to the attentions of the experts.

The fact is, however, that the majority of place-names, in almost every parish, did not evolve in that distant past. It would be impossible to say exactly what percentage came into being during the period of Middle and Modern English, during the last six or seven hundred years, but it must be considerable. I recently traced a map of the township of Honley, dated 1838, and found myself writing over one thousand place-names onto the copy. These included fields, wells, woods, lanes, farms, moors and other features of the landscape, and yet it was far from being a complete catalogue of Honley's names: not included were more recent names and many that had come and gone in the centuries before 1838. It serves to remind us that the English landscape is intensively named, and that many of these names are not of ancient origin.

When I turned to the section on Honley in the relevant volume of the English Place-Name Society series, I found that it lists ninety-one names in the township, of all types; only three of those were supported by evidence from before 1300. For forty of the names listed there was no evidence at all, and a further nineteen had been noted only in 1843. Etymologies were offered in just over twenty cases. This should certainly not be taken as typical, but it identifies what scope there might be for Honley's local historians, whose task it is to accumulate evidence for all the hundreds of names not included. Sometimes that information will then have to be passed over to the experts, but there are many more examples where the context itself will make the meaning clear.

There are therefore two distinct areas of place-name study open to local historians. Where the earliest, important names are concerned they can help to uncover new evidence and provide vital, non-philological information. They can do exactly the same for names that have developed in the Middle English and Modern English periods, but in these cases, provided due care is taken, it may also be possible for them to offer meaningful explanations. I hope now to illustrate how both these tasks might be carried out and start by looking at how A. H. Smith dealt with some of the major names in my own part of west Yorkshire, in part two of *Place-Names of the West Riding of Yorkshire* (1961).

Major Names

When we use the volumes of the English Place-Name Society the first thing we need to take into account is the way in which the material is organised, for it must be suspected that the arrangement is one that has more to do with editorial convenience than with philology, which can be very misleading for the local historian. In what seems like an order of descending importance we have wapentakes or hundreds (the sub-divisions of the county), then ecclesiastical parishes and townships, often what we might now call 'villages', where the territorial divisions are based on nineteenth- and twentieth-century sources. Under the name of each township come 'other major names (printed in small capitals), each treated separately', and these are followed by so-called minor names 'dealt with summarily in a single paragraph'. Finally we have the field names, divided into two categories: (a) 'modern field-names recorded since 1700'; and (b) 'medieval and early modern field-names recorded since before 1700'.[1] The immediate concern is that such a classification relies too heavily on nineteenth-century sources, ignoring the changed status of some place-names and hampering the accurate identification and explanation of others.

Status

For readers who are not familiar with the old West Riding it is important to know that many of the parishes were large but sparsely populated and that each contained several townships. There was moorland in the west where they bordered on Lancashire and they were separated from their Yorkshire neighbours by swift-flowing streams in deep-cut valleys, although these streams were not always the exact boundaries. This was true of Huddersfield which for much of its post-Conquest history consisted of three townships: Huddersfield itself, Slaithwaite and Quarmby. By the nineteenth century there were six townships and Smith duly named these as Huddersfield, Slaithwaite, Lindley, Longwood, Scammonden and Golcar, obviously unaware that the last four in the list had no independent status before 1800. Previously they had all been sub-divisions of Quarmby, which he listed under Lindley – misleadingly for historians.

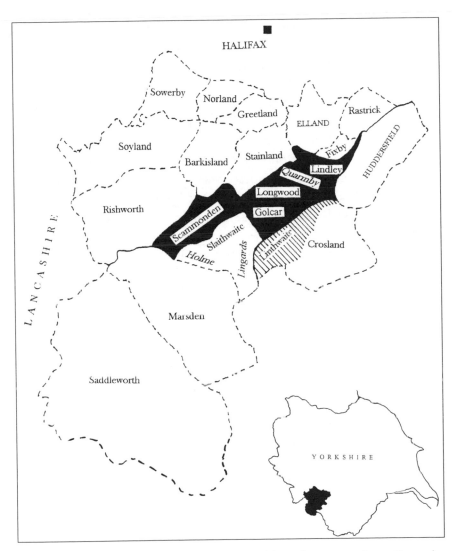

1. Quarmby: From the thirteenth century, and into the 1700s at least, Quarmby included the territories of Lindley, Longwood, Golcar and Scammonden, all of which later had independent status. In the same period parts of Linthwaite, across the River Colne, were also said to lie in Quarmby, e.g. Cowlersley (1497), Wiggin Cross (1591) and Flat House (1676). In 1597 Longroyd Bridge, across the same river, was maintained at the expense of Huddersfield and Quarmby.

This is no place for the complicated arguments that would make that point, but it is important to realise that accurate knowledge about Huddersfield's history depends on the identification.[2] The township is the context within which local historians work, it is the unit for taxation and communal farming; its inhabitants were responsible for their own poor and their own highways. Quarmby was already an estate at the time of Domesday and a vast territory through Tudor and Stuart times. The first 'official' evidence of its relationship to the other four territories was in the hearth taxes of the 1660s and 1670s, when they were all listed as 'quarters' of Quarmby, not as townships. Smith's failure to identify it as a major place-name does not affect the etymology he offered, but it masks the leading role of Quarmby in Huddersfield's development and certainly affects the historian's search for source materials and their interpretation.[3]

His entries on another territory in the parish are even more misleading. Bradley is a common place-name found in many counties, and the etymology 'broad clearing' poses no major problems. The Bradley near Huddersfield was another Domesday estate and it had independent township status as late as the thirteenth century. It declined in importance soon afterwards, however, perhaps because it became a grange of Fountains Abbey, and was absorbed into Huddersfield, where it continued to be a distinctive territory, at least manorially. After the Dissolution a gentry family called Pilkington acquired the abbey's Bradley territory, which was enclosed within a ring fence, and operated it as a woodland estate into the early 1800s. This early history and status may not seem to be the etymologist's concern, however significant it is for local historians, but Smith's failure to recognise Bradley's status is misleading and he compounded that by confusing it with several similar place-names.

From the 1500s the former township was often referred to as Nether Bradley, that is 'Lower' Bradley, and Smith stated that this was 'to distinguish it from Bradley Mills', a locality in Kirkheaton parish on the other side of the river. These were in fact fulling mills, apparently established in the mid 1500s, and they acquired their present name a century or so afterwards, when the miller or mill owner was a certain Mr Bradley. They were not in any way connected with Nether Bradley, which was given that name, at least in documents, to distinguish it from

Over or 'Upper' Bradley in Stainland, some six miles to the west. It is a distinction that probably owed something to the power and influence of the Savile family, who had interests in both places. Unfortunately, Smith also assumed that Bradley Mills was an ancient place-name and in support of that he quoted a reference to Bradley mill, dated 1195–1215. That was a mistake, for the mill referred to was a corn mill in Nether Bradley, not Kirkheaton.

These are not isolated problems. The truth is that mistakes sometimes arise simply because the expert philologist has never visited the places that he is writing about, which means that local historians who use the volumes must get into the habit of checking the references carefully. That is particularly true of any place-name which is duplicated in one area. Other important local names for which incorrect evidence is given include Edgerton and Egerton, the two Linthwaites, the two Shepherd Thornes and the two Marsdens, one of them in east Lancashire. It is not just Huddersfield that has been badly served, for there are similar problems when we look at neighbouring Bradford.

Girlington

This is one of several Bradford place-names that have been the subject of academic debate. It describes a part of Manningham township now swallowed up by the spreading city of Bradford. Smith treated it as an ancient settlement site, comparing it with the north Yorkshire place-name Girlington. He suggested that it meant 'Gyrla's farmstead', from an Old English personal name, whereas Dr Feilitzen thought the first element might be an unrecorded Old English word that would have been the antecedent of 'girl'. The debate about its possible meaning was totally divorced from its history.

Three early spellings were put forward as evidence that the locality was an ancient settlement site, dated to 1412, 1615 and 1658, and yet not one of the three references has anything to do with Girlington in Bradford: they refer instead to Girlington in north Yorkshire and to Grindleton in Ribblesdale, formerly spelt 'Gyrlington'. A chance reference to Bradford in the earliest document was no doubt responsible for the first and most important error, but the people mentioned in it were from Lancashire, so the Bradford reference was probably to Bradford in that county. The 'Gyrlington' referred to was clearly Grindleton in lower Ribblesdale. Some of the most obvious and informative sources were simply not consulted.

There is, for example, a superb map of Manningham by Robert Saxton, dated 1613, and there were just fields then in the area now occupied by Girlington. These are not named on the map but they were the property of a certain William Northrop, one of three Manningham men with that name: Girlington is not named in the survey that accompanies the map. The Bradford historian William Cudworth wrote of Girlington that it was an estate purchased in 1850–52 by the Bradford Freehold Land Society and then put up for sale in 250 lots. The aim was that purchasers would hold sufficient property to qualify as '40s. freeholders' and be entitled to a county vote. The abstract of title to the land takes its history back to 1782 when 'five closes in Manningham, formerly in one close called Girlington', were named as having been the property of William Northrop, deceased: in 1743 the name was Girlington Intacks.[4] Clearly Girlington was the name of an enclosure and had never been a medieval settlement: it was more probably a transferred name, directly from Girlington in north Yorkshire or indirectly via one of the two families whose surnames derived from that place-name or from Grindleton.

Greengates

Similar problems affect many more Bradford area names. Undercliffe, for example, is another suburb of the city, just one mile from the centre, and it is included among the major names, although for much of its history it had only topographic significance. Smith's earliest evidence is for 1606 but the deed he quotes refers to 'Hundercliff' as a field. Actually, because of its location, it is mentioned occasionally in local records from the fourteenth century, but, even as late as 1822, it was merely a tiny hamlet. The entry for Thornbury, another suburb, is even more confused, for it quotes just one reference, for 1547, and gives the etymology as 'fortified place overgrown with thorns'. The reader is then invited to compare it with Thornborough near Allerton Mauleverer some twenty miles away; yet a glance at the source will confirm that the reference is actually for Allerton Mauleverer. Names of suburbs in a city of such late growth as Bradford need to be looked at much more carefully and the clues can often be found in title deeds and maps.

The now busy suburb of Greengates, situated three miles from the city centre, will serve as an example. It lies in Eccleshill township and was first recorded in 1631 as 'the nether common called Greengates'. The origin of 'gate' in this case is significant, for in Yorkshire the word could have either an Old English or Scandinavian origin and the two meanings were somewhat contradictory. Celia Fiennes summed up the outsider's reaction when she wrote 'I observe the ordinary people ... in the northern parts ... tell you its a very good gate, instead of saying it is a good way, and they call their gates *yates*'. Usually a 'green gate' was a way across a common, but, in this case, the plural was employed consistently and the name derives from the gates at the northern and southern extremities of the green, where it was crossed by a lane running from Eccleshill to Apperley.

There was also 'a newly built house' there in 1631, with land taken from the green – clear evidence that it was under pressure from an expanding local population. By the 1650s, when the parish registers were referring to where people lived, they described families called Briggs, Swaine and Kitchen as 'of Greengates', and there is a small group of houses on a map of 1705 that marks the site of the growing community. The map relates to a dispute about water rights, as the green or common was opened up to further building and enclosure, and one deposition actually mentions the 'Lower Common Close' where the plaintiff kept his cattle. The defendant was alleged to have maliciously diverted the water 'out of its Ancient Current' and another tenant had dug a ditch 'on purpose to drain a Bogg in Common Layne'. These were routine complaints, but they illuminate the transition that was taking place in this part of the parish.

Place-Names and Boundaries

In other cases it is the significance of duplicated names that is not commented on, particularly those which are located on important watersheds. Huddersfield is in a hilly part of the Pennines and boundary disputes in the 1600s suggest that it was customary then for the watershed to be looked on as the dividing line between townships. That was not always so, for in my own township of Lepton there are settlements on each flank of a ridge which carries a major highway: Little Lepton to the south and Great Lepton to the north, each situated close to a source of fresh water. Elsewhere though major ridges define the western and eastern limits of the district and two places called Whitley mark the eastern boundary, one in Kirkheaton parish and the other in Thornhill; to the west are two Lindleys, one in Huddersfield and the other in Halifax – belonging to different wapentakes. In these cases the distinguishing prefixes, Upper and Lower, Old and Nether, are relatively late, and the inference is that the original settlements straddled the ridge, as they did in Lepton, and were later separated by major boundary changes. That may not be the etymologist's concern, but the presentation of the evidence for the places named Whitley and Lindley masks the fact that each of these names occurs twice, in adjoining townships – and the potential significance of that for the historian.

In other cases the spellings for an important locality appear under different headings. For example, Haigh in Quarmby was a distinctive territory as early as the twelfth century when it passed into the possession of Fountains Abbey, and it gave rise soon afterwards to the prolific local surname Haigh. Some spellings for the place-name are correctly listed under Haigh House in Longwood, of which territory it was a detached part, but others appear incorrectly under either Haughs in Golcar or Haughs in Lindley. It is worth remembering that all three places were actually in the ancient township of Quarmby discussed earlier.

Etymological Problems

At other times the failure to identify major localities correctly leads to what must be wrong etymologies. Smith's only evidence for Holme in Slaithwaite, now Lower and Upper Holme, is a single Ordnance Survey reference of 1843, and he derives the name from 'holmr' meaning a water meadow. In fact Holme was a major hill-top settlement, referred to in charters from about 1200, when it was occasionally credited with 'vill' or township status. The earliest spellings include Houwom, Howom and Haume, and these seem to point to a Scandinavian dative plural 'i haugum' meaning 'on the hills', a meaning which exactly describes the situation of the present hamlets. In other words, Holme in Slaithwaite can be compared etymologically with Holme on the Wolds in Yorkshire's East Riding. The surname Hawme, which derived from the Slaithwaite place-name, was also absorbed eventually by the more common surname Holmes.

Yateholme is another place-name in the area which seems likely to have been misunderstood. Domesday Book refers to two local vills named 'Holne', one clearly represented by modern Holme, near Holmfirth. The other 'Holne' has been traditionally identified by both historians and place-name specialists as Yateholme, a single farmhouse until its demolition in 1937. Archaeologists have discovered no trace there of a medieval settlement, and it must also be said that the place-name evidence for such a settlement is weak. In fact, the modern spelling 'Yateholme' has no great antiquity and I have found no reference to the place-name itself earlier than 1434, even though the court rolls are extant from 1274 with relatively few gaps. Typical spellings for the 1400s, and even as late as the 1600s, are Yhatom, Yatam and Yatum, and these appear to point to a dative plural of the word 'yate', our modern 'gate', certainly not to 'Holne'.

Liley Hall is a timber-framed house, high on the hill that now marks the boundary between Huddersfield and Mirfield. It is an old ridge route and the site of several hamlets that can be traced to the late twelfth and early thirteenth centuries. Smith had several references to Liley from 1589 but none with 'Hall' as the second element until the nineteenth century. He thought that it probably meant 'flax clearing' – 'with a common loss of -n- as in Lillands', a locality in Rastrick just a few miles away.

A family called Thurgarland lived at Liley from 1493 until the early 1700s, and for much of that time they enjoyed gentry status. That appears to have changed by 1709, when Richard Thurgarland, a tanner, sold the 'capital messuage called Lyley' to another tanner from south Yorkshire. The original deed of purchase, back in 1493, shows that an earlier Richard Thurgarland had acquired the house by marrying Beatrix Lyley, the daughter and sole heiress of William Lyley. At that time the property was called Lyley Place, so named because it was literally the Lyleys' place, but it became Lyley or Liley once the Thurgarlands were in occupation.

The solution to the meaning of Liley, as both a surname and place name, is in the numerous charters and deeds that refer to the Liley family. They were in that area from the twelfth century and it is possible to take their name back to the spelling 'Lile' in the early 1400s and then even earlier to 'de Lisle' or 'de Lile'. In those documents where the name was latinised it was usually 'de Insula', confirming that it derived from the French word for an island. The 'de Insula' family was of considerable status in the West Riding in the middle ages, holders of a fee that included property in Harewood and Beeston. It is worth noting that in Glover's Visitation of 1612 George Thurgarland of Liley claimed descent from 'William de Insula of Lyle'.[5]

The Shelley place-name Ox Ings was taken by Smith at face value, that is 'ox meadows', but this form of the name was the work of map makers, from Greenwood to the Ordnance Survey. It is certainly not known locally, where the written and spoken forms are Ozzings. In fact, Smith had the spelling 'Osanz', dated 1381, but chose to interpret it as an Anglo-Norman influence, failing to notice 'Ozings' on the Jefferys map of 1775 and parish register spellings such as Ozyns. The etymology is clear from unpublished documents, which refer to Osanplace in 1411, when John Osane was living there.[6] This Shelley family is on record for almost two hundred years and we can be reasonably certain that the progenitor was John, son of Osanna (c. 1250).[7] This confirms the origin as the female name Osanne, which derives from 'hosanna' and may have been given to a girl child born on Palm Sunday.

Interpretations that are based on late evidence are almost bound to be speculative and Grimwith, in the township of Appletreewick, is a good example of how the picture changes as new evidence comes progressively to light. The first spelling until recently was Grymwith House (1540). This was said to derive from two Norse words and mean something like 'goblin wood'. Grimwith alias Grymouth Houses, recorded in 1601, alerts us to an alternative spelling and this proves to be the one we need to explain. A family called Grymmoth was living in Appletreewick in 1473 and they descend from the de Gyrmouths taxed in the village in 1379. The typical spelling in the period back to 1296 is de Gyrnemouth. Grimwith House was the family's home, but the element 'house' did not long survive their departure.

The recently published accounts of Bolton Priory identify this place as a stock farm in the early fourteenth century, and there are annual references to haymaking and to the various herdsmen employed there. In 1306 clearances were carried out which involved digging ditches, putting up new walls, mending old walls and repairing buildings. It was a busy and important medieval settlement and the later spelling Grim-with was clearly a piece of popular etymology. The earliest spellings of both the surname and the place-name are remarkably similar to those of the Norfolk place-name Yarmouth.

A Major Place-Name Ignored

Given the scope of his eight volumes on the West Riding, it is hardly surprising that some important place-names escaped Professor Smith's attention and that others were placed in the wrong township, but the failure to make any comment on the etymology of the 'Pennines' is a strange omission. The name is certainly not in the detailed index he provided, even though he felt bound to use it in his introduction, and I cannot find it in the text. He wrote of the West Riding as ranging 'from the marshlands of the south east through the great industrial and urban area of the coalfield ... itself a hilly and well-wooded landscape, to the Pennines in the West', so it cannot be that he gave the name no thought.

Perhaps it was omitted because it does not belong exclusively to Yorkshire but, if that were what determined a name's inclusion in the county volumes, he would also have had to omit several district and river names, like Bowland and Ribble, both shared with Lancashire. In fact no county editor seems willing to comment on the origin of 'the Pennines', and it is absent also from Cameron's *Place-Names of Derbyshire* (1959) and Ekwall's *Place-Names of Lancashire* (1922), an apparent conspiracy of silence.

There are though one or two writers who have found space for it, if somewhat hesitantly. Margaret Gelling, perhaps the most respected voice in modern place-name studies, thought the name was probably Celtic, beguiled no doubt by the 'Pen' prefix. She linked it with the Malverns, the Cheviots and the Quantocks, evocative hill names which take us back to a pre-Anglo-Saxon landscape. The late Kenneth Cameron, another great place-name scholar, who was born in Burnley in the heart of the Pennines, was not of that opinion. He dismissed the idea of a

Celtic origin and described the name as 'a forgery', saying that it was attributed by Charles Bertram (1723–65) to Richard of Cirencester, a twelfth-century monk, although 'where he got the name from is unknown, nor do we know any name for the whole range before the eighteenth century'.

The view expressed by Cameron is one that has been popular with a range of other writers over the last ninety years or so, certainly with James Johnson, who thought it had 'no ancient history' (1915) and with John Field 'a late name, the earliest record being of eighteenth-century date and almost certainly a deliberate invention of one William (sic) Bertram'. It would be tedious to repeat all the similar views expressed in books on place-names, views which found clear expression in an article by D. Robbins in an issue of the *Pennine Magazine* in 1985. This essay had the title 'Britain's Biggest Con Trick'. The claim was that the name had been invented by Charles Bertram, the man already referred to, when he was teaching in a naval college in Copenhagen in the 1700s. Bertram was lonely, it is said, and to ease the tedium he compiled an account in Latin of all that was known of Britain in Roman times, and of surviving Roman remains, attributing the work to a monk called Richard of Cirencester.

Bertram's important 'find' attracted the backing of the scholar William Stukeley, who translated the text and had it published. Alpes Pennini was one of the names in the text allegedly coined by Bertram, whilst Alpes Pennies Montes appeared on one of the maps. This term was not his only invention. It is said that many of Bertram's imaginary names of Roman stations eventually found their way onto the Ordnance Survey maps. Indeed, traces of his misleading influence continued well into the twentieth century and he was, according to the *Dictionary of National Biography*, the cleverest and most successful literary impostor of modern times.

If we search for the very first references to the word Pennines, it is true that it seems to go back no further than the early 1800s. I first came across it in a geography book of 1876, in which the author referred to 'the great range of hills called the Pennine Chain', but the term had been chosen even earlier by Conybeare and Phillips for their *Outlines of the Geology of England and Wales* (1822). They mentioned the Alpes Penini, and quoted Richard of Cirencester's chronicle as the source, saying 'we shall therefore henceforth call them the Penine Chain'. H. E. Wroot, in an article about the Pennines, in 1930, commented on Bertram's forgery but added 'now because a general name is convenient our hills are Pennine to the end of time'. Arthur Raistrick, in *The Pennine Dales* (1968), also stressed how useful the name was, saying that Defoe had found it convenient to refer to them as the English Andes and that 'Bertram's pseudo-discovery gave them a name which was at once accepted'.

So the term Pennine Chain was an invention, if not exactly Bertram's, and it soon became more popular than Penine Alps, used as a literal translation by J. A. Giles in 1841. In fact, other writers had already described the hills as a 'chain': Marshall in 1788 and Aikin in 1796; the latter also describing them as 'a back-bone through all the north of England'. Reading these works it is easy to understand how useful the new name Pennine Chain would be for geographers and travel writers.

There the matter might be closed, except that other nineteenth-century writers, local historians in particular, seldom took advantage of this useful new term. For Morehouse, in 1861, the 'extensive mountain range was called the English Apennines', and that phrase is found also in James (1841), Hunter (1819) and Whitaker (1816). Nor was it a phrase that they had coined, for local historians and travel writers had used the analogy, if not the exact words, for centuries. Defoe, credited by Raistrick with the term the English Andes, had also written of 'these mountains ... that they may be said to divide Britain, as the Appenine Mountains divide Italy' (*c.* 1724). The diarist Thoresby described Ingleborough, incorrectly as it happens, as 'the highest of our English Apennines' in 1694, but even he was not the first; the great antiquary Dodsworth likened the range to the Italian Apennines on more than one occasion, especially when commenting on the sources of Yorkshire's rivers – the River Don, for example; 'Dun riseth in the upper part of Peniston parish nere Lady Crosse which may be called our Appenine because the Raine water that falleth sheddeth from sea to sea'. The date here is uncertain but is likely to be in the 1630s.

The first references I have noted, however, take the idea back into Elizabethan times, to Camden, who likened the Yorkshire town of Skipton 'hidden and enclosed among steep Hilles to Latium in Italie, which Varro supposeth to have been called because it lyeth close under

the Apennine and the Alps'. More pertinently he made a direct comparison between our northern hills and the Italian range, drawing
attention to the lack of a unifying name:

> the North part ... riseth up and swelleth somewhat mountainous, with
> moores and hilles, but of no bignesse, which beginning here runs like as
> Apennine doth in Italie, through the middest of England ... even as far as
> Scotland, although oftentimes they change their name.

There is no doubt that Camden's work was widely read, so it is probable
that Bertram was just one of many who directly compared the two
mountain ranges, and then took advantage of the idea when he composed his forged chronicle. He cannot be credited with inventing the
name, for its use clearly goes back long before the eighteenth century,
and we cannot be certain that Camden was the first to make the allusion.
The chances are that it was a commonplace among travellers who were
familiar with the two countries.

5

Minor Place-Names

The major contribution that the local historian can make to place-name studies is in the field of minor names, many of them coined in the Middle English period. Here he or she might hope to find the sort of detailed documentation that makes speculation unnecessary. The court rolls of the manor of Wakefield are such a source, with almost a complete run from 1274 to 1925. Two series of these have been published, eighteen volumes in all, but, substantial as these are, they account for only a fraction of what is available, and such is the detail in the unpublished material that we can establish with great accuracy the chronological sequence to settlement in the manor. What follows is an account of one such hamlet that had its origin before 1350, some two centuries earlier than the previous place-name evidence had predicted.

Medieval Fulstone

Six miles to the south of Huddersfield, surrounded by great hills and moors, lies the small town of Holmfirth, the main settlement now in a region of scattered farms and hamlets. The landscape around the town is famous as the setting for the long-running television series *Last of the Summer Wine*, but for much of its history it was a remote and inhospitable part of Wakefield manor, a forest region known as the Graveship of Holme, comprising eight separate territories. These sub-divisions of the graveship were extensive but thinly populated, and they had only hamlet status, that is to say they enjoyed a degree of autonomy but were not townships. Their names were Austonley, Cartworth, Fulstone, Hepworth, Holme, Scholes, Upperthong and Wooldale.

Fulstone is a tiny place, no more than a couple of miles from Holmfirth as the crow flies, its few attractive, stone-built cottages set on the rim of a terrace, high above the valley. It seems curiously abandoned and has an air of somehow having missed out on the industrial revolution that transformed its neighbours. It is an ancient place, founded by Anglian settlers and recorded in Domesday Book, but it has no church or chapel, no public house, no school and no shops, in fact no discernible amenities of any kind, and the sense of arrested development is further emphasised by the beautifully preserved open-field system which lies beyond it, the ancient divisions marked by well-maintained dry stone walls. There is no written history to enlighten us about what happened here, but the clues are in the place-names.

This present account deals first of all with the names of just three localities in the territory: Butterley, New Mill and Ebson House, places which are closely linked both geographically and historically. Each of the names is relatively easy to explain etymologically but more satisfying than that is their exact 'meaning', which begins to emerge once the documents are studied in detail, and their joint significance, as the solution of one name leads into the next, an unfolding story of the early 1300s in which locally important individuals are identified, and light is thrown on a flourishing community. As that success is revealed so we begin to understand what may have happened to Fulstone all those centuries ago.

New Mill

The populous village of New Mill lies in the valley bottom, a few hundred feet below Fulstone and less than a mile away. In the 150th anniversary souvenir of its church there was an interesting article which touched on various aspects of life in the village in the 1830s and 1840s. The picture which emerged was perhaps not dissimilar from that of many of its neighbours: there were inns and beer-houses, several textile mills, a school, a chapel and, of course, from 1831, the fine new church which in more ways than one provided the community with a heart and an identity. It had not always been so. New Mill means literally 'the new mill' and in one sense the history of the village is the story of how that mill was established, how it acted as a focus for settlement and development, and how, eventually, the words 'new mill' came to signify the community itself.

The original mill was a corn mill, erected just before 1315, the year when it is first recorded in the manor court rolls. It was 'new' by comparison with the manorial corn mill on the River Holme which had served the graveship's scattered population for some years. The foundation of this second mill, on a feeder stream of the river, was a response to major developments in this southern half of Holmfirth, and that is first brought to our attention in 1307. In the roll for August that year there were over sixty entries for 'new' land that had been taken from the waste, a total of more than 150 acres in all. Such activity was unprecedented, and the clearance continued, bringing more and more land into cultivation. Some rolls from this period have not survived and the full extent of the operation cannot be calculated, but even so it is clear that some of the hamlets in Fulstone were among the places most affected. As more land came under the plough there would have been a real need for a new mill to be built, if only to ease the pressure on the old corn mill. It would also have been a financially attractive proposition for the lord of the manor and those who farmed it and its location so close to Fulstone would have made it convenient for tenants in the southern half of the graveship.

Butterley

Where Butterley now stands there was once only woodland but, at a very early period in Fulstone's history, probably before the Normans arrived in England, settlers had already cleared some of the trees and converted the land to rich, butter-producing pasture. That is the traditional interpretation of the place-name and it finds some support in the present location of the hamlet, set amongst green fields which slope gently down to the woods by the stream. We have no records to confirm that meaning, nor to tell us just how old the settlement might be, but it must surely have existed long before 1275, when there are references to tenants called 'de Butterley'. In that year, for example, Herbert de Butterley made a complaint against Richard de Fouleston, saying that he had beaten him so severely as to draw blood. The evidence of the rolls makes it clear that these were by-names rather than hereditary surnames, and they simply tell us where the two men lived.

For us now the name Butterley means the hamlet, a group of grey stone cottages clustered round a rather grander house erected by John Kay in the 1740s, but it must formerly have been an extensive territory, its boundaries roughly defined by the present highways to the east and north west. When the clearances were being made there, from 1307, eight acres in Butterley were listed in four separate, named localities: they were described as 'under the nabbe', the 'grene', the 'kerre' and the 'stiel'. These are difficult features now to identify and the 'stiel' or stile was no doubt a transient feature, as was the 'grene' which could have been any patch of uncultivated land. However the 'nab' was probably the scarp slope above the hamlet and the 'kerre' or marshy area may be where today's Carr House stands. The tenant called Herbert de Butterley who lived here is the key to the third of the place-names under consideration.

Ebson House

There are several references to Herbert de Butterley after 1275. His was by no means a usual first name and it had the pet form Hebbe, so it is not difficult to pick him out in the rolls. For example, in 1285 he was fined 12*d.* for allowing his beasts to stray, and he served on a manorial inquisition the following year; but these are among the last direct references to him and he may have died soon afterwards. Before he did so though he acted as surety for Thomas de Butterley, when he took 9½ acres of new land in Fulstone in 1286. Such clearances were rare at that time and it is worth noting that the family's interests were not confined to Butterley where they had their home. There is a gap in the rolls between 1298 and 1306, but then we almost immediately encounter references to Herbert's descendants, Richard, Robert and Thomas, three men who all had the by-name 'son of Herbert'.

These three were all involved in the large-scale clearances which began in 1307, and Richard in particular seems to have had a special interest in the Fulstone lands. For example in 1313, when he was described as Richard son of Hebbe, he surrendered '12½ acres with buildings' in Fulstone to his daughter and then took possession of them again for the term of his natural life. In 1332, Herbert's grandson Thomas paid 4*s.* when he inherited this property, part of which was named as a dwelling house. He was named as Thomas, son of Richard, son of Hebbe. These might seem tiresome details but what they tell us in total is that 'Hebbeson House' was already in existence, some 250 years before any direct reference to the place-name has been noted. It might be claimed that the name would only have developed later, during the occupation of succeeding generations of the family, but that cannot be so, as we shall see.

The references which confirm that 'Hebson' had become a hereditary surname unfortunately also tell us that it cannot have survived much beyond the Black Death of 1348–49. In 1350, for example, Alice, the daughter of Thomas Hebson, took possession of a cottage and six acres in Fulstone. The fact that she was identified as his heir means that no male Hebsons survived: in 1351 Agnes, the widow of Thomas Hebson, paid 12d. for licence to marry a man called John Alcock, and he was later named as Alice's guardian, with control of her property until she should come of age. She was the great grand-daughter of Herbert and the surname in Fulstone must have died with her. The place-name survived, however, and the hamlet of Ebson House is still there on the sloping side of a hill which looks down on the field system and on Fulstone itself. It is a landscape that confirms the early decline of Fulstone and the emergence of New Mill as the focal point in the township.

There are numerous names of similar hamlets in and around Holm firth, such as Choppards in Wooldale, which was the home between 1298 and 1333 of Robert Chopard, a man who moved into the graveship from Wakefield. Close by is Totties, where William Totty lived from 1314. Neither of these by-names survived the Black Death and the inference once again is that the hamlets were established roughly about the time the 'new' mill was built, two and three hundred years earlier than the direct place-name evidence.[1] There is a slightly different picture in Austonley, another hamlet in the graveship. Here much of the initial clearance was carried out by a family that took its name from the locality. Gilbert de Alstanley gave 2s. in 1307 for two acres at 'Dobberode' and the 'Lonehende', the latter now part of Gibriding Lane, that is Gib or Gilbert's clearance; close by was Mocock Place, named after Mocock or Matthew de Alstanley, Gilbert's son. At the end of Gibriding Lane, and higher up the hill at the limit of cultivation, is the ruined shell of a farm called Bartin. It derives from a diminutive of Bartholomew, and commemorates the transfer of land there in 1509 to Bartin Brodehede by his father John.

Lost Place-Names

Some of the most distinctive surnames in west Yorkshire derive from place-names that cannot now be found on the map and, in many cases, the settlement site has not even been identified. When that happens it always leaves a question mark over the name's origin and that is disappointing for family historians, who like to visit their exact 'ancestral' home. The Ickringills, for example, are told that their surname derives from Ickering Gill in Beamsley near Skipton, a name which means 'squirrel ravine', and there are certainly references in early deeds to such a place. In 1329 'Ecorngill' in Beamsley was a vaccary or stock farm, in the possession of the Mauleverer family, and it was still a farm in 1518 when John Franklayn was the tenant. In works on place-names though it is simply said to be 'lost' and, as we cannot visit a place of that name now, or see it on a map or local signpost, I suppose it is lost.

In other cases there is not even a mention of the place-name. People called Cordingley or Hemingway cannot visit places with those names, nor can they find them in any of the reference works, certainly not in the volumes published by the English Place-Name Society, and that is even more disappointing. In fact the proof that they derive from place-names rests on the tiny preposition 'de', which is found in the earliest references to the surnames: Richard de Hemmy(n)gway was fined for trespassing in Hipperholme in 1309 and Richard de Cordonlay lived in Bowling in 1379, so we are inclined to believe that these names originated somewhere in the Brighouse and Bradford area. There is no proof of that, but attempts to discover possible sources outside the county have also been unsuccessful and we are no nearer discovering where the settlements of Cordingley and Hemingway once were. Hamlets such as Bottomley and Shackleton may now be not much bigger than they were in the middle ages but at least they can still be visited by the many families called Bottomley and Shackleton.

Occasionally the place-name responsible for the surname is not 'lost' but merely difficult to find. For a long time Cowgill was mistakenly thought by the American branch of the family to derive from Cowgill near Dent, and there are several identical place-names in other parts of the Dales that further complicate the issue. The evidence of the surname is therefore a vital clue in the identification; it was already quite widely dispersed by 1379, with examples in Nesfield, Malham, Arncliffe and Threshfield, and that distribution is not as random as might at first appear. Three of those villages are on the fringes of Malham Moor and it is there in Bordley that we find Cow Gill, a tenement that once belonged to Fountains Abbey. The connection can safely be inferred since the place-name and the surname were both originally 'Colgill', nothing to do with cows therefore but probably the Scandinavian personal name *Kolli*.[2]

The link between surname and place-name can also be difficult to trace if the place-name has changed fundamentally in the last six or seven hundred years. Murgatroyd in Warley was the home of the Murgatroyds for centuries, but by the early 1700s it was being referred to as Murgatroyd alias Hollins and it is Hollins that is now on the map. The initials of the Murgatroyd family are still, however, on the massive lintel of the fireplace at The Hollins. In the same area Rawnsley survives as Cliff and Stancliffe as Scout, whilst farther south the Micklethwaites owe their name to a settlement in Cawthorne now known as Banks Hall; it was already 'Bankes alias Mikelthwaite by 1580'. I can think of no satisfactory reason why such distinctive place-names should be abandoned in favour of something more ordinary.

Local historians can do a great deal to throw light on such origins, by searching through court rolls, title deeds and the like. The surnames Crabtree and Waterhouse will illustrate the point. Crabtree was said by Richard McKinley to be 'topographic' in origin, simply because he could find no possible place-name source, but Crabtree was 'de Crabtre' in Sowerby in 1391, so it may derive from a locality with that name mentioned in Bradford court rolls in 1355. Its exact location is not known but it was almost certainly close to where the Crabtrees lived. Waterhouse is more difficult, for it flourished in Skircoat near Halifax for centuries and is traditionally associated with that parish. Because there is no local place called Waterhouse there have been some wild theories about the surname's origin, notably the suggestion that it came into the area from Lincolnshire. In fact the surname and place-name are both recorded from an early date in Golcar, a territory some miles from Skircoat but in the same manor. The locality was in Crimble Clough, close to where the brook runs into the River Colne, and it is the most likely source of the surname.

Littlewood and Hinchliffe are Holmfirth surnames which also demand careful 'detective' work by the local historian, although both are recognised more generally as having west Yorkshire origins. It is usual to say that Hinchliffe derives from Hinchliffe Mill near Holmfirth, but that is not the case and the mill owes its name to the fact that it was tenanted for generations by members of the Hinchliffe family. William Hyncheclyff was there in 1503 and another William Hinchliffe 'of Hinchliffe Mill' was the 'fuller' in 1646. The locality which gave rise to the surname is referred to once in the court rolls, in 1307, but Holmfirth was a vast territory and it is not clear from the context exactly where it was. Fortunately, a more specific reference turned up recently in some deeds I was working on in Kansas. Hinchliffe was given there as a boundary marker in a perambulation of Netherthong, which was in a different manor. Nevertheless its immediate neighbour was Upperthong and this township was in Holmfirth, so we know that the medieval hamlet was on the boundary between the two and can work out with reasonable accuracy where it must have been.

Identifying Littlewood was equally satisfying, especially as it is listed incorrectly under Wooldale by Professor Smith. There is no place called Littlewood now in the Holmfirth region, but it was prominent enough in the thirteenth- and fourteenth-century court rolls and was even said at one time to have 'vill' or township status. Many of the references were to new land being brought under cultivation in 'Littlewood' and the inference is that it was a territory rather than a settlement site. For example, in 1274, John de Lyttlewode gave 3s. 4d. for licence to take 14 acres of land in Littlewode from Geoffrey his father.[3] Similar entries occur until 1317 but not later so the possibility is that clearance on this scale finally removed the 'little wood' from the landscape. The evidence suggests that Lower and Upper Woodhouse in Cartworth emerged in that period as settlements in the former wood.[4]

The few place-names discussed above are examples of just some of the 'lost' Pennine settlements. There were many others that gave rise to surnames and then either disappeared from the records or suffered a significant change in status, e.g. Bairstow, Binns, Gledhill, Hollingrake, Ormondroyd and Sowden. It is not a topic that has received much attention but one possibility is that the so-called Black Death of 1348–49 was responsible, not simply because so many people died but because those who survived may have been able to move to areas where the land was more productive. There is a hint of that in the distribution of certain surnames before and after 1349, most obviously in such cases as Fixby, Hipperholme and Shibden, which relocated to Rothwell, Pontefract and Normanton. Less obvious was the migration into south Yorkshire of names such as Fulstone and Hogley and moves made by the numerous Hepworths into areas around Almondbury and Kirkheaton.

A Riverside Name

There are certain place-names that we traditionally associate with the riverside and in the north 'holme' is one of the best known of these; a word of Scandinavian origin that is usually interpreted as 'water meadow'. However, it can also mean an island, as it does frequently in the Lake District; Belle Isle on Windermere was formerly called 'The Holme' and then 'Long Holme' only being given its modern name after Isabella Curwen purchased it in 1781. Durham was originally 'Dunholm', that is 'hill island', an apt description of the city built on a rocky hill above the River Wear. 'Holme' also described higher, dry ground in a marshy area, as at Levenshulme in Lancashire. In other compound names such as Axholme in Lincolnshire, it tells us where there was once an island. In fact the area is still referred to as the Isle of Axholme even though the waters have long since receded.

Much less well known is 'steaner', an archaic word that was formerly in common use in Yorkshire, perhaps as late as the 1750s. Its meaning can be deduced from the contexts in which it occurs; in 1581, for example, Thomas Pilkington sold some land by the River Calder to his neighbour Mr Armytage and it is described precisely in the conveyance as 'one parcell of lande and water, contayneinge ... one acre or thereabowtes, commonly callid a steanor, adioyninge and lienge alongest the sowth syde of the Callder'.[5] In the 1600s the same word was used frequently by witnesses at the quarter sessions when they were discussing flood damage. In 1649 it was claimed that the current of the river at Horbury was impeded by 'a banck, sandbed or stayner', and that it would be necessary to cut through the obstruction to restore the flow to its former channel.[6] A similar recommendation was made five years later in Leeds when a 'stainder ... cast upp by the vyolence of severall great floods' had put the bridge there in danger.[7] The last reference of this type that I have found was for 1718.

A steaner was therefore the debris cast up by a river in flood, composed of sand, stones and gravel, or a piece of land covered with debris that had been isolated by a change in the course of the river. A map of 1598 shows such a steaner in a significant semi-circular bend of the River Calder, the type of bend that geographers call an ox-bow: it was 'in controversye', its ownership debated by the landlords on either side of the river. In 1625 there was a similar dispute in Rastrick about a steaner that was said to consist of land 'won and encreassed ... by force of the river, some at one tyme and some att an other'. The problems that such flooding could cause over the years are made plain in a memorandum:

> Note also that the said River hath made in former ages great alteration of Landes for that there is two closes of Mr Lacyes beinge by Southe the said River which be parcell of Sowthowram and other two closes of Mr Thornhills which lye by Northe the said River and be parcell of Rastricke. Which closes are accounted as forced from their severall Townshippes by alteracion of the said Ryver.[8]

So a flooding river might alter its course and separate a farmer from some of his land, making access extremely difficult. Court rolls of the period contain numerous references to such pieces of land and to the by-laws that required tenants to defend their closes by erecting 'wears' or water banks. Many neglected to do so and six tenants in Ossett were fined 6s. 8d. each in 1664 for 'not wearing' their lands. These wears, or weirs to use the modern spelling, could be substantial structures, made of piles that were 'hooped' and 'shoed' in special circumstances, presumably with iron, and they were bound together by hazel wands. They are mentioned in township records from 1340 to 1840 and one that was built in Deighton was designed to protect 968 square yards of land on a river front of 140 yards. It was calculated that about 350 piles would be required, not counting 'hedgewood', and it would cost £100.

Flooding had been an annual hazard in these Pennine valleys throughout the documented period, regularly destroying bridges, houses and riverside fields, but it was less apparent in the 1800s, possibly because of improved draining and the diverting of excess water into the canals. The use of steaner as a place-name element reflects this change for we

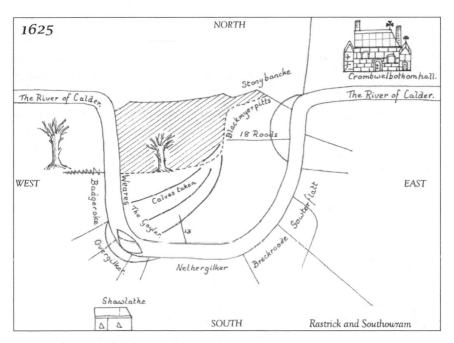

2. The steaner and 'blackmyerpitts' on the River Calder at Rastrick.

find 'elynstener' in Horbury in 1348, a 'close called the Steynour' near the Calder in Mirfield in 1494 and a close of Widow Bothomley's on the Colne 'called the Steaner' in 1672. After that, as the word fell out of regular use in the 1700s, it was frequently spelt Stannard or Stennard and then, finally, Stanyard. Perhaps the best-known of the place-names that derive from this word is Steanard Lane in Mirfield which runs along the river bank. In 1999, when plans were approved in Mirfield for massive sand and gravel extraction near Sands Lane, access to the site was to be via Steanard Lane.[9]

On some of the maps that I located there were steaners that had survived and been brought under cultivation and I noticed that in several of these there were places described as 'pits'. The most explicit names were 'Blackmyerpitts' and 'Carr Pitt'. I soon found similar minor names in documentary sources, together with some inconclusive evidence of their exploitation. The only explanation I can offer is that these names identified sections of the steaners where alluvium or black earth was being extracted, with the aim of improving the quality of the land elsewhere in the parish. Methley inhabitants had a right of way to the 'town mires' in the early 1500s and were ordered to cleanse a ditch between 'the Myers and the Stener' in 1518.[10] In 1755 a Mirfield diarist listed 'black earth', up to twelve feet deep, as one of the township's useful commodities.

This vocabulary of the Calder and its affluents is the key to colourful events and practices that were once a familiar part of our ancestors' lives. Each of the words discussed gains from being studied in its local context, telling us far more than the etymology in isolation. The volume of *English Place-Name Elements* (1970) informs us that steaner derives from an Old English word, and means 'stony, rocky ground', although Professor Smith in his work on Yorkshire at least put the word in a riverside context.

Wood Management

One of the commonest place-name elements in west Yorkshire is 'spring', typically said in reference works to have two meanings.[11] Used of water sources it requires no comment, for the word is still part of our everyday vocabulary, but in the sense of 'plantation' or 'copse' it has dropped out of the language and survives only in place-names or in documents that have to do with wood management. In fact 'spring' is the key to an almost forgotten but colourful part of our history, and the dictionary definition is no real clue to the word's former importance. Spring woods were coppices, felled at regular intervals and sold for the most part to charcoal burners, working in partnership with tanners and sawyers. This tradition is well documented, from the 1400s into the nineteenth century, and its decline since then is evident in the sign outside the Spring Grove public house in Kirkburton. This shows a spring of water gushing out from under a grove of trees, the publican and artist clearly unaware that the 'spring' was a coppice wood.

It is difficult to discuss 'spring' in isolation, for it was just one word in a vocabulary that lost its relevance as wood management declined, but the principle of coppicing that it described is simple enough. Spring woods were crops, managed in order to provide different local industries with exactly the kind of wood or timber they needed. The leases use a wide variety of terms for trees, calling them stovens, wavers, lordings, blackbarks and poles, all terms that our ancestors once understood perfectly but which are now familiar to just a few specialists. Gregory Spring is the name of a wood close to where I live, an ancient coppice connected with a farm called Gregory, but local people are unaware of that, assuming that there must once have been an important spring of water in the wood.

Many of the words associated with 'spring' have also left their mark on surnames and minor place-names. The 'barker' or tanner was so called because he used the bark stripped from oak trees – although the process itself was locally called 'pilling'. He needed it for the tannin that helped to turn animal hides into leather and it was first stacked or 'pearked' outside the wood before being removed to the 'bark house'. There are several places named Barkhouse near former spring woods. Once the barking was complete, the 'collier' or charcoal burner had access to the coppice, making his 'pitsteads' on a platform of level ground close to water. The cut timber had to carbonise rather than burn, so the stack was covered with sods or 'hilling' so that air was excluded as the 'coling' took place. The surname Collier, and place-names such as 'Collier Hagg', refer to charcoal burning rather than coal mining. 'Hagg' incidentally was an alternative dialect word for a copse or part of a copse.

The coppice cycle varied from one region to another, depending on what was required locally, but in west Yorkshire most of the charcoal was destined for nearby iron forges or furnaces, and this is reflected in the pattern of minor place-names, with 'Smithies' or 'Smithy Places' sited close to 'Springs'. Amongst the field names that we expect to find in those regions are 'Cinderhills' and 'Orepits', although the latter might survive as 'Toppits'. Other minor names derive from the open places within the woods, called 'plains', 'laundes' or 'cockglades', where wood-cock were netted or grazing was sometimes allowed. 'Reins' were narrow strips of woodland, often on steep slopes, and these were coppiced along with the springs. It is a rich and varied vocabulary but so specific that, when we find several of these minor names together, we can be sure which industries were linked with the management of the woods.

Transferred Place-Names

In New England there are many reminders of home for the tourist from Old England, not least the place-names. Boston and Plymouth are near neighbours here, not at opposite ends of the country, and within a radius of ten or twelve miles lie Winchester, Cambridge, Chelsea, Reading and Wakefield. Less familiar generally but evocative for travellers from East Anglia are Dedham, Lynn, Malden and Braintree, all consciously commemorating the links between the two countries. The effect can be disconcerting, for while these names certainly remind us of home we don't expect to see them so close together and it is easy to feel disoriented. Much the same can be true in Australia, which actually has its own New England: if I journey south from Ipswich in Queensland I pass through Warwick and Tamworth before reaching Newcastle and notice many more familiar names en route.

It is not a one-way process. In England there are fields and farms called New England in a dozen counties and we also have Newfoundland, Virginia, Philadelphia, Quebec and Bunker's Hill. From Australia we have borrowed Van Diemens Land, Ballarat and Botany Bay, and from other parts of the former empire Spioncop, Zululand, Pondicherry and Barbados. The wars that we have had with our European neighbours mean that we are familiar too with Alma and Inkermann, Waterloo, Dunkirk and Blenheim. We have streets called Carolina, Florida and

1 Oscar Wilde posing as himself. He indirectly owed his unusual first name to the Scottish poet James Macpherson, whose Ossianic fragment 'The Death of Oscar' became popular in Europe. Napoleon expressed his admiration of the poet by calling his godson Oscar, and the boy later succeeded to the throne of Sweden. Oscar Wilde's father was King Oscar's physician. (*National Portrait Gallery*)

2 The Pennines, Gordale Scar near Malham – an area of Scandinavian settlement. Most of the topographic place-names derive from Old Norse words. For example 'dale' means valley and 'scar' means cliff. Other common Scandinavian elements are beck (stream), fell (hill), foss (waterfall) and gill (ravine). (*George Redmonds*)

3 The Pennines, Crummack Dale. There are several places named 'Crummack' in the north, and the word is thought to have a British origin. It means crooked and probably referred here to the twisting hill called Long Scar. (*George Redmonds*)

4 Mankinholes, in the south Pennines, is said to derive from an Old Irish personal name 'Mankan'. It gave rise to a surname as early as 1275 and in east Lancashire this became Manknell and Mangnall. These have been wrongly said to refer to the 'mangonel', a medieval war engine that threw stones. (*George Redmonds*)

5 New Street, Huddersfield, 1966. The town is of recent growth and has no ancient street names. When this street was cut through the fields, in the late 1700s, it was first named Southgate, which would have hinted at a longer history. In the end New Street prevailed. (*Huddersfield Examiner*)

6 Bulstrode Buildings, Kirkgate, Huddersfield. In a sense both these names were 'transferred'. Kirkgate was chosen arbitrarily, *c.* 1800, in imitation of towns such as Leeds and Wakefield; it replaced the older Town Gate. Bulstrode was a surname, derived from the village of that name in Buckinghamshire. (*Huddersfield Examiner*)

7 Shuttle Eye Colliery on Grange Moor, Lepton, closed in 1971. The name is possibly a reference to the very thin seams of coal worked there. Earlier pits in the same area had the names Nineveh and Mount Pisgah, both drawn from the Bible. (*Huddersfield Examiner*)

8 The White Horse, Lepton, in the early 1900s. The sign of the white horse has been in use since the late middle ages and is a traditional heraldic emblem. A galloping white horse may go back only to the accession of George I in 1714. (*George Redmonds*)

9 The Kirkstile Inn near Loweswater, Cumbria. Formerly each farm and hamlet had access to the 'kirk' via the 'kirk gate', or footpath, and the 'kirk stile'. The inn may be on the site of a former church house, where 'church ales' once raised money for the poor and the church's upkeep. (*George Redmonds*)

10 Lepton Common and fields. Beyond the 'whins' in the foreground are fields that were enclosed by Act of Parliament in the late 1700s. Beyond them is the ancient assart of High Royd, probably cleared of trees in the thirteenth century. One of the enclosures, set at an angle to the others, is named Overthwart. (*Huddersfield Examiner*)

11 An ancient and solitary oak on the Arlingham peninsula, Gloucestershire. Oak Field, Oak Tree Close and Oak Tree Meadow are common English field names. There are also numerous small settlements named Oak or Oakes, some dating from the middle ages, that may have been sited near such prominent trees. (*George Redmonds*)

Nevada and houses that identify such holiday destinations as Marbella and Torremolinos. More exotic choices are Samarkand, Inyanga and Kowloon, inspired by more intrepid trips abroad or armchair-based day-dreams.

In much the same way place-names are transferred from one part of Britain to another, perhaps predictably so where houses, inns and streets are concerned. So we have a Llandudno in Cornwall, a Polperro in Bradford and a Pen-y-ghent in East Barnet. The 'Nottingham' public house in Plymouth has a sign showing the castle and coat of arms of the city of Nottingham, and may have been named after a street or a ship, whereas the 'Leeds and Liverpool' at Brierfield in Lancashire is a reference to the nearby canal. The royal associations of Sandringham, Balmoral and Windsor have made these names popular and other common choices include Bath, Chester and York. London, Land's End and the Isle of Wight are found often enough as the names of fields and hamlets and I am familiar in Yorkshire with Pendle Hill and the Isle of Man.[12]

Just occasionally we come across a contemporary comment on such names. In 1677, for example, two Bradford tenants were ordered at the manor court to 'repair their water Banks on both sides of the Isle of Mann' – doubtless a nickname here for a steaner! In Mirfield, in 1651, the overseers of the poor were called on to provide accommodation for an old woman and the parish register records that they 'bulded her an house at a place above the Lee Grene Pits, which said place is called Letell London': it survived as Little London City. It may have been a standing joke, for there are nine other Little Londons in the old West Riding; not one of them is recorded before the nineteenth century.

Each county dictionary has examples that are less ephemeral and have more complicated histories, but not everything in such cases is as it seems. Leedstown in Cornwall is not a straight borrowing from either Leeds in Kent or Leeds in Yorkshire but a village founded in the nineteenth century by the Duke of Leeds, a major local landowner. New Grimsby, in the same county, was actually 'Grymsey' in the 1500s and derives from the Scandinavian name for the whole island of Scilly. The 'b' is first recorded in 1652 but it is likely that its acceptance in the modern place-name owes something to the influence of Grimsby in Lincolnshire.[13]

Where most transferred names are concerned it is obvious that the etymology is less interesting than the circumstances surrounding the transfer. We should like to know more about the exact date when the name was given and the motives of the name-givers, and these facts are not easily arrived at. With names like New Grimsby in mind, we should also like to be certain that we are dealing with a genuine case of transferral. It is in such matters that the local historian has a part to play, and that will hopefully emerge in the following examples.

Nineveh

Nineveh is a transferred place-name found in many parts of England, from Westmorland in the north west to Kent in the south east. Most writers say that places were given such names because of their remoteness from the farm, or their location on a parish boundary far from the centre of the village. In fact Kenneth Cameron called them 'nicknames of remoteness'.[14] No doubt that explains many of the late field names coined during parliamentary inclosures, such as Australia or New South Wales, and it makes very good sense where some of our numerous Botany Bays are concerned. It may also explain the more exotic Nineveh, but it is dangerous to categorise names in this way and there is one Yorkshire Nineveh that may have originated in quite different circumstances.

The old highway that gave south Yorkshire access to the Calder Valley follows the line of the ridge between Grange Moor and Liley Hall at an altitude of about 700 to 750 feet. Nineveh is now the name of an old house that stands immediately to the north east of the road at the point where it runs close to Whitley Park, with Cockley Wood behind it and Nineveh Plantation across the way. There is evidence of old coal workings both in the wood and just beyond the farm. The place-name is at least two hundred years old for it occurs in 1799 in the Whitley estate accounts. That date is significant for John Field believed that most of the Ninevehs were probably named in the early nineteenth century, when the ruins of the ancient Assyrian capital were being excavated and the name was in the news; but that cannot explain Nineveh in Whitley. Nor can it explain Nineveh Close in Holbeck, near Leeds, shown on a map dated 1762, so the inference may be that the individuals who coined these names were familiar with the place-name through the Old Testament, particularly those references in the Book of Jonah, chapter 3. An Old Testament source would seem more likely in the nonconformist strongholds of the West Riding.

It is not just the origin that we should question. A fine old grandfather clock, in the possession of Mary Parry, has a strong connection with Nineveh, for it has come down to her through the Kitson family who were tenants there in the mid 1800s. As it was made by John Halliwell, a Wakefield clockmaker, it may be almost as old as the place-name, for he appears to have stopped production by 1820. The real interest in the clock is the delightful picture above the face which shows an old coal pit worked by a horse gin, for it surely commemorates the colliery at Nineveh. Indeed it seems likely that Nineveh was initially the name of the colliery, especially as there was another named Mount Pisgah just a few hundred yards away.

Clitheroe

Clitheroe Wood and Farm are place-names in Honley, a township and chapelry in the ancient parish of Almondbury, and they serve to remind us of a long-forgotten piece of local history. The place-name has its origin in decisions made by the three commissioners of the Honley Inclosure Act in 1782, who proposed to 'divide, inclose and improve' the extensive commons and wastes of the township. That was acted upon in 1788, and it took account of the rights of the governors of the Free Grammar School of Clitheroe in Lancashire, who were the impropriators of the rectory of Almondbury. As such, they were entitled to all the great and rectorial tithes of the commons of Honley and also had the right to a sum of £3 11s. 6d. arising out of earlier titheable inclosures.

To compensate the governors for their loss of the tithes, the commissioners awarded them substantial sections of the common and these allotments, one of twenty-five acres and the other of seventy-five acres, are shown as the property of the school on the inclosure map of 1788. A map of 1838 has the name Clitheroe Wood on part of the smaller allotment, the remainder of which consisted of a farm and a dozen or so fields. These are the buildings now called Clitheroe Farm.

The place-names may be said therefore to date from about 1788 but the association with Clitheroe School goes back almost to the Dissolution. Henry VII had previously granted the tithes of Almondbury to the College of Jesus in Rotherham, but, after the college had been dissolved, Philip and Mary granted the rectory to 'the Free Gramer Schoole of Cliderhow'. The tithes were a source of lasting and well-documented contention, but most local historians have concentrated on Almondbury's role in these disputes, ignoring the various chapelries that were also involved.

Honley's grievances came to light recently when I was given access to the private papers of the Green-Armytage family. One of the relevant documents is undated but written in a seventeenth-century hand. It records a meeting of the inhabitants of Honley who claimed that a tithe was 'going to be laid upon all Landhoulders ... upon potatiss and Turnips' and that no such demand had ever been made before. They were of one opinion – that it was 'unlawfull and Imposing', and a second meeting was arranged to decide on a course of action. Sadly we have no record of the later meeting, but the scrap of paper that has survived reminds us that distant 'Clithrah fre Scool' was once a reality to the townspeople of Honley, a reality that was forgotten only when the tithes were sold to the lords of the manor in about 1860. The only reminder of those three centuries of history is the name of Clitheroe Farm.[15]

6

Field Names

The study of field names is of relatively recent origin and some of the earlier county volumes of the English Place-Names Society series contained no data on the subject. The first volume to do so was *The Place-Names of Northamptonshire* (1933). Since then the amount of material has increased so dramatically that it is not unusual in a modern publication for several hundred names to be listed for an individual parish. Normally such names consist of two elements or words; the second of these, now often referred to as a 'generic' term, is usually a word such as 'close', 'field' or 'croft', easily recognised as a characteristic field-name element, even by the non-expert. The first element, or 'specific', has much greater variety and will define some special feature of the field to which it refers. In different ways each of these can help us to interpret the historic landscape of a community.

For that to be possible the principles that are taken for granted in other branches of place-name study have to be adhered to and that means that ideally each name must be supported by a series of examples covering its linguistic history. It should also be possible to find it on a township or parish map, so that we know exactly where it was located and the names of neighbouring fields. We can then study it in the landscape, so that we are familiar with the topography and the soil, the shape of the field, its dimensions and its position vis-à-vis the other fields. Even where the land has been built on, some clues to its history may remain, perhaps in the names of modern streets and houses or even in the street pattern. The question of its meaning is fundamental to our understanding of its place in the township story, but that interpretation is enhanced if we can relate it to adjoining fields and buildings, and learn more about the elements involved.

Such names are of interest to the linguist for the information they provide about our ancestors' language in general and its regional variations, but they can also throw light on many other aspects of the past,

particularly topics such as clearance, enclosure and local farming practices. They may tell us directly about former owners and occupiers,
vanished industries and buildings, and provide clues about plants, wild
animals, folklore, pastimes, legal disputes, boundaries and archaeological
features. What we need to keep in mind is that such names have been
used predominantly by those who worked the land, and it is not unusual
for the spellings to reflect that. In other cases the names themselves will
have been replaced; but, even if that is not the case, we cannot expect
that the fields will have been untouched by time, their size, shape,
function and boundaries unaltered over the centuries. Moreover, as the
field names reflect the progressive clearance and exploitation of the land,
they will date from different periods: a few may go back well over a
thousand years but others will be relatively modern.

Spelling Changes: Popular Etymology

My collection of field names for Lepton alerted me long ago to the
pitfalls that lie in wait for us if we jump too readily to conclusions, and
I can make that point by reviewing the evidence for a name that I first
encountered in the form Surgeon Flatt. The generic 'flatt' posed no
problems, for it is a common element in that hilly region, often associated with level areas of the former open-field system. Nor did I initially
see 'surgeon' as a major problem and I bracketed it with minor names
that have 'doctor' as the first element. It was just one name in a group
of several that had to do with a property in the Lascelles Hall area of
the village, however, and it soon became clear that 'surgeon' may not
have been the original first element. Indeed, in a document of 1554 the
field was referred to as 'a close called Sir John Flatt', and this easily
predates the earliest references to 'Surgeon Flatt'. Although the trail of
evidence ends there, speculation does not, even though it is possible
that 'Sir John' commemorates a member of the Lascelles family who
lived locally until c. 1434. As the Lascelles family had previously made
important grants to the Knights Hospitaller – the Knights of St John –
it could be argued that St John Flatt would be a more logical explanation
of the name.

A second Lepton name in this category, with a better documented
history, is Thurgory Lane, found on maps if not on signs. Local people

who walk on the lane say they are 'going on the Oggeries', although one or two feel that it should somehow have an initial 'H' and they pronounce it 'Hoggeries'. Asked about its possible meaning, they usually point to the fact that pigs were once kept at the farm at the end of the lane. In fact charters of the thirteenth and fourteenth centuries make it clear that it was originally 'Thorgar's mound', possibly a burial mound, and, as 'Thorgar' has a Scandinavian origin, the place-name may be very ancient indeed. The modern pronunciation results from the assumption by local people that the initial 'Th' is really for 'the', as in the dialect, and it must have persisted at all levels because the written form is seldom seen.

There is one final intriguing point of general interest in this name and that is the consistent use orally of the plural, with the word 'lane' omitted – local people never walk on Thurgory Lane, always 'on the Oggeries'. A map of 1720 shows that Thurgory was originally an enclosure, with several sub-divisions by that time, and these were bisected by the lane that now bears the name. It seemed possible to me that this division might explain the plural usage, although deeds from the 1800s referred to Thurgory Closes and not to Thurgories. It was not a matter that I gave much thought to initially but, in 1999, whilst I was working in Kansas on the Kaye deeds in the Kenneth Spencer Library, I came across an early thirteenth-century charter for Thurgory.[1] It confirmed an earlier grant to the Knights Templar by Ralph the son of Hamund, a Lepton chaplain, and the two acres in question were said to lie separately in 'two assarts called Thurgorhoues'. The name of the lane would certainly have come later, so the residents' use of the plural may go back to the middle ages, preserved in the vernacular.

An Old 'Street' Name

Lilycroft Road is now the name of a road or street in Manningham, the built-up part of Bradford referred to earlier, and it is interesting because it can be identified on Robert Saxton's map of the township for 1613. There were fields where Lilycroft Road now is and one of these was John Denton's 'Lilliecrofte meadowe', with a house in the croft and two more close by. It has previously been suggested that the field was named after a member of the Liley family, whose surname appears on

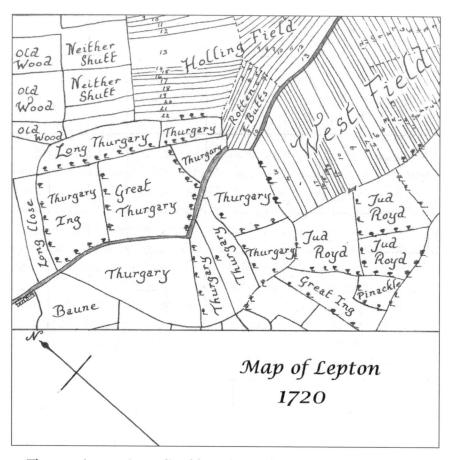

3. Thurgory in 1720; its medieval boundary still obvious despite enclosure.

seventeenth-century deeds for Bradford and could be spelt Lilly, but they were not Manningham residents and there is a more plausible alternative.

First, however, it should be made clear that 'croft' is a term often associated with the earliest history of a community. It was not just a general word for a small field but almost always an enclosure linked to a house. A tithe dispute of 1554 defined the term as it was customarily used in the diocese of York:

> and ... by the order of the Courtes ... thos be onelye Croftes and called Croftes which have a house belded [builded] upon thiem or joyninge to thiem or to be joyned to a house and inclosed from other common feldes.[2]

Manningham was not a 'village' in the conventional sense and it had no nucleated centre even in 1613. The population was still scattered at that time and Lilycroft seems likely to have been the site of an old settlement that predated the Black Death. It was probably a piece of land held by the Lilling family, for it was named 'Lyllyng Croft' in the court roll of 1411 when it was held by Adam Atyhate. It was a close where the tenants of Manningham had common rights every third year, and a manorial inquisition of 1340 takes the history back even further. At that time it was a tenement claimed by John and Robert Attyhate but had previously belonged to a certain William Lillyng: when he died without male heirs the property passed to his daughter Agnes, who then also died without an heir. As a result of the inquisition the jury decided in favour of the plaintiff, William son of Adam, a grandson of Thomas Lillyng. That seems to explain the meaning of Lilycroft, but the etymology of the surname Lilling remains obscure. One strong possibility is that it derives from Lilling in north Yorkshire.

Generics

The definition of 'croft' in the legal dispute of 1554 emphasises how far our modern understanding of such generic terms differs from that of our ancestors. Nowhere is that more apparent than in the word 'field' itself. As the suffix of place-names such as Chesterfield and Hatfield it is thought to have meant 'tract of open country', one that was free of woodland. It can be compared therefore with the Dutch word *veldt* and is believed to have referred to quite a large area.

As villages began to farm their land communally the word acquired a new extended meaning, descriptive of the arable lands in which each man had a share and where there were no permanent fences. As these open or 'town' fields were progressively enclosed and subdivided the modern meaning of a fenced-in plot developed and the generic 'close', of French origin, became very popular. The process of enclosure was usually piecemeal and it differed considerably from one parish to another. In some cases it started soon after the Black Death of 1349 but was not complete everywhere even by the nineteenth century, after the parliamentary enclosures. Where the generic 'field' has survived in minor names it is often therefore our best clue to the location of the former arable lands. In fact, there is usually a story behind each 'close', however straightforward the name might be etymologically.

The Generic 'Close': Clearance and Enclosure

From hence the inclosed fields in Mirfield make one grand Parterre; the thick planted hedge-rows seem like a wilderness or a Labyrinth; the houses interspers'd look like so many several noble seats of gentlemen at a distance.

Rev. J. Ismay, 1755

Some place-names have such self-evident meanings that writers pass them by quickly, as if they are scarcely worth a mention. What could possibly be interesting, for example, about a field called New Close? Once we have settled that it refers to a piece of newly-enclosed land there seems little more to say. Yet nothing could be further from the truth. The elements 'new' and 'close' may have obvious etymologies but they can both pose problems and the combination of the two, although commonplace, is a not insignificant reminder of some farmer's distant battle with the landscape. In fact each 'new close' commemorates a temporary victory in a long-running campaign; one that began when the first men cleared away the scrub and trees in order to plant grain or provide protection for stock.

Enclosures are of course very much older than the word 'close', which came into the language from French and is first recorded here after the Norman Conquest. It is frequent enough in field names from the thirteenth century but much commoner from the fifteenth century. Its popularity reflects the history of enclosure, a history that is different from one community to another. Not all the pieces of enclosed land were called closes; some were assarts or 'royds', cleared by individuals and individually named, and others were ancient 'crofts' which had adjoined the houses of the first Anglo-Saxon settlers. Open and unenclosed was the communal arable land or 'field', with each tenant holding strips in different parts of the township.

Only when the community decided to rearrange these holdings and allow individuals to exchange strips with their neighbours was it necessary to erect fences and thus enclose the land. A title deed of 1630, for property in the township of Honley, refers to 'seaven closes as the same adioyne one to another ... lately enclosed in severall, and hedged out and from the common feildes there'. An important word in this text is 'several', much closer to its original Latin meaning, and referring to land held *separately* or individually, not in common.

In that deed, as in many others, the relationship between the act of enclosure and the erection of fences or 'defences' was explicit: few people now associate fences with our ancestors' need to defend their property against invasion by wild animals or a neighbour's stock, but that meaning was uppermost in their minds. To 'close' was to enclose. In other earlier documents there is mention of three strips 'in the common felde, unclosed and unfenced' (1554), and land near to the house 'closed with olde walls' (1517). It is important to remember that communal enclosure in this earlier period was a significant act, a milestone in each township's history, and symptomatic of more fundamental changes affecting the individual's status locally and in society more generally.

Even within the village the process of enclosure was usually piecemeal, carried out at different times and in different circumstances, often completed only by Act of Parliament in the eighteenth or nineteenth century. And that process could be reversed; the above reference of 1554 to 'unclosed' land in the common field is taken from a dispute at the ecclesiastical court over tithes, and the question that followed it asked 'how it chansed that they [the three strips] were lade opyn in to the felde again and for what cause the hege was pluked downe'. In other cases the same word 'close' refers not to enclosed parts of the town's arable field but to clearances from the manorial wastes or commons, as more land was brought under the plough. The historian's attempt to understand the history of the English landscape depends very much on the accurate interpretation of field names such as New Close.

In my own village of Lepton there is one deed of 1625 which clearly had to do with open field enclosure, for it refers to 'a close called Neweclose, heretofore taken forth of the Furlong Feilde'. Another, dated 1553, mentions a field called 'Souremore or Newclose', where the inference must be that the newly-enclosed land had been taken from the moor, notorious for its acidity. The alias suggests that the name may have been relatively new at that time but we cannot be certain and have to be careful what conclusions we draw. 'New' is a relative term, as we are reminded by such names as Newton and Newark which are both found more than once in Domesday Book. So, if a place-name is to be really meaningful, we need far more information than is contained in those two references. Just occasionally a document provides exactly what the historian needs, as the following extract from an Ilkley deed of 1592 shows:

> Three score yeares ago the said percell of ground was called by the name of the Westwood ... so it was called till about fifty yeares ago that the same was enclosed and ever since the same hath been called by the name of the New Close or Oxeclose or Intacke or what other name pleaseth them.

The place-name was apparently unstable but 'new' here clearly referred to about 1540 and we learn a great deal from the discussion about the history of the enclosure. For example, it was said that before the ground was enclosed the tenants 'did get wood and brakens there without any interrupcion' and that they 'were verie bushey grounds, growen full of thornes, hollings and other woods and brakens' – just enough detail to hint at the back-breaking toil that lay behind the words 'new close' in this case. An account book, kept by a farming family in the nineteenth century, tells an even more compelling story.

New Close in Crosland

It was 4 July 1818 when William Sykes, a Crosland farmer, wrote the words 'Expences of New Close' in his account book, an entry which is the first recorded reference to an enclosure with a three-year history. The details emerge only after a painstaking search through the records but, in its way, it is a heroic tale and one that must have numerous parallels the length and breadth of the country.

The inclosure of Crosland Moor (a spelling preferred by the commissioners) had taken place some years earlier, in 1803. Not all the land was cleared and developed immediately, however, and Jonathan Wilkinson appears to have sold the rights in his 'parcel' to William Sykes in May 1815, for £5. It was referred to in their agreement as an 'intake', that is land taken in from the moor by enclosure, and William was 'booked as tenant for the same at Whitley Hall and got possession of it the same day'. In addition to the 'purchase' price, he had to pay a yearly rent of £1 1s. 6d. It seems clear from the accounts that the intake was subdivided over the next two or three years and progressively cleared and brought under cultivation. We cannot therefore be certain which of the earliest entries refer specifically to the piece of land that would eventually be called New Close, but it is clear from the beginning that William had embarked on a formidable task.

From the daily accounts it is evident that the year 1816 was one of unremitting toil for the whole family, for work on the intake was going on side by side with the building of a new house and all the usual farm labour. The first task was to enclose the intake, and the records show that William spent over eighty days building the dry stone walls, getting the stone either from the land or carting it from a quarry near by. At times he was helped by Ely Dyson and Mark Crosland, and part of his agreement with them was that his wife would lodge them and cook their meals. At the same time the moorland vegetation, much of it gorse or 'whin', had to be removed and burnt, and this was followed by what was called 'push plowing', that is paring off the turf with a simple plough. This was operated by manpower rather than horsepower and the implement used was similar to a pointed spade, with a flange at right angles to the blade and a cross piece which was pushed by the operator's body. Ploughing by this method has been described as 'the most slavish work in husbandry'; on difficult terrain a second man had sometimes to be harnessed to the plough.

Entries in 1818, which clearly refer to New Close, record the 'leading' and spreading of soil, clearing roots from the land and stones, some of them 'earthfasts', and fetching lime from the kiln. The moorland soil was after all extremely acid and large quantities of lime were required to sweeten it. In March alone at least twenty-eight sacks were carted and 'slecked', that is broken down in water. Even then the land had to be levelled or 'fayed down' and the 'clots' broken up before it was provided with drains and prepared for the first crop – 'fettled for taties' in William's words. Finally 'yate dearns' or gate posts were purchased and New Close was ready, at a cost of £109 13s. 9d. according to the accounts.

Intake

We have already had a glimpse of the labour involved in 'taking in'. The dictionary definition of an intake as 'a piece of land taken in or enclosed from a moor' does not do the word justice, however accurate it is etymologically. Something of the work and the practices involved emerges in the documents that mention 'intakes' from the Tudor period to the present day. The hard work is implicit in a lease of 1611 which noted the expenses of Thomas Brooke 'taking in, enclosing, fencing and reducing into husbandry one piece of barren ground'. A Barkisland document the same year tells us more about other aspects of 'taking in', when it describes a new enclosure of four acres as having been staked out in such a way as to make measuring it an easy task: 'to witt into two squares and one triangle'. A second enclosure by Michael Lome, later referred to as Lome Intacke, had no water supply and the lease stipulated that he should therefore 'have a Current made from the Springe ... for the use of his grounde'. In other words a stream running down from Cross Well should be diverted through the intake, but the agreement required him to take due account of the freeholders' right of access 'in somertyme ... for wateringe of their Cattell'. These parcels of land 'were measured by the Roode of Seaven yeardes (being accomptid the great Measure)', another reminder of local practices.[3]

It was an on-going process that transformed the Pennine landscape. Although it was seldom written about specifically, there are one or two passages in the records that are enlightening. In Slaithwaite, for example, a township never enclosed by Act of Parliament, the upland landscape is bleak, the almost treeless slopes patterned with dry stone walls. Over a hundred hamlets and cottages are scattered across the great ridges and the Earl of Dartmouth's steward described these in 1805 in the following words:

> A great portion of these hamlets have been cultivated from Moorland by the present tenants and their Forefathers within the last Century: and the Buildings have been chiefly erected by them with a little Assistance in wood or money from the Noble Owner. However, there still remain large Tracts of Moor Land ... patches of which are annually taking in [sic], with leave of his Lordship's Agents and cleared of Rocks and large (what are there called Bolder) Stones, at great Labour and Expence. With these Stones, when broken, the fences are formed and will take a Man a great portion of the winter to clear an Acre fit for Cultivating ... on these spots it seems very good Policy to advance the Improver a little money to build himself a Cottage as he is always willing to pay a good Interest for it.[4]

There is an account of Marsden, the next township up the valley, written almost two centuries earlier, that captures rather more of the impact this dramatic intake landscape could have on the outsider:

> The town, which I call that where the chappell standeth, lieth low and under greate hills, coald and moorish mountaines from whence by the conflux of watters thence descendinge ... are made two litle rivers which unitinge together ... runne with greate force and violence like unto the catadups of Nilus, in the bottome of which are to be seene nothinge but greate stones and some of them a wayne loade a peece. By this watter, upon the sides of the winding hills are seated theire scattered dwellinges, some higher to the hills, some lower to the watteres shelter ... they live hardly ... and daily enclose and improve grounds out of the rude mountaines above them.

The writer had been sent to Marsden with the task of ascertaining what the customary practices and rents were in the manor but he retired, shaking his head no doubt, saying that he could not learn what they paid an acre as the people claimed that 'acre' was not a term they were familiar with in that context. His rueful comment on that piece of innocence was 'these are more subtill people than ignorant'.[5]

Specifics

Not all field names are as apparently bland and unpromising as New Close. Many have quite fanciful names, such as Chopping Bill, Heater,

Cocked Hat and Leg of Mutton. The inspiration in these cases seems likely
to have been the field's shape, whereas the quality of the soil or the sheer
hard work involved for the farmer may have been responsible for Greedy
Guts, Bare Arse, Featherbed and Purgatory. In other similar cases it may
simply have been the nature of the terrain that was responsible: local
names like Curdle Churn and Clatter Collocks seem to indicate an
uneven or bumpy surface,[6] whereas Treacle Nook and Pudding suggest
waterlogged land. Even here not everything is what it seems and isolated
spellings can be misleading. My first impression where Turmoil Ing in
Almondbury was concerned was that it fell into the Purgatory category,
but a sequence of earlier references proved that it developed from
Turnbull Ing. William Turnbull had been the tenant in Elizabeth's reign.

On the whole these colourful names are apt to tell us less than those
with a more commonplace specific, simply because we are unlikely to
find out much about the circumstances in which the name was coined.
That is not always true, for we may have a contemporary explanation,
as in *c.* 1745 when Thomas Wright wrote in his autobiography 'we were
entering a field – called the Gravemaker's Close because at that time
the gravemaker of Bradford Church farmed it'. Hearsay may be less
reliable. In a discussion about the tithe of a field called Hardy Flatt, in
1556, a witness called John Etton commented that he had heard old men
say that 'one Hardye wif did give the said Hardie Flate to the Priorie
of Kirkham, to thintent to have everie daye newe brede of the said daie
it was baked, and that she choked of the firste mouthefull and dyed'. It
is a good story, but is likely to have been embroidered over the years
and probably all we can be reasonably certain of is the link with the
Priory and the Hardy family.

Tenter Croft

There are certain field names that occur over and over again, principally
because they are descriptive of the everyday farm buildings or relate to
usual crops and common practices. These can be slightly more obscure
if the dialect word is used. Laithe Ing or Croft are common because
'laithe' is a northern word for a barn and there are numerous crofts
with the specifics 'haver' or 'bigg', the northern words for oats and
barley. Near the corn mill we expect to find Milne Close and by the

mill race Goit Ing, the latter a reference to the 'gote' or water channel. The tendency in west Yorkshire to diphthongise the vowel in such words is responsible for 'goit'. In these cases it is usually possible to locate records which tell us more about how the names developed.

One of the most popular specifics in areas where cloth was being made is 'tenter', a reference to the tenter frames that were erected near the clothiers' houses. These were usually made of wood and set up in the open air so that the finished 'piece' could be dried evenly, the cloth being fastened to hooks in order to give it the right tension. To be 'on tenterhooks', that is to be in painful suspense, is a figurative use of this word, recorded from the 1400s. It may be even older, for there was a 'Tenturgerde' or tenter garth in Pontefract in 1322. We can expect to find such names in the towns, with their guild-based cloth-workers, but priorities were different in the rural areas that were beginning to take over the industry in the 1400s and it is there that we find the first examples of field names such as Tenter Close or Tenter Croft.

It is not known for certain just when the first tenters were brought into use in these rural communities, but the element occurs in field names from 1414 at least and by the 1600s it was quite common. The tenter represented an 'industrial' invasion of farmland and this conflict of interests is reflected in documents of the period. For example, there was controversy between a father and his son in 1575 over 'the occupacion of certaine howsinge' in Sowerby, and part of a complicated agreement was that the son should have 'one tenter rowme where there is one tenter nowe standinge in the crofte upon the south end of the howsinge'.[7] From that time it may well have been known as Tenter Croft.

The phrase 'tenter room', that is space for a tenter, was used commonly from this time, as disputes developed about how the croft that lay close to the house should be used. This invasion of land that had traditionally been given over to the production of food was on a relatively small scale but there is no doubt that it created tension and some men were convinced that their rights were being threatened. A typical lease of 1653 specified that a certain John Cowper should have possession of a field called Laith Croft, with the exception of 'one Tenter rowme in the upper end'. There a clothier called Richard Dison was given leave 'to fix and sett one Tenter', but there had to be 'sufficient wayes and passages to and from the said tenter at all times'. In another lease, of 1651, the lessee was allowed 'to erecte, sett up and use two paire of tenters ... within the Crofte before the dore of the messuage', but the length and breadth of this 'room' were clearly specified.[8]

When Richard Williamson of Huddersfield died, in 1686, he left one tenter to his son-in-law and the other to his son. As the first was said to be 'broken and ready for setting up' and the other stood 'upon the wast in Huddersfeild', the inference is that tenters need not be permanent fixtures and that they could be erected on common land, presumably with the consent of the lord of the manor. It was a practice that lasted into the 1800s:

> Memorandum. This first Day of November 1813 John Kinder of Greave in Netherthonge has paid me One shilling as One of the Lords of the Manor of Meltham for the priviledge of putting down a Tenter near Gilbirks in the said Manor and also agrees to pay One Shilling Yearly for the standing of the said Tenter untill he has Notice from any of the Lords ... to remove the same and no longer.[9]

In Huddersfield, where cloth-making was carried out on a large scale, an estate map of the 1770s shows that areas close to the town centre were set aside as tenter grounds. These were divided into 'gates', or rows, and rented out to the principal cloth-dressers. It was a development that was possible only after the balance had shifted in favour of the manufacturers. George Borrow's father was a soldier stationed in the town during the Luddite disturbances of 1811–12 and the boy passed these tenter grounds on his way to school, later referring to them in *Lavengro*. As cloth production became a more important part of the local economy, so the number of tenters increased. Indeed, by the middle years of the nineteenth century, their locations were large enough and permanent enough to be shown on Ordnance Survey maps.

Not surprisingly the element is productive of field names. It was occasionally used on its own in the plural, as at Killington in Westmorland, and even more rarely it was the generic. Broad Tenter, for example, was the name of a house built on the green in Huddersfield, first recorded in the 1590s. No doubt it took its name from a tenter ground near by. More predictably 'tenter' as a specific was linked with a variety of words that referred to enclosures, including the common elements close, croft, field and flat and the more regional garth, hey and ing.

Tenters located on waste land gave rise to the names Tenter Banks, Tenter Green and Tenter Hill, whilst Tenter Balk referred to the location of a tenter on unploughed land in the open field. The rare Tentergate in Knaresborough dates from the early 1400s and seems more likely to be a street name than a row of tenters.

Husbandry

The specifics 'lime' and 'marl' occur in numerous minor place-names and they draw our attention to important local industries, and farming practices more generally. The words remind us that as more land was cleared, in regions where the soil was acid, both commodities were needed to sweeten it – and neither of them was readily available locally. The exploitation of these resources was beset with problems that lasted until canal and railway transport eased the difficulties and expense of carriage. We have very little evidence for the medieval period, but minor names such as 'Limpit' in Ferry Fryston (*c.* 1212), and 'Merlepytte' in Roundhay (1341) show that extraction was taking place then. Lime was also being burnt from a very early date, as evidenced by 'Limekilne' in Barwick in an undated twelfth-century document. There are other isolated references to the carriage of both lime and marl, but only over very short distances.[10] The Roundhay marl pit was visited by 'strangers', with their carts, from the 1340s, and it remained a manorial commodity into the seventeenth century at least.[11]

The picture is much clearer from the 1500s, when so much new land was being brought under the plough, and the demand for lime and marl increased. As we have seen, the places where these could be obtained are easily identified, sometimes from the records and sometimes from the minor names, but they are not always evident from the solid geology. Glacial drift meant that limestone could be extracted in many parishes away from the limestone areas and the key to that may be in title deeds, especially leases. In 1620 four closes of land in Bingley were leased to Michael Dobson 'with authority to dig there for lyme-stones, and to burn, sell and dispose of them'; in 1630, in Draughton, several men were granted the 'liberty to digg and gett Lymestone ... and lead and carrye awaye the same ... at all tymes of the yeare'. Significantly one of the fields was called Kilne Close.

The fact that these leases mention the sale and carriage of the limestone hints at commercial exploitation rather than individual use. Proof that this was the case emerges, somewhat surprisingly, in later quarter sessions records. Two petitions made by the inhabitants of Bingley provide the information. In 1699 they stated that 'for a long tyme ... great quantities of Lyme Stones' had been 'gotten promiscuously' in the parish, 'by means whereof the ground was digged upp and very much impaired'. This had attracted 'abundance of poor people', presumably on the look-out for employment, and that in turn had increased the burden on the ratepayers. Just eight years later they brought the issue up again, saying that, although Bingley had no market and was not on a major highway, a great many labourers were employed there, 'digging and getting Lime'. It was claimed that they spent 'a great parte of their wages idly and at undue seasons in the alehouses'.

Bingley was a long way from the limestone regions, in that part of the Pennines where clearance had accelerated through the 1500s, so no doubt much of the lime was burnt there before being despatched to other parishes. In the 1600s more than one highway in the region was referred to at the quarter sessions as 'a common way for Carrying Lyme' and witnesses incidentally mention working 'at the Lime Kilnes'. In 1704 John Walker of Bingley claimed that several times he had had 'quantities of Coales stollne from his Lime Delfe' and a witness described as a 'lime burner' said he had seen a man called William Robinson leave a lime delf with a 'scuttlefull of Coales, with a little fire on the top of them'. He was carrying it on his head!

If we turn now to how the lime and marl were being used, there is information in a variety of documents from the 1500s. Marl was a calcareous clay, used as a fertiliser, and Camden noted how yellow it looked in the places in Yorkshire where it was 'being cast and spred upon the fields', helping to increase corn yields. Mr John Kaye of Woodsome put well over one hundred loads of it on the demesne fields between 1577 and 1582, but he frequently used lime also. In those instances where more precise details are given the proportion was usually ten loads of marl to one of lime, but it may be that liming was a regular activity, whereas marling was carried out immediately after new land had been cleared. According to his son John Kaye had 'marlyd and stubbyd Ryshworth Yng and the Mylner Hill ... and made yt plowghable and sett in yt of marle and Lyme xxxiii loods'.

The most interesting entries in John Kaye's farming accounts for those years concern his clearances. He tells us how he 'dyd stubb a pece of the Carr ... callyng yt the Great Stubbing', and also land next to the Foxhoils which yielded 'above an hundrith loads of great stone'. It was hard, back-breaking work for the labourers who had to cut down and stub the trees, cart away the stone – some of it for fences – and spread vast amounts of marl, lime and 'soope ashe' on the newly-won land. When the 'Ladie Roods and thre litle Clossis adioyning' were cleared, he spread four score and eight loads 'loods of Pomfrett marle' on them, that is marl from Pontefract. A bridge had to be built in the park just to provide access for the loaded carts. In 1617, when the tenants of Marsden were recorded making their intakes, the new enclosures were 'made the more fruitefull by lymestone burnt and fettched as farr as Pontfract and Knottingley above 20 miles off'. The land there was said to be 'soe cold and backward' that it would 'beare nought but grasse, oates and pease'.[12]

Apart from minor places named Limepits there are numerous fields with Limekiln as the specific. Typical final elements are Bottom, Close, Field, Furlong, Grange, Ground, Hill, Ing, Lane, Meadow, Pasture, Piece, Sleight and Wood. The abandoned kilns are a characteristic feature of the landscape. 'Lime' is the first element in field names with the following generics: Close, Croft, Field, Garth, Grassings, Meadow and Piece. Several Calder Valley highways still bear the name Limers Gate, reminding us of the moorland intakes and the carriage of lime over the hills on pack horses.

Marl Pit is also a common minor name, on its own or as a specific. Yorkshire examples include Marlpit Drain, Marlpit Hill and Marlpit Lane. Field names with 'Marl' as the specific occur in many counties and typical generics include: Acre, Churl, Close, Croft, Earth, Field, Hay, Ing, Intake, Lands, Lont, Marsh, Piece and Pighell. It is likely that most of the field names originally had 'Limed' and 'Marled' as the first element and that it later gave way to 'Lime' and 'Marl'. In Yorkshire that development can sometimes be traced to the seventeenth century. A field named as le Marled Close in 1636 had become Marle Close in 1720.

7

First Names

The academic approach to first names in the English-speaking countries has changed dramatically in the last few years. Formerly it was seen as the etymologists' field of study, and a succession of dictionaries explored the linguistic origins of our traditional names, a heritage that could be traced back to Anglo-Saxons and Scandinavians and then to the invading Normans and their allies from Flanders and Brittany. In the aftermath of the Conquest the growing name stock was increasingly brought under the influence of the Christian Church so that through the Bible and stories of the saints English speakers came to employ names of Hebrew, Greek and Latin origin.

To these were later added names from Classical antiquity and the medieval Romances, part of a continuing influence from other parts of Europe. That influence was sometimes the direct result of immigration and trade but it also took place more subtly through royal and aristocratic connections. More recently Celtic names have spread far beyond the borders of Scotland, Ireland and Wales to become a popular part of the English name stock, their 'foreign' origins sometimes unsuspected.

That variety is apparent in any list of the most popular names. In 1925, for example, the top ten names for boys in England and Wales were John, William, George, James, Ronald, Robert, Kenneth, Frederick, Thomas and Albert. Of these William and Robert had Germanic origins but had been taken into Gaul by the Franks and then brought here by the Normans. They almost immediately became popular and have remained so for centuries. Also of Germanic origin were Frederick and Albert, but their introduction was more recent: occasional examples of Frederick in the Tudor period can sometimes be traced to men from the Low Countries, but it became an 'English' name after 1714 with the Hanoverians on the English throne. Albert, on the other hand, was almost unknown until Queen Victoria married Prince Albert.

Of the apostles' names John is Hebrew and Thomas Aramaic, both brought into prominence during the religious revival of the twelfth century. James was also Hebrew and actually shared a common history with Jacob, but its use probably had more to do with the cult of St James of Compostela than directly with the apostle and martyr. George is the name of England's patron saint but it was rare in the fourteenth century; it seems to have become popular only after 1415 when George's feast was raised in rank by Archbishop Chichele. The now unfashionable diminutive Georgie was very popular in the early 1500s. The two remaining names, Ronald and Kenneth, had both spread into England and Wales from Scotland, but whereas Kenneth was Gaelic Ronald appears to derive from Old Norse, sharing a common origin with Reginald.

The top girls' names in 1925 were Joan, Mary, Joyce, Margaret, Dorothy, Doris, Kathleen, Irene, Betty and Eileen. These are rather less traditional, although from the same name stock. Margaret and Dorothy are both saints' names with Greek connections, the former meaning 'pearl' and the latter 'gift of God'. Also Greek are Doris and Irene, neither of them known here until the nineteenth century, and, strangely, so are Kathleen and Eileen, Irish variations of the better-known Catherine and Helen. The Hebrew origins of Joan and Betty are not straightforward: Joan was a female alternative for John and Betty was a diminutive of Elizabeth, found in both the Old and New Testaments. It became a name in its own right about 1700. Joyce is something of a mystery, apparently a Celtic name borne by a seventh-century Breton prince. It was used occasionally for girls in the 1500s and then came back into fashion late in the nineteenth century.

Leslie Dunkling was the first writer to put the emphasis on name usage rather than on etymology. In *First Names First* (1977), he based his comments on name counts that covered the period from 1850 to 1975. He also discussed what he called 'real' meaning as opposed to etymology, suggesting that our reaction to a first name depends on the associations it has for us and who we know with the name, personally or historically. We are certainly influenced now by whether a name is in or out of fashion, and are apt to make judgements about age, appearance and even personality purely on those grounds. It was Dunkling's theory that a name can arouse a powerful response in us that has nothing to do with its origin and early history, and that such reactions can be very individual or more stereotyped.

In *Everyman's Dictionary of First Names* (1983), which Dunkling wrote in conjunction with William Gosling, the authors went one step further, criticising previous writers for dealing with names 'in a rather haphazard way', particularly for failing to gather accurate information about their popularity at different periods. The authors' own nationwide name counts, which were described in the Introduction as 'massive', covered the period from 1600, although only for sample years up to 1800. Sadly that statistical evidence was not published. Scott Smith-Bannister also took the question of first name popularity very seriously and, in *Names and Naming Patterns in England, 1538–1700* (1997), he provided the reader with frequency tables for both boys' and girls' names at ten year intervals for the period indicated in the book's title.

In his case, however, the quantitative analysis was merely the basis for an investigation into how children acquired those names, and the part played by parents and godparents in the choices made. It has long been known that children were named by or after a godparent in the later middle ages and Smith-Bannister's concern was to show how the balance then shifted, allowing the parents more control. He was absolutely right in his concluding remarks to reproach previous writers for either ignoring or being unaware of the role of the godparents in name-giving, but it is disappointing that the impact of this practice was not illustrated through examples of some less common names, for that has important implications for genealogists in particular.

An even more recent book by Will Coster has the role of the godparent as its main theme. It uses evidence from parish registers, wills and other documents to explore the institution in depth, demonstrating how it interacted with other social and cultural factors. This is a thorough and revealing investigation into the spiritual communities that were a fundamental aspect of our ancestors' lives and it touches briefly and tantalisingly on the ways in which that affected name-giving.[1] It has been a common assumption that first names were chosen by the natural parents. They were certainly an important influence in the process, initially at gentry level and more generally from the late 1600s, but before that the choice of name was influenced more by the godparents.

Coster looked more closely into how this custom affected the use of Bridget as 'a relatively uncommon female name', commenting on its use for one of the daughters of Edward IV in 1480 and then examining a localised number of examples found in Bickerton from the mid-sixteenth century. He traced this to Bridget Gascoin, the widow of the lord of the manor, showing how her name was passed down the generations, following this with comments on the possible influence in this process of the godparent's social standing. From the point of view of genealogists and local historians, this is clearly a topic of major interest, and it was the central theme recently in my *Christian Names in Local and Family History* (2004).

Part of this was an investigation into the use of first names within the close-knit groups that characterised Tudor society, it being possible to show that it was the gentry who enriched the national name stock in the 1400s. There were some quite striking innovations: the Cliftons of Nottinghamshire introduced Gamaliel, Ezekial and Silvanus, long before these were taken up by Puritans, and the Tempests of Bolling Hall near Bradford had Tristram, Rainbrown and Troilus. All these unusual names then had distinctive regional histories. Families such as the Cliftons and the Tempests were drawing inspiration from literature and the Old Testament, and it was not long before other families revived names from their past and even turned family surnames into first names. The pedigrees of gentry families prove how important surnames were to them in the Tudor period, as their role in society changed, and it can now be seen that they attached similar importance to certain first names. These were not confined to the family but passed on to kinsmen and neighbours through the godparent relationship, so that in a short time they became as distinctive as a suit of livery, identifying people within the same social and spiritual group.

As a result, individual families could be responsible for quite different naming patterns in neighbouring regions or even neighbouring parishes. These could persist for several generations and they are most obvious if the name in question was unusual. Typical examples include Conan (Yorkshire), Hamlet (Cheshire), Ughtred (Lancashire), Anselm (Gloucestershire) and Anker (Nottinghamshire). These names were not common throughout those counties but only within certain kinship groups and restricted geographic areas. But it was not just true of unusual names: for parts of the sixteenth and seventeenth centuries even names like Michael, Paul and Godfrey could have distinctive local distributions. Some of them then passed into the wider society and became generally popular, whereas others had only a brief and very local influence.

By the 1550s other innovators were emerging, some of them zealous ministers, and through them whole parishes were drawn into revolutionary change. In Sussex, for example, several ministers favoured phrase-names, notorious even in their own day. These include Sin-deny, Abuse-not, Hate-ill and Learn-wisdom. Of a similar nature were Obey, Refrayne, Repent and Magnify.[2] The virtue-names such as Charity and Prudence were more popular innovations, perhaps because they had precedents such as Grace and Constance which helped them to be accepted and pass into the name stock. Only a small percentage of Puritans opted for such names, but the practice was so distinctive that it brought ridicule on the movement. Other Puritan groups reacted in a different way. Halifax parish was unique locally for a time because so many ordinary families preferred names from the Old Testament, and several of these, Jonas and Abraham for example, remained much more popular there than in surrounding parishes or England more generally.

Not surprisingly the importance of godparents as name-givers began to decline by the 1700s and parental choices became more important. Nevertheless, most of these were still made from within the stock of conventional names and it would be a long time before parents felt completely free to give their children whatever name they wished. As a result, some first names continued to be distinctive right through the nineteenth century and a few were almost family-specific. The idea that we might trace a first name to a particular family or group of families is exciting news. In fact, first names is a study that promises to be a rich field for the genealogist and historian, for it throws considerable light on surname origins and offers us an insight into our ancestors and spiritual kin. The accounts that follow are meant to illustrate these aspects of the subject.

Godparents

Those registers which provide information about the godparents are testimony to the impact of this naming practice. In Kirkburton, for example, the names of godparents are given for only a very few years. They start in September 1556 with the baptism of Isabel Hynchclyfe: her two godmothers were Isabel Batty and Jennyt Hynchclyf. The second baptism is that of Robert Denton, whose godfather was Robert Fyrth, and the third Ralph Jesop, whose godfather was Ralph Greve. In a high percentage of cases the newly baptised child bore the name of one of the two godparents of the same sex, but because most of the first names were not particularly distinctive the influence of the practice within the parish would not stand out. There are examples, however, where children were given more unusual names, such as Arthur and Gervase, and the godparents on those occasions were Gervase Storthes, a local gentleman, and Arthur Binns, a prominent clothier. Both these names went on to be relatively popular in and around Kirkburton, during a period when they were generally uncommon.

Some wills provide similar evidence. In 1541, for example, Peter Dyneley of Whitkirk, near Leeds, made the following three bequests in his will:

> Item to Peter Helde, my godsone, one olde freside jacket.
> Item to Peter Webster, my godsone, one shorte gowne.
> Item to Peter Hall, my godsone, iijs. ivd.[3]

Peter was the chief of the apostles and the first bishop of Rome, but his name was never particularly common and it might be expected that it would have fallen completely out of favour after the Reformation, if only because it was so closely identified with the foundation of the Roman Catholic Church. That did not happen, although its use declined to a certain extent in the 1600s. Peter Dyneley was an unmarried priest and he may have seen his godsons as carrying on his name. In any case they had been given the name before the Dissolution, so it is unlikely that he was making a political statement. Later though it is noticeable that a number of Recusant gentry families favoured Peter.

Although we know a good deal about godparents from such sources, there is a lack of good evidence for the years before 1538, when parish registers first came into use. The following reference is therefore of special interest for it concerns the rare first name Bertram. In 1475 Bartram Dawson, a tailor and hosier, was enrolled as a freeman of York and he subsequently served several offices in the city. He was a chamberlain in 1490, sheriff in 1497 and mayor in 1510. Despite such credentials, he was the subject in 1506 of an inquiry set up to investigate rumours that he was 'a Scottysshman borne' – a particularly ironic accusation as he had raised money for a campaign against the Scots in 1497, when he was sheriff. In evidence it was said that Bartram 'was gotten and borne in the ... pariche of Bamburght' in Northumberland, and that his godfather was Bertram Fenkyll of Newham, a yeoman.

We can safely infer from the information in the freemen's rolls that Bertram Dawson would have been born about 1450 and the evidence that he shared his name with his godfather at that early date is useful, particularly as the man was a yeoman and not a gentleman. Bertram was especially uncommon in Yorkshire at that time and it is worth noting that several other Northumbrians connected with the county also had the name. Bertram Dawson's Northumberland origins are clear from his will, where he made a bequest to 'Bawmbeburgh kirke'. It seems as though the ambitious tailor may have had an accent that fuelled the rumours.

Spelling and Pronunciation

One of the problems we have with first names is that they were usually written in Latin in earlier centuries and we are not always sure what the English spelling and pronunciation were. Most names are not difficult: in a typical population list for 1379 we have Johannes (John), Willelmus (William), Alicia (Alice) and Margareta (Margaret), straightforward examples in which the Latin endings -us and -a clearly indicate the sex of the name bearer. This was essentially a written convention and there is no suggestion that the final letters were pronounced. It is useful in cases where a name could be given to either boys or girls, such as Philippus and Philippa, but there can be problems when the early latinised form is identical to a name borrowed more recently from abroad.

For example, in the same roll of 1379 we have the girls' name Emma, and that is the spelling used in most dictionaries. It is actually the form we employ now and is said to have come into fashion as recently as the eighteenth century, inspired by Matthew Prior's poem *Henry and Emma* (1709). It is doubtful therefore whether the medieval English name had a final 'a', but we are encouraged to think that it had when a dictionary describes 'Emma' as 'a short form of the medieval ... Ermintrude'.[4] The common diminutive of the original English name was 'Emmot' and the surname that derived from it was Em(p)son, so perhaps the medieval name was simply Emme, the spelling found in one fifteenth-century English text.[5] I suspect that there are other names listed in our dictionaries which betray similar confusion.

Christian, Christiana, Christina, Christine

These first names have separate entries in the most recent dictionary of first names and they are all said to derive ultimately from 'christianus', 'follower of Christ'. It is worth looking, therefore, at the history of the word 'Christian' in English. Its earlier history in Greek and Latin is responsible for the initial 'Ch', but the modern spelling is said to date only from the sixteenth century, when the English word 'cristen' was assimilated to the Latin 'christianus'. We have evidence of that in 'christendom' compared with 'christianity' and in the verb 'to christen', that is literally to 'make christian'. Of course the common noun and adjective could apply to both men and women and that is reflected in the history of the first name; in 1377 Cristinus Sausmaker was a resident of Carlisle and in 1381 Cristina Fulbrook lived in Berkshire. The likelihood is that both were addressed as 'Cristin'.

It seems worth asking therefore how many names there actually were in the middle ages, and we can begin with the spellings Christiana and Christina which are both found in the records. The evidence suggests that these were not separate names. In 1379, for example, a lady in Daventry had her name recorded twice, on the first occasion as Cristiana Neubold and on the second as Cristina Newbold. In Noseley in Leicestershire Robert Gowtby's daughter had her name written first as Christiana and secondly as Crystina. From other evidence in the poll tax returns it seems likely that the way it was written down may have been a matter of scribal preference: in Cumberland, for example, the girls' name was invariably entered as Cristiana whereas in Canterbury it was always Cristina. Whether it began with 'C' or 'Ch' again seems to have depended on the scribe.

On the face of it the by-name and surname evidence appears to point to a distinction, for Christian and Christin have both survived, although the latter is rare. P. H. Reaney dealt with them separately in his dictionary, deriving them from the distinctive first name spellings. However, the history of individual surnames is much less decisive. Christian is predominantly a surname found on the Isle of Man or in the coastal counties of north-west England, but most of the early spellings there represent some form of Cristin. From the 1400s, when the Gaelic 'Mac' was still in use, we have Mac Crystyn, Mac Christine and Mac Cristen, but there is one early Christiane in 1499. Nevertheless the latinisation of the common noun appears to have influenced the conventional spelling of the surname, and Christian has been the usual form since the 1600s.[6]

Christian was a frequent girl's name in the fourteenth century, much more popular in some districts than in others. In 1381, for example, in the Berkshire village of Long Wittenham there were eleven women called Cristina, whereas in East Garston, with a roughly similar population, there were just three. In Dorset it was the third most popular name overall but came no higher than twentieth in Staffordshire. It was not ranked at all in Derbyshire. As a boy's name at that time it was exceptionally uncommon, but a few examples are recorded from the mid 1600s, well before Bunyan gave the name to the male protagonist in *Pilgrim's Progress* (1684).

Withycombe noted the spelling 'Kyrstyan' in 1450 and compared it with the Scottish Kirsty. In fact vernacular spellings in Yorkshire such as Kyrshen (1556) and Kyrchyan (1558) are very similar. In the final syllable these seem to be parallel to Cristin and Christian and the variations are recorded into the mid 1600s. The distinction between the formal and the vernacular is nicely made in 1557, when Christeana, the daughter of Charles Stone was baptised: her godmother's name was given as Kyrchyn Wood. Family historians need to keep reminding themselves that most first names had vernacular pronunciations as well as pet forms and diminutives, and that these can all be masked by the formal use of Latin.

Adam: Some Surname Origins

Adam, on the other hand, never seems to have been given the -us ending, at least in my experience, although it had a Latin genitive form 'Ade'. It is another name that was far more popular in some districts in the

middle ages than in others. In 1377–81 there were a few counties where
it was scarcely used at all, notably Essex and Gloucestershire, whereas
in north-west England it was very common: only the traditional names
such as John, William, Thomas, Richard and Robert were more frequent
there.

Nevertheless Adam had several important English pet forms and
diminutives. All these have survived as surnames. The most common
were Addy, Adcock, Adkin or Atkin and Adinet, a double diminutive,
and the probability is that these were used to express affection or status.
They would have been useful also in communities where Adam was a
popular name, and particularly when a father and son were both called
Adam. The diminutive in such cases may simply have meant something
like 'junior'. Adkin in particular seems to have been employed in that
way, for instance Adekyn Bron of Ossett was the son of Adam Bron in
1286.[7] That practice may help to explain the origins of other characteristic
north country surnames, such as Atkinson, Hopkinson, Jenkinson and
Wilkinson.

It is when we look more closely into the early use of Adam in one
district that several points of interest emerge. In Yeadon and Esholt, for
example, a manor three miles south of Otley, it was a moderately
common first name in the fourteenth century, used by at least sixteen
families in a tightly-knit community. In the court roll of 1363 John the
son of Adam de Ottelay accused Adam de Mikelhagh of trespassing on
his lands, and a similar action was brought by Adam Piper; in May 1376
the three assessors were Adam de Yedon, Adam Walker and Adam
Carletonman. On the face of it all these men appear to have surnames,
but that was not the case. Their second names were mostly by-names,
some of them in the process of stabilising as surnames, and the manorial
records are detailed enough for us to see the role that Adam played in
that process.[8]

Adamson

A clerk called Adam de Ottelay was a tenant who died in 1345, after
which there are several references to his sons. John, the son of Adam
de Ottelay, has already been mentioned in the case of trespass in 1363,
and the unstable nature of his name is apparent later in the roll when

Alice, the wife of John, son of Adam was fined for a minor offence. Also described as a 'son of Adam de Ottelay' was another clerk with the first name Nicholas, but he had a number of by-names, including 'de Ottelay' and 'the chaplain'. His relationship to John is implicit in an undated deed whereby John Adamson of Otley gifted certain lands to Nicholas Adamson of Otley, chaplain.

Adinet

In general there are relatively few references to this double diminutive of Adam, but it was apparently something of a favourite in this manor.[9] Examples there include Adinett Wodward (1370), Adinet del Forest (1379) and Adynet, the son of Adam Walker (1403). More interesting than these, however, is Adinet, the son of John de Yedon (1376), who may of course be the same man as Adam de Yedon, mentioned earlier, but there is no confirmation of that in the rolls. Between 1377 and 1400 he featured regularly in the affairs of the manor, usually called simply Adinet de Yedon but also referred to as Adinet the Forester and even just as Adinet.[10] In any case it seems likely that he was dead by 1400 when his place in the list of tenants was taken by 'the wife of Adinet de Yedon'. From 1403 she appeared as Joan Adynetwyf, but there is no reference to her after 1406 and no obvious heir, so we presume that she too had died.

The other prominent Adinet in the manor was Adinet Walker. He was the son of Adam Walker and was admitted in 1403 as the tenant of a messuage and lands called Norcroft. The property was actually in Hawksworth, a locality adjoining Esholt, and it was still in Adinet's possession in 1443.[11] John Adinet of Norcroft succeeded him and thereafter Adinet was a hereditary surname in that part of Yorkshire, spreading to Ilkley, Harewood, Arthington and York. The curious aspect of its history is that in the sixteenth century it developed the alias Addinall or Addinell. It can be compared with Edward Burnett alias Burnell (1595).[12]

Both Addinall and Addinell were still concentrated in Yorkshire in 1881. In the census that year there were just over a hundred people so called and over eighty of these lived in and around York.[13] It remains almost exclusively a Yorkshire surname and Adinet appears to be extinct.

In this case the first name Adam, via an unusual surname alias and a rare diminutive, established a link between families now called Addinall/Addinell and the progenitor Adam Walker. Six hundred years ago he held a property called Northcroft or Norcroft in the township of Hawksworth.

Some Old Gentry Names

Among the names that the gentry chose to revive in the fifteenth century were Arthur, Charles and Leonard. These are so familiar to us now that we might be surprised to discover that they were almost unknown in the 1300s. One or two families reintroduced ancient Norman names that we would find obscure and which may have been equally obscure to their contemporaries. I imagine that they had come across these in their family documents (they were after all constantly consulting their title deeds). The Arthingtons, for example, chose to distinguish themselves by using Searle and the Vavasours revived Mauger, but these were successfully reinvented over the next few generations as Cyril and Major, with differing degrees of popularity among their tenants. Other very unusual names found in the pedigrees of the gentry and then among their tenants are Hardolph, Asculph and Malin, and it is the last of these that I shall look at now.

It is a particularly difficult first name to identify and seems unlikely to be a version of the Old Testament name Mahlon, although it was eventually confused with that name. Otherwise that would be an attractive possibility, for it is first recorded in that part of Nottinghamshire where Ezekiel, Silvanus and Gamaliel were revived in the late 1400s. David Hey discussed the name in his interesting account of the seventeenth-century emigrant Mahlon Stacy in *Aspects of Sheffield* (1997), and he noted the discrepancy between the late spelling Mahlon and those recorded in the 1500s. He was of the opinion that it might have its origin in the surname Malin.

It was in the sixteenth century that the gentry began to use surnames as first names and there were families named Malin in both south Yorkshire and Derbyshire in the middle ages. The surname was never prolific but it appears to have survived as later references to it are found in those areas. It could be spelt Malin or Mallin and is a pet form of

Matilda, not Mary as has sometimes been said: Mallinson is probably the best known of the surnames that it gave rise to. When it was thought that Malin as a christian name was first used in 1566, it was logical to think that the Stacys might have coined it to commemorate a marriage between themselves and a family surnamed Malin, for that fashion was establishing itself at that time. However, the discovery of a much earlier reference to the first name makes the surname theory most unlikely. Malin Marckham of Retford in Nottinghamshire died in 1515 and the circumstances mean that he must have been named in the 1400s, several generations before surnames were being used as given names.[14]

It may be therefore that the later history of the name has to some extent obscured its origins, for it is the use of Malin by the Stacys and other south Yorkshire families that has attracted most attention. David Hey recorded its use by no fewer than nineteen Sheffield families, most of them in the period 1620–50, but a few well into the eighteenth century and one as late as 1763. In Sheffield the last Stacy known to have borne the name was the Malin baptised in 1723, who was apprenticed to a cutler in 1738. The Mahlon Stacy who emigrated in 1678 died in New Jersey in 1704, but he was succeeded by his son, another Mahlon. Rarely can a personal name have so clearly identified an emigrant's English place of origin, although these American spellings prove that Malin was by then thought to be the Old Testament Mahlon.

The relative popularity of Malin in south Yorkshire, after about 1550, should not blind us to the significance of the reference to Malin Marckham in 1515. Of course this is not in itself very helpful, for it tells us nothing about the earlier history of the personal name, but it confirms that it was being used by the Markhams, who were an established gentry family; and it points to a possible origin in Nottinghamshire rather than Yorkshire. It might also be argued that such a name was more likely to have originated with a gentry family than with the Stacys, lower down the social scale, especially in the late 1400s. Once that has been accepted the Nottinghamshire evidence assumes more importance. For example, Mahlon Stacy's mother was from Eastwood in Nottinghamshire and he married Rebecca Ely of Mansfield in the same county. Moreover, David Hey's footnote to the hearth tax returns of 1672 alerts us to the fact that two Malins were listed in Derbyshire and six in Nottinghamshire. Clearly the name was well established in the latter county. Perhaps it is there that we should expect to find even earlier uses of Malin, either in the Markham family or in gentry families with whom they were linked. Hopefully that would help us to establish Malin's earliest history and origin.

Original

The unusual name Original has been the subject of much discussion. It was first used in the sixteenth century and one theory was that it had been coined by Puritans and referred to 'original sin'. Camden suggested that it was 'from the Greek *origines*, that is borne in good time', but Charles Bardsley rejected that idea, maintaining that it was given 'in the early part of the sixteenth century, in certain families of position, to the eldest son and heir, denoting that in him was carried on the original stock'. His examples of the families amongst whom it was used included the Babingtons and the Bellamys, who had estates in Nottinghamshire and south Yorkshire. According to Bardsley, the first Original Bellamy was baptised in 1539, 'far too early a date for the name to be fathered upon the Puritans'. There were at least three generations of Original Bellamys, one of them dying as a prisoner in York Castle in 1632.

Most of the other early examples of the name occur in areas where the Bellamys were influential landowners. Origynall Walshe was baptised in Braithwell in 1570 and the name was used after that by several families both there and in Nottinghamshire. These include the Wilsons, Midgleys, Ashleys and Gilbys, but this local custom was apparently short lived, and one of the last recorded was Originall Byron of Stokeham near Tuxford, who died in 1647. Elsewhere there was an Originall Todd in Howden in the 1580s, and a prisoner called Originall Lewis who was transported to the island of St Christopher in 1635.

There is, however, a quite different chapter in this name's history, traceable to a Wooldale family called Bower. In this case the name had no direct connection with the Nottinghamshire Originals but developed as a variant of Reginald. This relatively uncommon name was a favourite with the Bowers of Wooldale from 1633, when Reginald Bower arrived in the parish and married Frances Broadhead. It was his descendant Reginald Bower of Horsewells who was responsible for changing the name, but what prompted him to do so is not known. It was possibly just the pronunciation: when his children were baptised in the late 1700s, the spellings he used moved from Reginal to Origenal; when his wife died in 1807 he remarried almost immediately and signed his name as 'Original'.[15] Perhaps he was making a fresh start. His descendants later moved a few miles into the Colne Valley and the name continued in use there into the early twentieth century. There was a millwright called Original Bower living in Lockwood in the late 1800s whose family records are held in the Kirklees archives.

Tedbar

This most unusual first name has been in use in the Kirkburton area for nearly three hundred years. A family called Tinker was largely responsible for this. The first Tedbar Tinker was baptised in 1711, the son of Abel who lived at Shepley Carr, but others were to follow, and any student of Kirkburton's history cannot fail to encounter the name in that period. As recently as 1992 there was a reference in the local newspaper to Ellen, the widow of possibly the last Tedbar Tinker. These Shepley and Shelley Tinkers were just one branch of a prolific and widespread family with a history in the Holmfirth area going back to the 1200s. Their connections ensured that some of their neighbours and kinsmen also came to use the name although it was never generally popular.

It was taken up in parts of Kirkburton parish by the Jackmans and the Tyases, in Emley by the Moorhouses and Hinchliffes, and in Nether-thong by the Hobsons. Further afield there was a Tedber or Tedbert Barrowclough in Garforth, who died in 1805, aged seventy-four according to the parish register. He had named his own first-born son Robert, and the probability is that he came from Kirkburton, where a Tedbald Barraclough, son of Robert, was baptised in 1740. For that to be true the Garforth man must have been sixty-four at the time of his death, not seventy-four, but the combination of given name and surname is so rare that the inference seems possible. The spelling Tedbald, which was also used occasionally by the Tinkers and the Tyases, is a vital clue to the name's origin and earlier history.

In the early 1700s Shelley and Shepley were part of the manor of Wakefield, and one of the major freeholders was a gentleman called

Tedbald Wallis who lived in Mexborough. This is a village eighteen miles to the south east, but there is no doubt that this man had Shelley connections. In the great manorial survey of 1709, for example, he is referred to as holding land in Shelley. A few years later he was accused at the quarter sessions of 'a fraud on John Hudson', in alliance 'with men of Shelley and Cumberworth'. I have found no other Yorkshire references to this unusual name, so the first Tedbar Tinker may have been named in his honour. Tedbald is actually a spelling of Theobald, first recorded in the Domesday Book, and its use by the Wallis family may go back much earlier than the example found in the 1700s, possibly in some other county. Alternatively it may have been a deliberate choice by somebody with antiquarian interests.

Surprisingly, perhaps, there were still over forty people with the name in England and Wales in 1881. Almost all these were in south Yorkshire. Tedbar and Tedber were the most popular spellings, but several variants were also recorded. These were Tedbor, Tedbert and Tedbuard in Dewsbury, Tedborough and Tedburn in Huddersfield, and Tedbour in Leeds.[16]

Oscar

The attraction for me in this less than common name is that its origin and history appear to be well defined. Its modern use dates back to 1759 when the Scottish writer James Macpherson published his poem 'The Death of Oscar'. This was a forerunner of a body of work produced over a period of four or five years which purported to be a faithful translation of an original Gaelic epic. Macpherson claimed to have collected the material for this on his travels through the Highlands of Scotland and attributed it to Ossian, the son of Finn or Fingal, a Gaelic bard from a vague and remote period in Scottish history. He successfully satisfied his readers' desire for something redolent of an earlier, simpler age, and the popularity of his poetry in Scotland was followed by a similar vogue on the Continent, where the cult of 'the noble savage' had helped to create a receptive audience. Among several German writers who were influenced by Macpherson was the poet Goethe, who quoted Ossian in *The Sorrows of Young Werther* (1774).

It was not long before the authenticity of Macpherson's sources was being questioned, and the redoubtable Dr Johnson was one of the poet's most sceptical critics, denouncing him as a liar. That scepticism seems to have been justified, for an investigation several years after Macpherson's death reported that he had fabricated much of the material. The poems actually survived that revelation and one of their greatest admirers was Napoleon, who bestowed the name Oscar on his godson in 1799. Oscar's father was the marshal, Jean-Baptiste Bernadotte. When he became King of Sweden young Oscar became the Crown Prince. As early as 1812 the name Oscar was entered in his honour in the calendar under 1 December, replacing St Eligius. He succeeded to the throne in 1844.[17]

According to the Danish scholar Torben Kisbye, much of the subsequent popularity of Oscar had its origins in the Swedish connection and he has traced its early introduction into Denmark to Swedish immigrants. Its increased use by Danes dates from 1848, largely, it seems, because King Oscar of Sweden sided with Denmark in its war over Schleswig-Holstein, a move that was greeted with wild enthusiasm right through the country. Swedish emigration is also credited with having brought about Oscar's temporary popularity in the United States in the 1870s, a phenomenon noted by Dunkling in *First Names First* (1977).

In England it is usual to attribute the name's more modest success, and subsequent decline, to Oscar Wilde. The writer's growing reputation in the early 1880s no doubt explains why the name was given in 1882 to my uncle, Henry Oscar Redmonds. That choice may throw some light on his father, who regularly gave his sons two names, one that was traditional and one that smacked of the exotic: Oscar had brothers called Charles Edgar, George Granville, Frederick Harcourt and Percy Leopold. Oscar's decline is said to date from 1895 when the writer was imprisoned for homosexual offences, but it remained traditional in some families: Henry Oscar's grandson is now Victor Oscar.

It is probably true that the immediate inspiration in England was Oscar Wilde, but ultimately the connection was almost certainly with Macpherson's poetry via the Swedish court, for Wilde's father spent some time there as physician-in-ordinary to the king. In fact he called his son Oscar Fingal O'Flahertie Wills, and Fingal was another Ossianic name that had passed into more general use in Sweden. In Celtic mythology Fingal was the grandfather of Oscar and another great hero.

Torben Kisbye was also of the opinion that Oscar's linguistic roots were not Germanic, although Withycombe and others have explained it as a compound of 'os' and 'gar', that is 'god' and 'spear'. These are certainly well-known Germanic elements and the name Osgarus is recorded in Domesday Book, but Kisbye offers the alternative explanation that Oscar first appeared in the Fenian sagas and derives there from two Gaelic words meaning 'deer' and 'friend'.

8

Inns and Public Houses

For centuries the public house has been one of the main focal points of the community and public house names hold a special place in our affections. In fact, they are so familiar to us that without them we might find it difficult to give accurate directions from one place to another. We need to remind ourselves, though, that the name of the house originally derived from the sign, an important symbol in the days when few people could read or write: it served to distinguish a house where a stranger might obtain refreshment from one that was an ordinary dwelling. In Methley, in 1384, Cecilia of Thorne was one of several women indicted for brewing and selling ale but failing to place an ale sign outside her house. She was also accused of selling it in 'dishes' and not by the measure.

Perhaps we should be careful though how we interpret the word 'sign' at that time, for it may have been nothing more than a decorated pole. The Romans are said to have had a bush outside a tavern, as a sign that there was wine for sale, and the 'bush' may have been just a bundle of evergreen leaves fixed to a pole. There are numerous references to such poles in England in the middle ages. For example, in 1465 Thomas Burton's wife was said to have sold ale when she had no ale-stake in front of her house, and in 1498 a similar sign was described as an ailswispe.[1] There is a similarity here with Scotland, where a wisp of straw on a pole informed the thirsty traveller that he was outside an alehouse. The last such reference that I have come across is in 1613, when Michael Jackson's wife assaulted a man with a pitchfork because he was 'cutting down her Ale-rod'.[2]

Of course, there had been pictorial signs before this, and by the 1600s, when the practice was probably becoming more general, some alehouses had both symbols. A poem of 1622 refers to one with 'a bush and sign' and the inference from an undated anecdote of this period is that the sign carried increased status: it mentions that a painter offered one hostess a sign if she aspired 'to the conceite' and wished to pull down 'her birch pole'. In 1673 a minister called Oliver Heywood recorded his disgust at a sign set up at the house of a man called Mortimer, somewhere on the road between Halifax and Bradford – 'an abominable, filthy sign ... a man and a woman pictured in a shameful manner'. It had been painted by John Aked who had been commissioned 'to draw it as lively as he could' and the fee was thirty shillings for the painting and seven shillings for the posts.[3] It was still common in seventeenth-century records to find a hostelry described simply as 'the house of' a particular person, but references such as 'at the sign of the Rose' were increasing.

The affection we have for these names cannot be doubted, for any brewery-proposed alternative is sure to meet with strong local opposition. It is as though people treasure each name's associations, seeing it as a link between past and present and a reflection of the community's local history. Indeed public house names do reflect many aspects of the community's past, sometimes its social and political history, sometimes its folklore. They can tell us about local occupations and industries, changes in modes of transport and changes in the landscape. Even when the name has no obvious resonance of that kind, we value it simply because we are familiar with it. It is surprising therefore that the history of these signs and names has attracted so little attention from place-name scholars. It is true that these topics are written about, at a certain level, in magazines and newspapers, and in books about pubs in general, but, understandably, these tend to concentrate on the anecdotal value of the names and seek little more than popular appeal. Relatively few serious books have been written on the subject and very few volumes of the English Place-Names Society series contain examples of the earliest names.

Recently there has been a more scholarly approach, and one or two books have gone some way towards providing us with a context for the subject. Dunkling and Wright have listed some 10,000 names in their *Dictionary of Pub Names* (1987), including examples from every part of the country, and they have brought a sense of evidence to bear in their discussions about 'meaning'. It is undoubtedly a subject that lends itself to flights of fancy. Most of us will have heard it said that the Goat and Compasses is a version of 'God encompasseth us', the invention of a particularly pious landlord in the seventeenth century. Dunkling and

Wright trace this 'etymology' to Anthony Trollope – who no doubt heard it from somebody else – and then consider two other more likely explanations. For example the arms of the Worshipful Company of Cordwainers has a chevron that closely resembles an open pair of compasses between three goats' heads and this could easily have given rise to the name. The Elephant and Castle has been popularly explained as a corruption of Infanta de Castile, but here the authors' interpretation draws our attention to the crest of the Cutlers' Company. This shows an elephant with a castle-like howdah on its back. These suggestions have the merit of being in the tradition of names based on coats of arms, and are typical of the reasoned approach in this useful reference work.

Barrie Cox goes one step further in *English Inn and Tavern Names* (1994), dealing systematically with his material and attempting to put the names that he has collected into a historical framework. These are from a fairly restricted area, and the evidence is uneven, but he shows us nonetheless how the names developed through the centuries. His conclusions are worth summarising. They take the documented history of the names back to the fourteenth century, and examples from the early period include many which are still familiar to us, such as the George (1369), Sun (1374), Angel (1435), Swan (1446), Crown (1465) and White Hart (1492). In his opinion many of these related directly to heraldry, being descriptive of the devices or 'charges' on knightly and royal coats of arms. The Crown, for example, symbolised power and the White Hart was a device of Richard II. On the other hand the George in earlier centuries must always have referred to St George, England's patron saint from the early 1400s at least, and the Angel is likely to be the archangel St Michael, whose cult was strong in medieval times.

Of course, in the middle ages it was also the custom for some private establishments to have 'inn' signs, and surviving names such as Gray's Inn and Lincoln's Inn remind us of those which once offered exclusive accommodation to students. Some family homes are also said to have had their own signs, and this practice may have survived into the seventeenth century. The Paston family, for example, widely known through the Paston Letters, had a town house in Norwich called 'le Prince Inne' and they took the sign with them when they moved to another location. Not all documents would make it clear whether such a name referred to a public or a private house.

Barrie Cox noted many early names where a symbol such as the Hind or the Cock was followed by a phrase involving the word 'hoop'. Amongst others he quoted the 'Belle on the Hoope' (1403) and 'le Cock in the Hoope' (1554), offering the suggestion that the heraldic charge in these cases may actually have been placed within a hoop. His explanation of this practice was that the hoop represented the end panel of a barrel or cask, either suspended, or cut in half and fixed to the inn wall. Presumably it might also be that a device was attached within a hoop from the barrel. It may be that this little-discussed practice was responsible for some names which incorporate the words 'hoop' or 'hope', such as the Hope and Anchor, although Dunkling has other explanations for this. Could it be also that the obscure phrase 'cock-a-hoop' had its origins in one of these inn names? One early dictionary reference certainly connects the phrase with excessive drinking.

Heraldry continued to be a dominant influence on the names that Cox collected for the centuries that followed, although, as he rightly pointed out, we shall need material for the country as a whole if we are to discover the earliest date for each name. From the period 1500 to 1549 he noted what he referred to as 'the armorial beasts', that is the Bear, the Boar, the Bull and the Lion. In the same period are recorded many compound names, using colours or having 'head' as the second element. These include the Blue Boar (1549), the Bull's Head (1518), the King's Head (1540) and the White Lion (1512). The Rose (1525), which he called 'the medieval primate among flowers', he judged to have been introduced because of its association with the Houses of York and Lancaster. There were other sources of inspiration. The Lamb (1504), which represented the 'Agnus Dei' or Paschal lamb, and the Mitre (1536), both of which seem to point to growing ecclesiastical influence.

In a fascinating paragraph Cox commented on the picture of the elephant with a 'castle' on its back, saying that the elephant motif is found in manuscript illustrations and ecclesiastical wood carving back to the middle ages. He quoted William Caxton, who wrote that 'an olyphaunt bereth wel a tour of woode upon his backe' (1486), and noted that the elephant is present in the arms of the Royal African Company, incorporated in 1662, as well as in those of the Cutlers' Company. He speculated that the medieval motif may go back to classical accounts of Hannibal's crossing of the Alps with his fighting elephants, in the attack on Rome, and played down the importance of Britain's later trading connections with India.

A motif with a more recent tradition is that of the Saracen's Head, recorded as a tavern name as early as 1463. Cox linked this with the eighteenth-century Turk's Head and the Blackmoor's Head of 1770, but I have the feeling that the latter may belong to a different tradition. There are 'Blackamoors' now up and down the country, from Wigton in Cumbria to Chessington in Surrey, and the word appears to date from Elizabeth's reign rather than the Crusades, describing black people and not Moors or North Africans. Ethiopian meant Negro at that time and there is a reference in Elland parish register, in 1601, to 'Isabella Aethiops *vulgo* a blackmore', a servant to Lady Savile at Bradley Hall. This girl was probably from the west coast of Africa, for it was becoming fashionable at that time to have a black servant dressed in bright livery. In fact many of the so-called blackamores were given English surnames, and the word occurs fairly frequently also as a nickname, presumably for a white person. Richard Hunte alias Blackamore was living in Ingleton in 1611, and Christopher Styles otherwise Blackamoor in Thorne in 1657.

Among the new names noted in the 1600s are many which might now be called traditional in type, such as the Black Horse (1674), King's Arms (1697) and Nag's Head (1677). Also the Three Crowns (1697) and Three Tuns (1680) continue a trend first recorded in 1538 to have names based on groups of three, a practice which may have connections with 'three' as a mystical or magic number. To understand the evocative power of the word we need only consider children's stories about the three bears or three blind mice, on the one hand, and the three wise men and the Holy Trinity, on the other. A more practical consideration is that groups of three were convenient for decorating armorial shields, and that too may have contributed to the popularity of such symbols. What might be called nautical names appear also in this period, perhaps reflecting the growth of English sea-power: they include the Anchor (1682), Mermaid (1677) and Two Dolphins (1675).

The Fleece (1687) and the Woolpack (1696) are two of the first names to allude directly to commercial interests, but they may sometimes also reflect the growing importance of cross-country travel. These themes soon accounted for many new names, such as the Coach and Horses

(1708), Horse Shoe (1726), and Old Pack Horse (1738). Once the Industrial Revolution was under way, increasing numbers of names referred to craft and trade interests, for instance the Bricklayers' Arms (1824) and the Axe and Saw (1846). New modes of transport made a particularly strong impact, introducing the Travellers' Rest (1811), Steam Packet (1824), Railway Tavern (1845) and Locomotion (1847). The Great Western usually commemorates the Great Western Railway, whereas the Great Eastern was inspired by Brunel's ship of that name, the largest in the world in the 1800s.

In the Pennine towns of Yorkshire and Lancashire many new names referred to the wide variety of occupations in the textile industry. Names such as the Spinners, Weavers, Dyers and Clothiers require no explanation, but others are more complicated. The Slubbers, for example, found in Rochdale and Huddersfield, takes its name from a process in which wool or cotton was prepared for spinning. The word first came into use in the late 1700s and its etymology is obscure. The Croppers, another Huddersfield public house, refers to the highly skilled workers whose job it was to shear the cloth in the finishing process. These were the men whose livelihood was threatened when shearing machines were invented, and who formed the backbone of the Luddite movement in west Yorkshire. One of their meeting places was the appropriately named Shears Inn in Hightown.

The Tim Bobbin in Rochdale, one of the inns where the turnpike to Huddersfield was planned in 1806, has a less direct textile connection. It was the nickname of a Lancashire dialect poet and artist, but derived from the bobbins around which the thread or yarn was wound. The making of bobbins was a thriving local industry, and the word became part of local lore. To be fit and well is still to be as 'reight as a bobbin': in the mill the children who placed the bobbins in position were known as bobbin 'liggers', and those who removed them were bobbin 'doffers'.

Local Features

Several of the names first noted by Cox in the 1790s had to do with what he called 'local features', and some of these might almost be described as place-names. He noted the Gallows and the Pump at that time, followed later by the Bowling Green, Elm Tree and Flash.[4] Of course all these names may be very much older than his first examples suggest, and that is particularly true of those that developed out of a very common feature such as a bowling green. The court rolls record the punishment of people playing bowls 'against the statute' from the early 1500s, that is on a Sunday, but there were doubtless bowling greens at that time in many villages. They are referred to frequently in the records in the 1600s. In 1636, for instance, there was a 'Bowlinge spott' in Almondbury 'sett forthe to bowle upon', and the by-laws prohibited tenants from driving 'with horses, cart or waine over the bowelling green'. In 1690 Joseph Hepworth of Almondbury was ordered to 'levell and make even one parcell of ground called the Bowleing Green' which he had 'lately plowed up'.[5] It would have been a logical place to have an inn, and my own first reference to the name is 1744, on a tombstone in Kirkheaton churchyard.

It is not unusual now to see names that contain the word 'cross' accompanied by a sign depicting a knight in armour, as though the inspiration was heraldic. That may sometimes be true and, when Cox recorded the name in 1571, he thought that it might go back to the Crusades. In other cases, however, it certainly refers to a standing cross, and Dunkling suggests that the Old Cross at Stapleford in Nottinghamshire takes its name from an ancient Saxon cross in the churchyard near by. Local knowledge can be vital in such cases. Close to where I live, there is an inn called the White Cross in Bradley, and another called the Green Cross in Dalton. Both occupy sites at cross roads that were once marked by standing poles or stones. These were known as 'crosses' and they explain the public house names, but the signs today are embellished with white and green crosses on knightly shields.

There are other names in this category which I feel might be of particular interest to local historians. For example, Dunkling and Wright have listed public houses named the Warren or Warren House in Kent, Devon and West Yorkshire, and there are likely to be others elsewhere in the country. The explanation offered by the authors is that these were 'all references to rabbit warrens which had to be filled in before the pub was built or which were to be seen near the pub'. I suspect that there is much more to the name than that, at least in Yorkshire, for the place-name is very frequent in the county, not always referring to a public house. This in itself implies that the 'warren house' was formerly a familiar enough feature of the landscape, and there are certain records which throw light on its function.

A lease of 1668 names the 'Warrenhouse or Lodge ... in Mirfield, late in the tenure of John Howmes, and all that Warren and Liberty of Warren for conyes upon ... the wast or common of Mirfield Moore ... with liberty to make burrowes for conies'.[6] Conies were of course rabbits, said to have been introduced into this country by the Normans. In the middle ages they were bred in specially enclosed areas of the manorial waste or common and were prized for their fur and for their meat. The right to breed them was jealously guarded by important landowners. Apparently it was only in the eighteenth century that rabbits were hardy enough to survive in the wild and, until then at least, they remained under the supervision of the warren keeper or warrener. The 1668 lease suggests that his warren house was the equivalent of the park keeper's lodge.

The quarter sessions records for the seventeenth and eighteenth centuries frequently mention offences committed in the warrens. In 1728, for example, three Longroyd Bridge men were accused of 'entring upon a warren upon Crosland Moor belonging to John Wilkinson of Greenhead and occupied by John Ellis'. They were then brought before the magistrates and fined heavily for hunting rabbits there 'with doggs and netts'.[7] The only other record we have of this warren is the name of the public house near by, better known for its connections with the murder of the manufacturer William Horsfall during the Luddite riots. At that time the Warren House was situated at the side of the old highway from Huddersfield to Manchester, as it began the steep climb over Crosland Moor. When a more direct road was built through the valley in the 1820s, the licence was transferred to a new public house, built to take advantage of both local and trans-Pennine traffic. That is the one listed by Dunkling and Wright in Milnsbridge.

A third Warren House stood on Lindley Moor, on the disputed boundary between Halifax and Huddersfield. It is some time since it was an inn, but the old name can still be seen painted on the front wall, a nice link with the past for passers-by, but a source of annoyance to the residents. It is difficult now to visualise the house in a moorland setting, for the area was converted to farmland in the early 1800s, but until then it was an isolated dwelling that served both as an inn and a warren house. The publican and warrener was Saville Crowther, one of several members of the family to serve that function. An earlier Savile Crowder was responsible in 1731 for the 'coney warren' on the Beaumont estate in Whitley.[8]

The fact that some warren houses became inns suggests that warreners may have sought to supplement their income by having the house licensed. When the waste areas were enclosed and the warren ceased to function, the warrener managed to survive as an innkeeper. At Lindley the transformation took place between 1806 and 1816, a period during which the moor was enclosed and a new turnpike road built near by. Many of the meetings of the trustees for these two projects were at the Warren House, and one large piece of land was set aside for the lord of the manor 'in lieu of warren'. Thereafter the inn was a warren house in name only.[9]

The Woodman or Woodman's Arms

The first example of this name was noted by Cox in 1846, and he linked it with names such as the Bricklayers' Arms, Shipwrights' Arms and Coopers' Arms, all associated with skilled workmen 'whose craft organizations used taverns as houses of call'. He described them as a significant new departure in hostelry naming in the nineteenth century, and wondered whether some of them represented the heraldic devices of national livery companies. Dunkling and Wright found the name 'everywhere' and noted about twenty-five in the greater London area alone. In their view the name was simply a reminder of the woodman's former importance.

No doubt the name is sometimes just an arbitrary choice, but in other cases it may be a more direct clue to a long-forgotten aspect of the local economy. For example, it is noticeable in the area in which I live that public houses called the Woodman are usually sited very close to former woodland estates. There is a Woodman in Emley, close to Emley Park, which once supplied great timber to local builders; a second Woodman, at Bradley, is situated on the boundary of the Pilkingtons' former woodland estate; and a third Woodman, at Thunderbridge, lies close to the site of Roche Abbey's Timberwood Grange. This territory was wood managed from the thirteenth century at least.

It is right that we should be reminded of the important role the woodman once had, and how much it has declined. Oliver Rackham has discussed the earliest history of woodmanship in Britain, starting in prehistoric times.[10] He credited the Romans with developing it in an organised way, in order to ensure regular supplies of both timber and wood for building and industrial development, and also calculated that their ironworks in the Weald would have been sustained by 23,000 acres of coppice wood. The traditions were undoubtedly maintained through the Anglo-Saxon period, and we have excellent documentary sources for the centuries after the Conquest. These emphasise how intensively the woods were then being managed. The decline began as woodland products became less important. In the old West Riding timber for building and fencing began to give way to stone in the 1500s, and coppice woods declined in importance when charcoal for the ironworks was replaced by coke. The process was accelerated by cheap imports, so that by the early nineteenth century the woodman was becoming a rarity, at least in some parts of the country. And yet most of the public houses named the Woodman appear to have been given the name in that period.

The Woodman at Thunderbridge, mentioned above, has been a public house for well over two hundred years, although the name has not been noted before the early 1800s. It was the inn where the trustees of the proposed turnpike road between Penistone and Fenay Bridge had their inaugural meetings, in 1776–77, but in the minutes of those meetings it is simply described as 'the House of Joshua Smith'. We do not, however, need to look very far for the 'woodman' associations; the inn occupies a key position close to a bridge and corn mill, and it is only a very short distance from Grange Farm, owned by Roche Abbey until the Dissolution. The part this territory played in the overall economy of the abbey is clear in the name Timberwood Grange. Timber, sometimes called 'great timber', was a more specialised term formerly, and referred to the trees set aside for major building projects.

After the Dissolution the new owners of the abbey's estate continued to manage the woods, certainly until after the first references to the inn, so the woodman's house would have been well known. We know almost nothing about it, although the court rolls for this part of the manor carry several references to a 'Thomas Wodeman' in the early 1300s. He had a son named Adam Wodeman, but this was probably an occupational by-name rather than a true surname, and there is no record of it after 1332. Nevertheless, their house is likely to have been on or close to the site of the present inn, which may have acquired its name and new function when the woodman, like the warrener, found himself out of work.

Grange Ash

It can be difficult to tell the story of any public house, and yet many of those in prime situations are likely to have been popular local venues for centuries. Several of the difficulties that the researcher faces emerge in a brief account of the Kaye Arms, an inn that stands high on the main road between Huddersfield and Wakefield. It is an isolated enough place even now, despite the continual traffic and frequent customers, but where the fields are today there was once moorland, and, in the past, it must have been lonely as well as isolated. Now, there is only the place-name Grange Moor to remind us of that earlier phase in its history.

Maps and documents tell us that the inn's present name is not very old, at least not if we compare it with the age of the settlement itself. In White's street directory of 1853 it was 'Kaye's Arms', and Robert Watson was the landlord. His home address was Grange Ash and, apart from the local minister Mr Bullivant, who probably lodged at the inn, he was the only resident named. Not very far away at Denby Grange, the source of the two place-names Grange Moor and Grange Ash, lived Sir John Lister Kaye, and it is his family that is commemorated in the present name. Just when it acquired the name is not certain, but a gazetteer of 1822 described it as 'Grange Ash, a public house in the township of Whitley'.[11] In local diaries and estate accounts for that period typical entries record visits 'to Grange Ash today', and that appears to be the earlier name.

Armed with that information we can immediately locate much earlier references. The licence of the Grange Ash was given to John Ness of Whitley at the quarter sessions in 1803; a lease of 1746 mentions 'Walter Kaye of Grange Ash, victualler', and the place-name is on Warburton's map of 1720. The fact that a man called Kaye was then the publican is intriguing – even more so when we find references to the place-name in seventeenth-century sources. The register for Kirkheaton tells us that in 1695 George Kay was at Grange Ash, and a legal document of 1667 names Joseph Kaye of Grange Ash. Generations of the Kaye family must have lived there, starting with 'John Kaye of the Grange Ash', whose daughter Susan was baptised at Emley in 1647.

I say 'starting with', and yet the probability is that the connection goes back even earlier. Unfortunately the documentary evidence is not precise enough for us to be sure that an earlier 'John Kaye of Grange' was actually 'of Grange Ash'. Tantalisingly the 'Grang Ashe' is shown on Saxton's map of the West Riding for 1577, hinting at an even longer history, but we are denied access to that because the parish register has not survived. It seems unlikely, however, that the association between the Kayes and Grange Ash goes back much earlier than 1577, for the Kaye family at Woodsome had purchased the Denby Grange estate after the Dissolution. Nor can we be certain that Grange Ash was a public house before 1746, although its location near to the manor house, on a major medieval highway, certainly invites that conclusion.

Ash Brow

Grange Ash was in a moorland area, where the boundaries of several parishes came together, so it may have been named after a solitary tree used as a boundary marker. We know from the documentary evidence that there were formerly peat pits on the moor, but the place-name suggests that there were trees also at this altitude, roughly 800 feet above sea level. On the other side of Huddersfield, in Sheepridge, which is also the name of a former area of waste, is the Ash Brow, another public house that appears to take its name from a solitary tree.

The present inn is at the side of the main road to Bradford, but this is a nineteenth-century turnpike, a long way from the medieval highway, and it seems unlikely to have been a public house for very long. Despite that it has an interesting history. The locality was formerly known as Cuckold Clough, a name that commemorates the deep-cut valley close by and the Cockwold family who lived there in the thirteenth century. That name is no longer used, and it appears to have been replaced by Ash Brow, a process that may have started 450 years ago. In 1543, a tenant called James Mellor took out a lease on 'the messuage called Cokewald Clough', and this remained in his family's possession for some time.

We know that the Mellors were soon granted permission to clear part of the surrounding common, for a deed of 1565 refers to 'land latlye enclosed of the waste'. More significantly, in 1633, after the Mellors had departed, their successors' small estate was described as 'lying upon a place called Sheepridge, of which ten acres doth abut upon Meller Ashe', that is the Mellors' ash tree. In 1789, when Huddersfield's commons were being enclosed, the Act referred to this section as 'the common called Ashbrow, across a valley called Cuckolds Clough'. Today the name Ash Brow is used for the district and for the inn, and it seems certain to be close to where the medieval settlement was; close that is to where an ash tree once marked the limit of James Mellor's hard-won intake.[12]

Sporting Venues

Cox noted that country inns were popular sporting venues towards the end of the eighteenth century, particularly for hunt meets and horse racing, and that link is commemorated in the Horse and Jockey of 1783. Later names were the Fox and Hounds, Hare and Hounds and Tally Ho. In fact there was a public house in Mirfield called the Hare and Hounds in 1755, but the name is probably much older than that, since hare-coursing in the Pennines and the Lake District has a long history. That regional interest in the sport is reflected in numerous public house names and I shall look briefly at some of these now. In the examples quoted by Cox the etymology of the names is not in doubt, but several of the north-country names do pose problems.

In Glenridding, a small place at the side of Ullswater, there is an inn known simply as 'Ratchers', and my first thought was that the name might commemorate a famous hound. The inn sign shows two hunts-men and a pack of beagles, so the link with hunting seems clear enough, even if there is no hint of exactly what Ratchers might mean. On the day of my visit the staff were unable to offer any help, except to confirm that the name had 'something to do with hunting'.

In fact there are numerous local references that help to explain the name. A document of 1514 mentions 'a grett multitude of dogges, both grewhondis and ratches', as though a 'ratch' was a specific type of dog.[13] A book on Cumbrian folklore lists 'ratch' as a dialect word, explaining it as a verb that means 'to ransack, to seize meat as a hungry dog does' – well illustrated in the phrase 'ratchan' about like a hungry hound'.[14] The *English Dialect Dictionary* offers the explanation that the noun 'ratch' is used, in the north, of a dog that hunts by scent, and gives it an Old English origin. Particularly illuminating is a Halifax diary, where we read that 'Gabriel-Ratches' was the name given locally to 'a strange noyse in the aire … as if a great number of whelps were barking'. The noise was a warning 'before a great death' (1665).[15] The painter of the inn sign might have made more of that.

A second puzzling name in this category is Whoop Hall, an inn near Kirkby Lonsdale, and again my first thought seems to have been wide of the mark. Because of the moorland near to the inn I associated it with 'whaup', the north country dialect word for the curlew. A similar place-name is Tewit Hall, common in the Pennines where 'tewit' is the dialect word for the green plover. The local explanation, recorded by Dunkling and Wright, is that the inn stands on the site of a former manor house known as Upp Hall. It was adapted to Whoop because of its links with the local squire and his pack of hounds. The cry 'whoo up' is apparently what the huntsman shouts at the death of his quarry.

Public House Nicknames

Public houses quite commonly have two names, one of which might be called a nickname, and these can often tell us something about former landlords. Typical examples in west Yorkshire, where by-names were once commonplace, are Wills o' Nats, Ben Ordle's and Nont Sarah's. They refer respectively to William Sykes the son of Nathaniel, Benjamin Iredale and Aunt Sarah. Such names can have a long history. I was intrigued when I first came to live in Lepton to hear a private house referred to as Mally Pashley's. Maps and documents helped me to establish that it was formerly a public house called the Three Crowns, and that Jonas Pashley was the landlord in 1800. Mally or Mary Pashley is likely to have been his widow. In Eldwick is Dick Hudson's, formerly the Fleece, an almost obligatory stop for walkers setting out across Ilkley Moor. Three generations of the Hudson family were innkeepers there from 1809.

In those days the publican was usually a person of considerable importance in the local community, and often something of a character too, and there is likely to be a story behind every such name. The Dyers' Arms at Slaithwaite sits high on the old road over into Lancashire, and its official name is interesting enough, for an estate survey of 1805 shows that there were several dye-houses near by. It is popularly known, however, as the White House, a name given to it because the walls were whitewashed annually, to coincide with the anniversary service at a nearby chapel. I was puzzled, therefore, to be told by local people, over forty years ago, that it had originally been called Alcander's, for that name had no obvious meaning. Later, quite by accident, I came across an undated newspaper article about Alcander Holroyd, a former land-lord who had been blessed with an inventive turn of mind. Perhaps his most famous exploit, in the late 1800s, was to invent a 'flying machine' and test it from the roof of the inn. Although it did not fly it gathered enough forward momentum to deposit Alcander in his own 'muck midden'. The licence passed first to his widow and then to his son, but it is Alcander, possibly 'Alexander', who is remembered locally.

Other public house nicknames derive from features of the landscape, and three examples close to where I live are Bumroyd, Slip and Kirk Steel. The 'Bum', as it is also irreverently known, takes its name from a field which was originally Burmonrode (1399), a clearance or 'royd' connected with the failed 'borough' on nearby Castle Hill. The Kirk Steel is the nickname of an inn by the bottom entrance to Kirkheaton churchyard, marking the point where the kirk gate, or footpath to the church, passed through a stile. These inns have the much grander official names of the Victoria and the Beaumont Arms, whereas the Slip may always have been so named. It is a name found elsewhere as early as c. 1750, and Cox interpreted it as 'slip in' – 'the earliest play on words found as a tavern name'. That may be the explanation in some cases, but the bit of Longwood where the Slip Inn now stands was described in 1812 as 'a slip of land beginning at ... Haughs Lane Top and extending thence ... about 300 yards in a line towards the Guide Stone at Raw Nook'. It is a steep climb, described by locals as 'up t'slip'.

The role of public houses has changed dramatically in the last twenty or thirty years, affected particularly by the new laws which relate to alcohol and driving. The clientele too has changed, and many pubs are now the chosen venues of young people of both sexes. These changes have had two obvious influences on the names. The first of these has seen breweries and publicans invent new and supposedly more fashionable names, often to the dismay of the regulars. The Commercial in Huddersfield, a town centre pub with a long and well-documented history, was renamed the Jug and Bottle with the aim of attracting younger drinkers, and it succeeded for a time. More recently, a victim of the fashion it had sought to capitalise on, it once again became the Commercial. The other tendency is for public houses to make their local nickname official, partly no doubt in a conscious attempt to preserve 'character' and resist the uniformity that has overtaken so many other 'locals'.

The increased success of small brewers may have contributed to this trend. In Linthwaite the New Inn was no different from dozens of other small village pubs, except that it had the unfathomable nickname the 'Sair'. The usual theories about what this means are based on the fact that the spelling approximates to the dialect pronunciation of both 'sow' and 'sour', but these are just speculation. According to the most popular version a former landlord called Eli Dyson neglected to pull clear water through the pumps after cleaning. Customers claimed that his beer was 'sair' and he became known as Eli o' t'sair. Now, however, the inn is officially the Sair, the name having been chosen by Ron Crabtree, an enthusiastic campaigner for real ale. He had purchased the New Inn as an outlet for the sale of his own traditionally-brewed beer.

9

Animals

Over a period of many years I have made a note of all the names of animals that I have come across in historical sources. Although such references are comparatively rare, the total number is now something over four hundred. They fall essentially into three categories, that is horses, hounds and cattle, with oxen accounting for fully half of the last group. I have no examples of names for sheep and pigs, nor even for domestic dogs, although animals kept for hunting purposes are clearly an exception. Wills and inventories have been the most fruitful sources for such names but, because I had other aims in my main areas of research, the material is very patchy, drawn primarily from the period 1350–1700. As a result I have only occasional and not necessarily representative examples for later centuries. For that reason the account that follows has severe limitations. Its modest aim is to awaken interest in the topic, and there is obviously scope for further collection in other areas, and over a much longer period.

Horses

Bayard was an Old French word for 'reddish brown' and, in the middle ages, it was used particularly for horses of that colour. In Chaucer's *Reeve's Tale* an escaped horse was variously described as 'capul', 'palfrey' and 'bayard', all of which, incidentally, were used as surnames in the same period.[1] Much earlier, however, Bayard was the name of the magic horse given to Rinaldo by Charlemagne, and, perhaps as a result of that, the word came first to have a mock-heroic sense, and then to signify blind recklessness or over confidence. It was used with that meaning in the seventeenth century by Milton and, more literally, by Scott in *The Lady of the Lake* as late as 1810, in a conscious attempt at local colour.

Early wills show how this word was combined with personal names, or possibly place-names, to identify favourite horses. In 1379 Robert

Swillington bequeathed two horses, one called Bartram and the other Bayerd de Bekwith, to his brother William.[2] In 1393 John Fairfax bequeathed forty shillings to a priest called Thomas de Cundall and also 'unum equum vocatum Bayard Nesfeld':[3] the Nesfields were of the Fairfaxes' kith and kin, and this name may be telling us that John had acquired the horse by gift or purchase from a member of that family. Bayard de Ripon was the name of a horse valued at ten shillings in the inventory of Thomas de Dalby, an archdeacon of Richmond who died in 1400. Also in the inventory, valued at sixteen shillings, was a second horse, 'vocato somer coquinae'.[4] In this case it is likely that 'somer' was again a French word, meaning a sumpter or pack horse, whereas the second part of the name means 'of the kitchen'. This could easily have been the surname Kitchen.

Less well known than Bayard is *Lyard*, which meant silvery-grey or white, another French word which passed into Middle English and had a number of related meanings. The earliest reference to it as the name of a horse is in 1347, that is 'unum de equis meis vocatum Lyardum de Ebor', meaning Lyard of York, a gift by Hugh de Hastings to William de Redenesse.[5] York in this case might be a surname, but seems more likely to refer to the place-name. There were many more, for example an ambling horse 'vocatum Lyard Rouclyff' (1393),[6] and, explicitly, 'a white horse called Lyard' in York in 1429.[7] In fact, similar examples occur into the early 1500s, including Lyard Gib (1452),[8] Lyard Otteley (1495),[9] Lyard Baraclogh (1503) [10] and finally Lyerd Banys (1508).[11] Possibly the most interesting of these is Lyard Gib, in which 'Gib' might be a surname but seems more likely to be the pet form of Gilbert, the only use of a first name in this way that I have noted. Of the above examples Barraclough and Baines were probably family names and Ripon, York and Otley place-names. They are likely to refer back to the purchase of the animals, identifying either the individual concerned or the market visited.

Bayard and Lyard occur frequently enough for us to assume that they were in general use, at least among upper-class families, to describe horses that were brownish-red or silver-grey in colour, certainly throughout the fourteenth and fifteenth centuries. There may, however, have been other less common names of the same type: in 1347, for example, Hugh de Hastings referred to his horse 'vocatum Morrellum de Tyrweyn',[12] which was almost certainly the French 'morel' meaning black. The tautological Blak Morell (1495) may indicate that this style of name was already becoming archaic.[13] The naming custom clearly had its origins in the Anglo-French community, but, as Middle English gave way to Modern English, it seems to have declined. It is interesting, therefore, to note that a parallel English custom remained in use for a century or more. The inventory of the possessions of William Conyers of Marske, in 1557, will serve as an illustration of this later development:

Item a gray horse callede Gray Taillor price	53s. 4d.
Item a horse callede Gray Craven	36s. 8d.
Item a bay horse callede Bay Coittes in the handes of George Conyers	53s. 4d.
Item a meare callede Gray Scott and an other meare callede Gray Craven	26s. 8d.
Item Roland Tophame of Carlysle for a hors called Gray Swan	£6 13s. 4d.[14]

This list contains several 'grays' and one 'bay' and there are many similar names in other sources, particularly for grays. These are found right through the sixteenth century and into the early part of the seventeenth century. There were also one or two names in that period with 'white' as the first element, which may suggest that Lyard had not been precise enough. Examples include Whit Fletcher (1562) [15] and White Smythefeild (1605).[16] Mr Cholmeley's mare Gresseld Evers, that 'ranne awaye' in 1617, would probably have had a gray or grizzled coat, and been acquired from the Evers family. He also had a black mare 'covered with black Palmes' in 1614, and the context here tells us that 'black Palmes' was a stallion. It had presumably been purchased from the gentry family called Palmes.[17] Much more difficult to interpret is a name where the first element appears to be 'green', that is, 'my best horse called Greine —' (1550).[18] Perhaps it was a young horse and green referred to its immaturity. Greenhorn, for example, used from 1650 as a word for somebody who is inexperienced, was the name of an ox in an early fifteenth-century play.

Horses were valuable animals, and they played a major role in the social and economic life of England in the middle ages. As a consequence horse-stealing was a major problem, and it was dealt with as a capital offence. It may be, therefore, that the main aim of the naming custom was to link the animals with particular breeders and markets, in the hope of making life difficult for potential thieves. That should not be taken to imply that all horses bore such names in the early period, for they did not, although the colour and the personal name were always important themes. Many of the recorded examples of one-theme names were of this type, such as Gresill (1434),[19] and Rande (1485).[20] Gresill was for grizzled, a relatively common name for animals of all kinds, and Rande was a surname. Indeed the horse 'Rande' was listed in an inventory where Thomas Rande was a debtor.

I have noted relatively few names of horses for the seventeenth century, but these include one or two that were based on surnames and might be thought to continue the earlier tradition. These include Lowther (1694)[21] and Sander Maire (1672).[22] Sander is for Alexander, and in this case could be either a first name or a surname. Most of the others, however, seem to be of a quite different character, more in the nature of nicknames. For example, the list which included Sander Maire also had 'one gray mare called Long Legs ... one bay maire ... called Thick Knee ... one gray mare called Blacklock and one white maire called Mad Brains'. Turke and 'yonge Turke' were stallions belonging to Richard Cholmeley, although the younger horse was gelded in 1615.[23] Two other names, Scueball (1647)[24] and Jockey (1694),[25] are both interesting lexical items. The first of these was given to a horse that was irregularly marked – usually white with brown or red; the second was a north-country diminutive of John, used in much the same way that Jack is, to address a stranger. It was also used for horse dealers, or more generally for anybody who worked with horses, and is first recorded in the modern sense of a professional rider in the mid seventeenth century. A long list of named mares, in the accounts of a Warwickshire 'horse enthusiast' (1691), contains many similar names in both categories, for example Smithson, Pudsey and Tempest; Dun Nag, Strawberry, Nipping Nell and Hollow Back.[26]

There appears to have been a relatively sudden change in the custom of horse-naming from the early 1500s, and it is interesting to speculate what part Tudor legislation might have played in that. Two Acts in particular are worth considering. The first, in 1555, was a response to the problems arising from the sale of stolen animals at markets and

fairs, and it gave rise to the holding of independent horse fairs. Two of
its provisions were that the toll-collector for the fair should record each
transaction, together with the colour of the horse and at least one special
identifying feature. In 1589, a subsequent Act laid out even more strin-
gent rules: these included public exposure of the animals between sunrise
and sunset, for an hour at least, and the identification of the vendor.
This was the responsibility of the toll collector or an 'avoucher', that is
some credible person who could testify to the vendor's honesty. Finally,
the law required the collector to enter into his book the names of all
the parties concerned. Extracts from the toll-taker's book for Adwalton
horse fair illustrate how this was put into practice:

> Richard Oxley of Harlington in co. York chapman sould one bay fillie with
> a starre and a snip trots unto John Whitticars of Rosendale co. Lancaster
> price iij*li*. xix*s*. John Abson aforesaid avowcher.

> William Jackson of Adle in co. York sheerman sould one grissell fillie with
> a white face trots unto Henry Ellis of Rigton in co. aforsaid price iij*li*. j*s*.
> Richard Wright of Headingley avowcher.[27]

Until well into the Tudor period, a great part of the Englishman's life
was governed not by the law but by customary practice, and much of
that practice was amended and made statutory in the new legislation.
It seems possible, therefore, that many of the names given to horses in
earlier documents were not names in the modern sense at all, but a
recording of facts that would identify the animals, that is their colour,
and either the vendor's name or the market where it had been purchased.
The examples quoted take that practice back into the early fourteenth
century, and the predominantly French vocabulary points to its origins
in Anglo-Norman society.

Before we leave the topic there are two other words connected with
horses that seem worthy of mention. The first of these is 'jennet', which
looks like early spellings of Janet, but is quite unconnected. It derives
from a Berber word that came to be used in Spanish of a light horseman.
In England it was transferred to the horse itself, and is recorded in
Yorkshire from the 1540s. In 1605 George Clifford, having named several
horses in his will, left his 'baye balde Jennett' to his 'lovinge brother'.
The second word is 'barbary', used of horses from the north coast of

Africa, and again connected with Berber. There appears to be an indirect link with the word barbarous and the girl's name Barbara, both of them ultimately from a Greek word for savage or uncivilised. In 1617 a north Yorkshire farmer noted in his accounts that one of his mares had been 'covered with a young barbara', so it could clearly be used of a male horse. The term was also used by Francis Boynton, a gentleman from east Yorkshire, and extracts from his will (1617) emphasise the important role that horses had in our ancestors' lives:

> Also I give my sonne Bellingham as a token of remembrance of my love
>   unto him my blewe Dand horse with a whyte racke.[28]
> Also I give unto my brothe Fairefaxe myne oune saddle nagge ...
> I give to my cozen Francis Frobisher £10 to buy him a geldinge.
> Also to my cosen John Norton of Wheldrake the elder younge bay Jelian.
> To my uncle John Norton the elder bay Jelian.
> Item to my cosen Thomas Appleyard my best broad mare.
> Item to my cosen Raph Fetherston my gray colt.
> Item to younge Tom Norton my barbary mare ...
>   and unto good Mr Brigges my parson a summer nagge.

Oxen

Most of the names of cattle I have come across are from wills in the 1500s. Although the total number is not very large, a significant percentage of them are recorded more than once: some were names used generally, for all types of cattle, whereas others were apparently confined to oxen.

A high proportion of the names given to oxen clearly referred to one or more defining physical characteristics, for example Broodhead and Brownbeard (1558), Grenehorn (1533), and Wythorne (1559). Topping (1558), may also belong in this category, as a name for an animal with a distinctive 'forelock'. More interesting than these, but of the same type is Burnett (1545) or Burnitt (1570), which occurs several times and may have meant 'dark brown'. In 1558, for example, Agnes Dawson left 'an ox called Burnett with halfe the plowghe geare' to her son.[29] Some oxen were named after other animals or after birds, probably drawing attention to their colour or, if only ironically, to their behaviour. Typical names are Lame (1553), Lyone (1556), Raven (1543),

Sheepe (1552), and Spinke (1572). The last of these may have been the dialect word for chaffinch, but an alternative explanation is discussed later.

Some may have a link with their owners. Mark (1559) is possibly the first name Mark, and all the following occur in Yorkshire as surnames, that is Harwoud (1580), Lakan (1553), Leming (1545), Lyghtbowne (1567), Palmer (1551) and Perte (1553). Several of these, however, have been recorded more than once, and the origin is not at all straightforward. Variants of Leeming, for example, occur five times, and a more plausible explanation is that the meaning here was the Middle English word for 'lightning' – an ironic nickname. Nevertheless, some of them, like the early names of horses already discussed, may have been intended to identify the vendor. More obviously 'nicknames', although we cannot rule out a surname link, are Darlinge (1556), Fether (1551) and Merryman (1546), whilst an extremely interesting name, almost impossible to explain at present, is Ysliman (1556).[30] It looks like the archaic word for an 'islander'.

The potential value of some of these names as lexical items emerges once they are examined in depth. The will of William Priestley, a Slaithwaite clothier who died in 1593, tells us that he had two oxen, called Goldinge and Hawke,[31] and both these names are of interest. Golding appears to have been a traditional name for an ox, for I have found it several times in wills. Examples include Bell and Golding in Fairburn in 1558,[32] and Goldinge, a 'stot' or young ox in Towton in 1560.[33] The name probably described animals which were light yellow in colour, and we can compare it either with 'Gowdie', a traditional name for cows in Scotland, or with 'golding', a dialect word for the corn marigold. In fact, Golding is also a surname, and a century ago it was particularly numerous in Wiltshire. It is said to derive there from an Old English personal name.

Although it is tempting to compare Hawke with Fawcan (falcon), which was what Edward Randell of Arkendale called one of his oxen in 1583,[34] the explanation may not be so straightforward. In fact, Goldinge's unnamed partner in Towton, in 1560, was said to have 'a white heade', and it may be that William Priestley's ox called Hawke was also white-headed. For example, Hawkey was a popular name in Scotland for a cow, well into the modern period, and its original meaning there was 'white-faced' or 'white-cheeked'.[35] It then came to be applied more generally to any pet cow, a sort of equivalent to Daisy or Buttercup. The origin of this word is obscure. It is said to be restricted to Scotland, or to Scotland and the northern counties of Cumberland and Northumberland; Stanley Beckensall has offered it as an explanation of a Northumberland field named Hawkeys Close. There, as in Scotland, it had come to describe 'a white-faced or pet cow'.[36] It may be worth noting that a name spelt 'Halke' is recorded in 1530, for this would readily become Hawke, but might point to an alternative origin.[37]

In fact, the word was in use much further south in earlier centuries, although it was recorded only in Scotland in the *English Dialect Dictionary*. There are numerous examples of it as an adjective in Yorkshire, including 'a hawekid quie' (1546),[38] and 'one hawked cow' (1576).[39] A 'quie' or 'why' was a heifer. Quite often, however, it was used in a way that seems to draw our attention to the main colour of the animal concerned, as in 'a black hawked stotte' (1550),[40] and 'a cow of Anthony Pratt's, red hawked in colour' (1613).[41] Most of these examples occurred in different parts of north and west Yorkshire in the sixteenth century, with just one or two in the early 1600s. The latest example is in 1618, when a skin sold to a tanner in Almondbury was described as 'one hawkt oxe hide'.[42] The inference clearly is that 'hawked' was in fairly common use in that period, probably meaning white-faced. Just how long it survived, and how widespread it was, remain uncertain, for the dates quoted reflect my own limited research interests, and I have examined relatively few wills after the mid 1600s.

Hawke has something in common with Tagge, which was a customary name for an ox in Yorkshire from about 1500 at least. Typical examples include 'towe stottes, the ane called Raven the other Tagge', in Castleford (1543),[43] and 'ij oxen called Fedder and Tagge', in Fairburn (1558).[44] The word 'tag' referred to the tip of an animal's tail and, more specifically, to a white-tipped tail. The *English Dialect Dictionary* seems to suggest, in this case also, that the word was not used outside Scotland, and it offers 'Taggie', and several variants, as a cow's name. Robinson's Scots dictionary confirms that it was still being used in Scotland in the nineteenth century.

In fact, this is another word that was in everyday use in Yorkshire, both as a noun and an adjective, well into the 1700s. Often the contexts suggest that it may have referred specifically to the white tip of the tail, although that is nowhere explicit. For example, in 1543, Christopher Naylor of Ardsley bequeathed 'a blake stott with a tage of the tale' to his son Thomas,[45] and in Huddersfield, in 1616, 'one black tagged oxe hide' was sold to a tanner by Mr Ramsden.[46] The first of these makes it clear that the 'tag' was not the tail itself, and that is confirmed in a much later reference. In 1707, George Bew of Selby bequeathed to his son Lancelot '1 tagtaild why' for his child's part.[47] In the same period there are other examples of cows and heifers with 'tagged' tails, and a very early north Yorkshire will mentions 'j bovem vocatum taggyd ox' (1458).[48]

There is an earlier, alternative, spelling of the word, that was also used as a name. In 1515, among the bequests of the incumbent of South Otterington, were an 'oxe called Lokwood, a kowe called Rosse', and 'an oxe called Takke'.[49] Later examples confirm that the last of these was a variant or earlier form of Tagge. In 1558, for example, Anne Emson of Newton Kyme named several animals in her will, that is 'ij oxen, Burnett and Lamme, a whyte mayre called Brocke' and two other oxen, 'the blacke and the tacked'.[50] In 1652 the inventory of James Stotherd of Gateforth listed several 'quies' or heifers, including 'a brouneish black and a blacke with a tacke taile'.[51]

Cows

The names collected in this category are almost all from the period 1485–1630. Although many of them are the same as those given to oxen, which may be what could be expected, there is considerable variety. Two wills, both of which list numbers of named cows, establish some of the characteristics of the group as a whole:

> Also I wit [bequeath] to Alison, my servaunte, ij kye called Nightigale and Luffly. Also to Johannet, my servaunt, a cowe called Tymelt. Also to William Marshall, of Bagby, a cowe called Sternelld with calfe. Also to John Squyer a cowe called Wright. Also to Agnes Chapman a cowe called Tydee [1486].[52]

> Also I bequeathe Agnes Diche my servaunte ... one rede cowe callid Cherie, one quie callid Nowt ... Also I bequeathe William Diche ij kie, the one called Sterneld and the other Browne ... Also I bequeathe to John Morton

one cowe callid Nyghtingegaile, with one quie cromble headid ... Also I
bequeathe Margarett Webster, Richarde my son wife, one cowe callid
Soneld. Also I bequeathe William Webster, son of Robert Webster, one
quye callid Whitefoote [1547].[53]

Here again we encounter a name apparently based on a surname, that
is Wright, and similar examples are commonplace. They include Benson
(1560), Bentle[y] (1658) and Parkinson (1559). It is also evident that the
colour of the animals was important, and to those names quoted above
can be added Allblacke (1588), Great Browney and Young Browney
(1588), Whytehorne (1557) and Whyte Rygg (1579), that is 'white back'.
The most popular name of this type, at least among those that I have
collected, was Cherry, often explicitly for a red cow. The earliest example
is 'my white hedded cowe called Chery' (1522).[54] On the other hand,
Sylver Topp (1545) occurred just once. Blackwald was the name given
in 1590 to 'one brounlye cowe',[55] and it may be that 'wald' here is for
'wall eyed' – a reference to the animal's eye colouring. Of the nicknames
quoted above both Tydee (Tidy) and the more popular Nightingale
survive as surnames.

It was suggested earlier that Spink might be the dialect word for the
chaffinch, but there is another possibility that would link it with Hawke
and Tagg, as a nickname descriptive of an animal's colouring. In 1551,
for example, Laurence Lyster of Gisburn bequeathed two black heifers
to Thomas Whittacar, and one of these was described as having 'a whyte
spynke of the backe', that is a white spot.[56] Adjectival uses of the word
also occur, for example 'one spencket qwye in Grinton' in 1570, and
'one blake spinkedd que styrke' in Marrick in 1600.[57] There are several
other variants of this word, including 'spanked' and 'spanged', and they
all seem to mean speckled or variegated in colour. The Spangled Bull,
which is the name of a public house in Kirkheaton, has a similar origin,
and I have noted animals described as Branded Spang and Red Spang
as late as 1832–40.[58]

In fact 'spangled' may help to explain what is possibly the most
interesting group of cows' names. The commonest of these is Sterneld,
found in both the groups which introduce this section. What links these
names is the adjectival suffix -eld, or something very similar, as an
alternative for the more usual -ed. It is found in the names Flooreld
(1588), Gawrelt (1566), Raggalt (1582), Soneld (1547), Taggelde (1588) [59]

and Tymelt (1486). Sterneld almost certainly refers to an animal with a
star as a facial mark, for 'stern' or 'starn' was an earlier form of this
word. It is found frequently in descriptions of both cattle and horses,
for example 'a little callfe with a starne' (1593),[60] and 'a blacke colte with
a white starne' (1578).[61] In several other cases the name might refer to
a distinguishing mark, sun-shaped or flower-shaped in Soneld and
Flooreld, and possibly gore-shaped or triangular in Gawrelt. The reference, 'a gowred cowe' (1558),[62] is just one of many that use the words
'gored' or 'gared'.

The name Tymelt remains a mystery, but Taggelde looks suspiciously
like 'tagged', that is with a white tip to its tail, the adjective from tagge
discussed earlier. Raggalt is not straightforward, however, for the word
has several pejorative meanings in dialect, notably as a word for a rogue
or rascal. It might also be a form of 'ragged', and have been used of a
shaggy animal. In either case the public house called the Raggalds, high
above Bradford, on an ancient highway used by drovers, may well
preserve the name. It is the formation of the suffix in these cases that
is linguistically of interest, for the words appear to be based on Middle
English -eled, a sort of double adjectival suffix.[63]

In more recent times we have become accustomed to hearing of cows
with names such as Daisy, Buttercup, Beauty and Blossom, but I have
found no examples of these, or similar names, in early Yorkshire records.
They can be found later, in the few nineteenth-century lists of cattle
that have come to light, and it is interesting, therefore, to speculate
whether they belong to a more recent tradition, or whether they have
a much longer history in other parts of the country. There is some
evidence of continuity in the period 1500–1900, certainly in the case of
Cherry, Nut and Whiteface, but the overall impression is that the naming
habits employed by our Tudor ancestors were very different from those
of the last two hundred years or so.

Hounds

My major source for the early names of hounds is a manuscript 'Dog
Book', preserved in the West Yorkshire archives at Wakefield. It contains
copies of seventeenth-century agreements that were entered into between Sir John Kaye of Woodsome and his tenants. These include details

about the keeping of hounds and more than one hundred names for the period 1690–1703.⁶⁴ Many of these are still in use, and it is immediately obvious that tradition has played a very important part in the naming process over the last three hundred years. From these lists, and a few additional names found in other records, it might be suspected that the tradition goes back very much further, but there is no direct evidence of that in the sources I have searched. Nor can I always be sure exactly what breed of dogs is referred to in the names I have found, for early records mention hounds, greyhounds and beagles, all used for hunting. Hares and not foxes were the chief prey.

In spite of those considerable reservations, the lists contain much of interest. For example, the earliest names of hounds that I had previously come across were those in the traditional Cumberland hunting song 'D'ye ken John Peel'? This was written in 1829, and four of the foxhounds' names, that is Ruby, Ranter, Ringwood and Bellman, are found also in the 1690s. The remaining name True may be paralleled by Trueboy, which is listed in the Dog Book and later sources. In the same category were Gameboy and Jollyboy, whilst Merrylass and Bonnylass referred to bitches. Merryman, it will be remembered, was a popular name for an ox in the sixteenth century, and it is found alongside Merrylass in the Dog Book.

We need only look at the histories and song books of local hunts to understand how names were passed down from generation to generation, as evidence of the animals' blood lines.⁶⁵ The animals' pedigree was obviously an important matter and the 'christening' of whelps is a custom that has survived. A local historian, called Ammon Wrigley, wrote about one such occasion in his *Old Saddleworth Days*, describing how the ceremony took place in a parlour, with the pack's huntsman at the head of the table. He was known as Allen o' th' Tinker's and wore his red coat, looking 'as dignified as a cardinal'. It was the task of the whipper-in, Joe o' Breb's, to hand the whelps to the huntsman, who then addressed each animal in dialect, warning it not to worry poultry and not to run after cats or farm animals. The 'nominy', as he called it, finished with the following lines and the actual 'christening':

> Theau mun run a hare as long as thi legs will carry thi.
> Theau mun keep thi nose cowd an' thi tail op,

An' theau munnot waste thi time marlockin' [frolicking] wi' cur dogs.
Awm beawn [going] to co' thi Plunder an' see theau'rt a good dog,
An' a credit to thi fayther an' o' belonging to thi.[66]

These details were then entered formally into a book and, where they survive, a clear picture emerges of each dog's history and ancestry. For example, in 1698 Sir John Armytage's Driver was 'got by his Drummer out of Sempster and she out of a Lancashire beagle of Mr Mitchel's and Mr Rook's Dido'. In 1820 five whelps named Fury, Towler, Jugolar, Ralleywood and Royal were born out of Blossom, and got by Jugolar of Holmfirth. Again most of these were traditional names. The hound Bluebell is listed in the Stud and Stock Book of Henry Lockwood as having been born 27 June 1904, 'walked by Sam Sugden and given to the Penistone Hunt in 1910'. She had 'a dark blue fleck', which no doubt partly explains her name, although there is also a Bluebell in the Dog Book of 1690. This is a flower we now associate with our woodlands in May, but the word originally referred to the harebell, and it is this that is likely to have inspired the name. Florence Lockwood, Henry's sister-in-law, wrote in her notes that Bluebell enjoyed many privileges 'because of her motherhood ... although she takes many a cruise round looking in at the cottage doors'.

We cannot be certain yet just how old many of these names might be, but a few are unusual enough to betray their antiquity. These include Whipster (a reckless fellow), Careless (care free), Giliver (the gillyflower) and Younker, a word of Dutch origin for a young lord. In other cases the age of the name means that we have to be careful how we interpret it: Ragman may refer to the devil; Bouncer and Ruffler to swaggering animals. In fact Ruffler is the earliest hound's name that I have noted, for it occurs in a will of 1578. Dainty is another name with an interesting semantic history, for it was originally a noun, a doublet of 'dignity', and came to mean handsome. Chaucer, for example, wrote of 'a deynte hors', and this sense is retained in some northern dialects. Other early names, which had to do with the hound's appearance, were Beauty, Comely, Fairmaid and Lovely, whilst Diamond, Jewell, and Silver comment on precious qualities. Some less desirable characteristics are implied in Dally, Doxy, Strumpet and Wanton for bitches, with Cruell, Gibsey, Drunkard, Madcap, Tipler and Tosspot for dogs.

In some cases the impression is that a name had been coined originally to celebrate an outstanding exploit, of the sort boasted about in many hunters' songs. Examples include Famous, Gallant, Marvel and Noble: others referred to the noise the hounds made during the hunt, Musick, Singwell and, possibly, Chanter and Sweetlips. However, Chanter could be short for Enchanter, and Sweetlips was apparently the nickname of a well-known prostitute and a Civil War gun![67] It is important to remember, in any case, that such names could pass down the generations and become part of a traditional name stock. They were more like the surnames of the huntsmen, providing evidence of their pedigree. Their meaning would in many cases be lost over several generations. Particularly numerous are names such as Caster, Leader, Ranger and Sweeper, which seem to describe the roles played during the hunt by individual animals. Something similar may be implied in the rather unusual Shearwood, Trimbush and Ringdale. The name Ringwood, mentioned earlier, would also fall into this category.

There are two remaining groups of early names which merit consideration, and the first of these concerns those drawn from the Classics. The most obvious of these is the name Roman itself, but the list also includes the names of emperors and gods, such as Caesar, Jupiter, Nero and Vulcan, with Juno, Venus and Fortune, possibly, used for bitches. Other names recorded in 1690, some referring to characters from antiquity of lesser stature, were Dido, Chloris, Phyllis, Phoenix and Pompey. Jovel may belong here, as a reference to Jove, but it could also be a name on the lines of Merrylass or Jollyboy. The impression generally is that such names may have declined in popularity over the years, but both Juno and Dido have been used until quite recently, and it would be important to have more names before jumping to that conclusion.

One way in which a few early names have been preserved is in the names of public houses traditionally associated with hunting, not just the ubiquitous Hare and Hounds. Most of these are found in the south Pennine area, and they no doubt commemorate long-deceased favourites. One of the best known is the Hark to Bounty, a lovely old inn located in Slaidburn, a Ribblesdale village formerly in Yorkshire. Other Yorkshire names of this type are Hark to Rover in Leeds, Hark to Nudger in Dobcross, and Hark to Mopsy in Normanton. The hound called Nudger is remembered also in a specially issued drinking mug,

and Mopsy, which was once a northern term of endearment for a young
girl, is in the Dog Book of 1690. It is also found as a cow's name as
early as 1536. Similar names in Lancashire and Derbyshire recall hounds
named Dandler, Lasher and Towler, and there is an isolated Hark to
Melody in Cumberland.

This brief account of a few names of animals from one English region
contains some items of interest as far as our social and linguistic history
are concerned. Ideally there should now be a more comprehensive
survey, one which examines the names of different kinds of animals in
every century for which there are records, and over a much wider area.
That could include other English-speaking parts of the world. The close
relationship that men had with their livestock and sporting dogs, through
the middle ages and Tudor periods, is reflected in both surnames and
animal names, but the latter subject has been largely neglected.

10

Unofficial Place-Names

As a boy, in the 1940s, I spent much of my free time in an area around the village of Tong, along with three like-minded companions. Tong was then an attractive village, midway between Leeds and Bradford, set in an undulating landscape of fields and woods. It was marked by industry, and bore the scars of coal-mining and quarrying, but there were no mills or factories and it managed to retain the feeling of a rural community, with a fine church and hall at its heart. It was the focal point of our wanderings and we seldom ventured more than three or four miles from its centre, not because we were incapable of walking greater distances, but because this was 'our' territory and beyond its ill-defined boundaries there were other territories, patrolled by similar groups of 'lads' who would have resented our intrusion. We prided ourselves on knowing every nook and cranny of the landscape.

I mention this only because I came to realise, long afterwards, that several of the place-names that we habitually used seem never to have been recorded in print and are not found on maps. One in particular that comes to mind is 'Peter Eaton', the name of a lane which the map now tells me is really New Lane, and which linked Tong Lane to 'Charley Pit', an abandoned coal-mining site. None of the mine buildings had survived, but there was an old pit hill, and a long brick-lined culvert through which it was possible to walk; there was also an intriguing, steep embankment which had once carried a railway, and a great open shaft with a gallery visible at one side, an irresistible attraction. We went 'up' or 'down' Peter Eaton with no thought for what the name meant or how it was spelt, and I have written it as we said it. It was never linked with 'lane' or 'road' and had no transparent meaning: I cannot remember thinking that it might have referred to a person, although 'Peter Heaton' now seems a distinct possibility.

It was not until much later that I realised how frequent such names are, or once were, and, when I first began to record them, it was more as an extension of my interest in dialect than through curiosity about their status as names. Yet this is an important class of names, sometimes akin to by-names or nicknames, and seldom discussed except at the very local level. The fact that they are not written down helps to explain that omission, and yet the truth is that these are not just anecdotal items, but names of enormous interest, throwing light on different aspects of social and economic history. My discussions with local groups have convinced me that many similar names must already have disappeared and, if we continue to neglect them, we shall certainly lose a significant part of our naming heritage.

Initially, I used this topic with adult students in evening classes, throughout south-west Yorkshire, as a way of arousing interest and stimulating discussion, and it brought to my attention hundreds of such names across a relatively wide area, sometimes with supporting anecdotal evidence. I have chosen here to call them 'Unofficial Place-Names', but that is not a generally recognised title, merely one of temporary convenience. The fact is that there is no distinct line between unofficial names and other place-names: a loss of status may mean that a formerly well-established place-name survives only at the 'unofficial' level, whereas increased status may put the unofficial nickname onto the map and into written records. Diaries and other personal documents may in any case preserve examples of some names that would not otherwise be recorded. No doubt some of the items that I have collected might be discussed under either heading.

Scapegoat Hill

In the old township of Quarmby, near Huddersfield, the land rises in the west to a height of over 1100 feet. It is a wind-swept spot, the highest area of common grazing in the township until it was opened up to settlement in the late 1700s. Part of the plateau is still covered with heather and other moorland plants, but a huddle of stone buildings clings to the rim defying the elements. Its present name is Scapegoat Hill, but chapel registers and tombstones prove that this first came into use in the early nineteenth century, gradually replacing the older name Slipcote Hill. We can only speculate about why the change took place, but this was a nonconformist stronghold and it seems likely that the first tenants who were offered land in this remote locality considered that they had been despatched into the wilderness, like the Old Testament scapegoat. The analogy must have tempted somebody to refashion the old and obscure place-name and Scapegoat Hill became its unofficial alternative. Now, it is 'official', and all memory of the original Slipcote has disappeared. Professor Smith's interpretation of it as 'sheep-cote hill' was unfortunately based on a misreading of Slipcote as Shipcote.

The Ocker 'oil or Ochre Hole

Several informants have offered me this name, which they consider to be unofficial, partly because of the dialect pronunciation, and partly because they have not seen it on any road sign. It is in regular use in the Fixby area of Huddersfield as the name of a locality on the former highway to Halifax, at a point where it passes through a shallow ford. In fact, it has not gone unrecorded, since Smith included it as Ochre Hole in his list of Fixby place-names: he had noted it on contemporary Ordnance Survey maps, at the head of Allison Dyke, the stream which soon afterwards crosses the old Halifax road at 'Ocker 'oil'. However, he offered no early evidence, and made no attempt to explain it, although the element 'ochre' is found over a wide area and may be more significant than has been thought. In Yorkshire, for example, there is an Ochre Dyke in Greasbrough, again listed without evidence, and further afield there are places called Ocre Kiln in Oxfordshire and Ochre Mine in Derbyshire.

A more thorough search shows that the Fixby place-name is referred to several times in township and quarter sessions records, both of which were formerly concerned with the condition of the roads. These include Hockerhole Lane (1688) and Oaker Hole Lane (1788), whilst in estate records the upper end of the dyke is named as Ocker Hole Clough (1811). It has to be classed as an official name, therefore, and I suspect that it achieved that status simply because it defined an important boundary along the former highway, not because the 'ochre hole' itself was very significant. Now that the highway is used only by very local traffic the name is preserved in its unofficial dialect form.

I have been given other 'ochre' names which I cannot find in any written source; Ocker Dyke in Berry Brow, for example. Such names always stimulate discussion among older people. They talk of the 'ocker watter' they were once familiar with, describing polluted streams or becks which, in their youth, were bright yellow or orange. One elderly lady said it reminded her of tinned tomato soup. Others called them 'iron streams', a name which draws our attention to the nature of the coloured earth that stains the water. This is a mixture of clay and hydrated oxide of iron, varying in colour from light yellow to deep orange – hence the reference to tomato soup.

In fact, these names may be reminders of an earlier small-scale industry, which supplied local clothiers with one of their dyestuffs. John Brearley, a Wakefield cloth frizzer, several times mentioned ochre in his memorandum books of 1758–62, noting places in the neighbourhood where it was 'mined'; at Outwood, for example, although the 'chief plase' was somewhere on the south side of the town. Interestingly he wrote that it was 'gotten in coal pitt sows' and sold by the horse load for 2s. 6d. These 'sows' were drains or adits, and his comment confirms the link with coal-mining suggested by the 'iron streams' in the area. The ochre was burnt near by, 'to give itt the right coalar', which may explain the place-name Ocre Kiln. At this stage in the process it was called 'Spanish Brown' and sent away to London. It was cheap to obtain, but its distribution from Yorkshire to other parts of the country caused it to be 'selled at great prises'. Much of it was bought in Wakefield by a 'groser' called Shackleton.[1] In 1689 the inventory of a Selby mercer contained references to several hundredweight of ochre, '4 stone of red occar' valued at 4s. and two hundredweight of 'rudd'.

Where the band of earth is particularly red it is referred to as 'ruddle' or 'raddle', and the discoloured water can be described as 'cankered'. As a result the number of official and unofficial names is greatly increased, and these appear to fall into two categories. Some almost certainly refer directly to mining activity, for ruddle had numerous uses as a pigment. By the nineteenth century it was being extracted on a commercial basis from shallow pits in south Yorkshire, and we are fortunate to have the whole process described for us in Walker's *Costume of Yorkshire* (1814).[2] It was the 'ruddle stone' produced in this way that was used until comparatively recently by west Yorkshire housewives to mark the edges of their steps and window-sills, and it indirectly helped the surnames Ruddlestone and Riddlestone to develop as variants of Riddlesden.

This was only ever a small-scale industry, and it is likely that ruddle had previously been extracted intermittently, from seams which were close to the surface, revealed in deep-cut cloughs or exposed by other mining activity. For example, the vicar of Mirfield wrote in 1755 of the 'ruddle or red chalk found in a quarry near New Hall in Hopton'. The place-names fall into two characteristic groups: on the one hand, Ruddle Pits, Riddle Pits and Raddle Pits, and on the other, Riddle Clough, Ruddles Gill and Ruddle Dike; they are recorded from the 1600s, and doubtless tell us where farmers obtained the ruddle that they used for marking their sheep. Typical references, mostly in sheep-stealing cases in the quarter sessions, are to animals being 'ridled on the head' (1688), 'marked with fresh redle' (1649) or 'marked with ruddle on the near buttock' (1669). The vowel seems to have varied considerably. The only spelling I have not found is 'roddle'. The phrase 'ruddling wafers' occurs in a Fixby estate account of 1810, and it tells us that ruddle was being used by the woodmen to mark certain trees.[3] In fact, the woodmen were working close to the 'Ockerhole Clough'.[4]

The stream names Canker Dyke and Ruddle Dyke were associated in people's minds with pollution, which occurred when earth was removed during coal-mining or quarrying. In a manorial survey of Elland, for 1779, one tenant's rent was considerably reduced 'on account of Floods daming the canker'd or rusted yellow water, which is very pernicious to this land'. A later writer indicates how such pollution might have helped an official name to disappear. He was commenting on a well in Ilkley 'called Canker Well now, but Pollard Well within our day, when it gushed out from the scarp' (1885). Neither name seems to have survived, and the same fate probably awaits the few unofficial names of this type still in use. Now that coal-mining has all but disappeared 'ocker watter' is rarely seen and 'canker dykes' are almost a thing of the past.

On t'Copperas

'Copperas' is an excellent example of a name which is now almost completely unofficial, and which I have not found in official Yorkshire sources as either a place-name or a place-name element. It was first brought to my notice by an elderly man from Birchencliffe, who said that he regularly took a walk 'on t' copperas' in Lindley and wondered what that meant. The dictionary told me that copperas is a sulphate of iron, much used in dyeing, so I hazarded a guess that there may once have been a dye-works in that area. Later, I read an account of a mill lower down the valley where the stream which filled the mill dam 'was quite clear until some copperas works were commenced above Birchen-cliffe', and which poisoned the trout in the stream. A trade directory for 1848 shows that William Sykes and Son were copperas manufacturers in that part of Lindley.

Several other copperas manufacturers were listed in nineteenth-century directories and local census returns and, as the enquiry widened, I was able to identify numerous small-scale enterprises in Halifax, Bradford, the Spen Valley and Penistone. I was told that the locality in Penistone, which was known locally as the Copper House, deserved the name because the windows caught the reflection of the setting sun! It was not the only 'Copper House', for I found another at King's Mill, near Huddersfield town centre. I have also noted how private houses or cottages have often preserved the name. In Honley, a house in Gynn Lane known as Copperas was said to have been a labourer's cottage next to a dye-works; Copperas House in Siddal, Halifax, was the home of Thomas Smith, who inherited a copperas works from his father and died in 1937.

Some earlier locations can be identified from other sources. For example, Coperas House near Elland was marked on the Jefferys map of Yorkshire for 1775, connected possibly with today's street name Cop-peras Mount. John Brearley noted that 'the[y] make coperas ... at Heland in Yorkshire', and the death of Mr Ireton 'at the Copperas house near Boothtown' (1739) is recorded in the Northowram register. A lady called Dorothy Jackson wrote to Mr Walter Stanhope of Horsforth in 1757, begging a favour as one 'consarned in a copres worke'. She said that she had heard 'that thar is a great maney in Leeds that deales in that way as itt is a great artickel in the deying way'. She wished to be put in touch with a 'substachel dealer' and be told 'which way itt will come the best to Leeds'. She also reminded him that he had known her husband in Horsforth, and assured him that his help would 'never be for gott'.[5]

The origins of the industry are obscure, but a reference by Camden takes its history in north Yorkshire back into the 1500s. In Guisborough he noted how rich the soil was with 'with vaines of metall ... earth of sundry colours, but especially of ocher and murray, likewise of iron, out of which they have now begunne to try very good Alum and Coperose'. There is also a Richmond will of 1577 which mentions 'two pounds of green coperas' – a clear reference to ferrous sulphate, or 'green vitriol' as it was also called. The 1668 inventory of a Slaithwaite chapman lists all manner of dyestuffs 'in the shopp', including 'Log wood, Fustick, bluegalles' and '24 quarters of copers'.[6] Slaithwaite was in Huddersfield parish so we can be reasonably sure that copperas was being used at that time by clothiers, possibly as a mordant for fixing the colours of dyed material. Quantities of 'coperose' were being imported into Hull as early as 1463, possibly for that purpose.[7] However it was not the only use, for a recipe dating from about 1700 claimed that copperas water would 'cure any reasonable sore or wound'. It is worth noting that the word is not mentioned in local accounts of the textile industry, so these unofficial place-names are the key to practices that were once widespread, and now appear to be forgotten.*

The Mangle House

I have found no reference to this place-name in any work on the subject, and the word 'mangle' does not appear to be listed as a place-name element, all of which suggests that Mangle House may not have been recorded as an official name, even though it is by no means rare at the unofficial level.

My attention was first drawn to the term when a lady sent me a letter describing the house she had once lived in. She wrote that it was known locally as the Mangle House and remembered her late father telling her that it had formerly been the location of the village mangle.[8] I was familiar enough with mangles as a child, when most working-class houses had one, but the idea that they could have been communal property, with villagers sharing in their use, intrigued me. So, I looked more thoroughly into the history of the word, and mentioned it whenever I talked to groups about local customs.

I was soon enlightened. The OED informs us that it was once

---

* For details of the recipe and an account of how copperas was produced see Appendix 2.

common, 'among the poorer classes of English cottagers', for one woman
to possess a mangle and earn her living by charging others a small sum
for its use. The question 'Has your mother sold her mangle?' was said
to be a derisory comment used by London street boys in the nineteenth
century. In Thackeray's *Vanity Fair* the butler announced his marriage
to a former cook 'who had subsisted in an honourable manner by the
exercise of a mangle'; in 1827 a Doncaster newspaper reported a case,
heard at the borough sessions, in which a lady named Mrs Booth was
described as somebody 'who keeps a mangle'.

The census returns of 1851 for Doncaster actually list several widows
or spinsters who were 'mangle keepers', so perhaps there too the occupation was reserved for a woman who had no bread-winning husband.
Typical examples include a widow called Mary Ashe, aged forty-two,
who lived in Church Lane and kept a mangle, and Jane Fletcher of West
Laithe Gate, mangle woman, who was also a widow, aged sixty-
seven.[9] One account of a 'mangle woman' was published in 1844. Her
name was Catherine Steward and, as a young girl, she had worked
happily enough in a Lancashire cotton mill before going into service.
When she married, she moved with her husband into a small house
and they had two children. Sadly, he died and Catherine was obliged
to take work in a nail factory, a job which made great demands on her
physically, and barely provided a living. However, a 'benevolent gentleman in the neighbourhood ... assisted her to purchase a mangle', and,
by means of that, she contrived to support both her children and an
ageing mother. When she later removed to Liverpool with her only
surviving son, she took her mangle with her.[10]

An entry in the *English Dialect Dictionary* suggests that 'the mengel
womman' was the person most likely to know what was going on in
the village. This was supported by a short paragraph I came across in
a booklet about the village of Lockwood. Here, the writer recalled, the
women would bring their wet washing to a house with a public mangle
room and 'while waiting their turn to use the mangle would no doubt
exchange all the local gossip.[11] Later, I was told by a lady that in North
Wales, particularly in the slate quarries, it was usual to make a collection
for the widow of a man killed in an industrial accident. It enabled her
to purchase a mangle and so ensure a living for her family.[12] That was
before the Workmen's Compensation Acts.

Such Mangle Houses may go back no further than the eighteenth century, for the mangle or wringing machine that we are familiar with, if only as a museum piece, is of relatively recent date. The upright mangle is said to have been invented in the nineteenth century, but there were earlier machines.[13] For example, I have noted a joiner's bill, dated 1773, which required payment of 1s. 6d. for '1 day mending the mangle with new rowlers',[14] and in 1774 a carpenter called Hugh Oxenham took out a patent on 'an entirely new construction', one that was designed 'to answer all the purposes of a mangle without the incumbrance of weight' (OED). As the entry implies, the word was much older than that, and it is said to share the same origin as 'mangonel' the medieval engine of war that hurled great stones at the enemy. Indeed, in its original form the mangle was a kind of oblong, rectangular wooden box filled with stones. This rested upon two cylinders, and it was worked backwards and forwards by means of a rack and pinion, thus rolling the cylinders over fabrics which were spread on a flat surface below. This type of 'engine' had been used in Italy, to press buckram, fustian and linen, as early as the sixteenth century.

In fact, if we move the investigation away from place-names for the moment, there is some evidence to suggest that there may have been 'mangle women' and 'mangle houses' well over two hundred years ago. A sequence of depositions in the quarter sessions rolls for Sheffield has to do with a woman called Ann Parkin, who was suspected of stealing a brass candlestick in 1789.[15] One witness said 'that she had seen Nanny Mangle (meaning the said Ann Parkin) put something that was yellow underneath her apron'. The insertion here of the words 'meaning the said Ann Parkin' was simply the clerk's way of establishing that Nanny Mangle was the accused woman's by-name, and the inference is that she was a 'mangle keeper'. John Sykes, writing of life in a Yorkshire village in the 1860s, said that 'Mangle' was an automatic nickname for any woman who owned one.

The Kirk Steel at Kirkheaton

In the chapter on inns and public houses I commented briefly on 'Kirk Steel', which is the local name of a Kirkheaton inn called the Beaumont Arms. It stands opposite the parish church, and means literally 'the church stile': I speculated that it may once have referred to an informal entry into the churchyard, at the end of the footpath to the church. These footpaths are called 'kirk gates' in early documents. As far as I am aware, the word 'kirk' is no longer used by dialect speakers in west Yorkshire, so I was interested to discover how old the name might be, and the circumstances in which it has survived. Needless to say it does not feature in lists of Kirkheaton place-names, although it occurs infrequently in certain types of records. Over the years, my inquiry into its history has raised one or two points of more general interest.

The first concerns the word 'kirk' itself, which is of Old Norse origin. As a regional word it was doubtless introduced in the late ninth century, as Danish settlers were converted to Christianity, and it remained in use in the counties of the former Danelaw well into the Middle English period. That is reflected in major place-names, such as Felkirk and Oswaldkirk where it is the generic, and Kirkleatham and Kirkstall where it is the specific. As the parochial system developed, in the Anglo-Norman period, its use as a specific in parish names, such as Kirk Smeaton and Kirkheaton, identifies where the church was located. Both these are recorded for the first time two hundred years after the Conquest.

It had a much wider use, and was part of everyday vocabulary in a number of regional dialects. There were several compound words, for example, in which kirk was linked with other Scandinavian elements, and we can chart their use through the centuries, to discover how the dialects fared compared with 'standard' English, at least in written documents. In Yorkshire, it is usual to find kirk, rather than church, in most documentary references into the early 1500s. We have 'the sacramentes of holy kyrke' at Elland in 1484, and 'Skypton kyrke' in 1491. In 1521 a Bradford man spoke of where he sat in the church as his 'stalle in the kirke', and Christopher Wilberfoss asked 'to be buried within the kirk' in 1533.

It is at this time, however, that we see the first outside influences on this distinctive local speech, especially where such terms as kirk greave, kirk gate and kirk garth are concerned. These were the local equivalents of the English terms churchwarden, church way and churchyard, and in Yorkshire documents they were used regularly until 1500, after which they start to be replaced by their English equivalents. Sometimes only half the term was affected, for example 'kyrk yerde' (1517), and 'churche grevis' (1539). An alternative local term for the churchwarden was kirk-maister and one scribe's dilemma is apparent in his compromise reference to 'the kirke wardens otherwyse callid the kirkmaisters' (1529). Of course kirk continued to be used orally for a very long time, but it seems likely to have fallen out of use soon after 1800. The Halifax historian John Watson was able to write in 1775 that 'a Church-warden is also called here a Kirkmaister', but the evidence of the *English Dialect Dictionary* points to the word's almost total decline in Yorkshire in the nineteenth century.

It is against this background that today's unofficial name Kirk Steel is of interest, for many of those who still use it are not dialect speakers, and it must have survived from the middle ages. Various spellings of the place-name, in the Whitley Beaumont estate accounts, point to compromises made by the clerks. They include Churchsteele (1654) and Kirkstile (1797). We know from such entries that it was a public house from 1781 at least, and that members of the Cowgill family were the landlords. The inn was the venue for important manorial and parish meetings, and, from the early 1800s, it became known as the Beaumont Arms. Nevertheless it continues to be called the Kirk Steel locally.

It is significant also because its survival draws our attention to the much wider use of the term, as an ordinary compound noun. From the evidence we can infer that there were some parts of the country where almost every church once had a 'kirk stile', just as they had a 'kirk garth' and a 'kirk gate'. In my own immediate area I find references to the 'church steele' of Almondbury in 1710, the 'churche stele' of Kirkburton in 1552, and the 'kirkstile' of Barnsley in 1493. Further afield there are references to 'the house at the kirkstille' in Stokesley (1497), and 'a howse at the kyrke stele' in Ecclesfield (1542). Others, too numerous to list here, are found in all three Ridings and in adjoining counties. Personal by-names take the use of the term back to the fourteenth century at least. For example, Richard at Kyrcstyle was a resident of Hayton in 1381, and Robert attekirkstiel de Wistow was made a freeman of York in 1314.

We are familiar with Kirkgate as a major street name in the northern towns, but less familiar with the term kirk gate when it refers to the rights of way that linked outlying hamlets and farms to the parish church. Nevertheless that is how the word is most commonly used in early documents, and it is clear that our ancestors were once familiar with it as an institution. In that context it is logical to see the kirk stile as the access into the kirk garth at the end of the kirk gate, and the inference is that there was often a dwelling close by. In large Pennine parishes, with their many townships, these rights of way figure frequently in the court rolls. In 1583, for example, three Elland hamlets affirmed their right to 'a way for bride and corse over the grounds of Thomas Bothomley, in the accustomed place'; in Kirkheaton, in 1686, it was emphasised that the 'church way' must be wide enough 'for three men to goe in a brest, accordingly as formerly hath bene' – wide enough, that is, to carry a coffin. In 1742, at the quarter sessions, when the path to Kildwick church was 'in ruin and decay', the tenants of Brunthwaite asserted their right to go there 'on foot and pass with corps and dead bodies to be interred'.

Terrace Houses

From the late eighteenth century capital originating from a wide variety of sources was utilized on an unprecedented scale for the provision of housing for the working population of West Yorkshire. Within half a century this trend was to transform the county's housing stock. In this period the single-storey cottage, the traditional workman's dwelling, began to be replaced by a new form, typically a two-storey house built in a terrace. During the late eighteenth and early nineteenth centuries such terraces became progressively longer ...[16]

By the early 1900s terrace houses accommodated a significant percentage of west Yorkshire's population. Much has been written about the developers; men such as Titus Salt who had 450 houses built for the families who worked in his mill, and Edward Akroyd, with his ambitious creation of a settlement near Halifax. These 'new towns' gave us the names Saltaire and Akroydon. Less well known is Ripleyville, the local name in Bradford for the several streets of houses erected by Henry Ripley in the 1860s. He had a thriving dye-works in the city and his workforce expanded, from eighteen men and boys in 1821 to one thousand by 1890. The street names in Akroydon were unrealistically evocative of England's rural market towns. They included Beverley Terrace, Ripon Terrace and Salisbury Place. In Saltaire Victoria Road and Albert Terrace paid homage to the Queen and her consort, but most of the remaining streets were unashamedly named after Titus Salt himself, his wife Caroline, and then his children, grandchildren and daughter-in-law, in order of birth or entry into the family.

Little seems to have been written, however, about the alternative names given to these terraces by the workers, and yet they offer us many fascinating insights into their humour, dialect and social perceptions. One or two of them are quite simply comments on where or when the houses were built. Titanic Row in Marsden, a terrace at Wood Top, was built in 1912. Slant Row refers to a terrace on the steep hillside at Underbank, near Holmfirth, whilst the more picturesque Shuttering Row describes a hillside terrace off Penistone Road. This is a useful dialect word, with a meaning not exactly paralleled in standard English. It is used to describe snow, 'shuttering' or sliding off a house roof, or coals being 'shuttered' or tipped from a lorry. When you open a cupboard where the shelves have been overloaded the contents are likely to 'shutter' out on you when you open the doors. The houses given this name do not have a common roof line, although they form a single terrace; they are built one below the other, as they 'shutter' down the very steep slope.

In other cases the names preserve small items of local history. Teapot Row in the Colne Valley presents no etymological problem, but its 'meaning' emerged when I met a lady who had been brought up there. She told me that the houses were put up during the building of the railway, and that the women who lived there regularly brewed tea for the navvies. She remembered that at least one of the houses was not under-drawn, and that railway sleepers had been used in the construction of the roof, 'with great nails sticking through'. She also wrote that 'the pattern of the beams had had to be arranged to accommodate the shortness of the sleepers and was most intricate'. Elsewhere the navvies are remembered in a number of place-names. There is the Tippins in Marsden, bordering the canal towpath, and a Navvy Row in Whitley that ended up as farm buildings.

Who can explain, though, why cottages at the top end of Occupation Road in Lindley are called Juggler and Poisem Fold? To 'poise' somebody in the local dialect is to kick them, so in this instance we can at least speculate on who might have been poised and who did the poising. Also obscure is Hicklety Bottom, the name of cottages near the Grey Horse

Inn, although to complicate matters this nickname itself had a nickname. Several older ladies in the village assured me that they called it 'Ticklety Bottom'. They were persuaded to recite a bit of doggerel verse that commented, disrespectfully, on the activities of courting couples in that place, but would not sanction its publication! Equally obscure is the name Ancient Lights, given to one end of Windmill Terrace in Berry Brow, but Bird 'oil in Skelmanthorpe has been explained. It was a small, disputed piece of waste ground in 1979, said by one parish councillor to mark the site of a row of cottages, where handloom weavers had once kept canaries. 'Oil for 'hole' is a common element in these names. For instance, places called Bell 'oil in Lepton and Golcar tell us where the handbell ringers practised; Buntin 'oil, the name of cottages between Millhouse and Thurlstone, may indicate that the houses were lavishly decorated with bunting on some special occasion, for this word was in regular use. On the other hand, Bunting is also a surname.

More often than not, nicknames of this type were the community's comment on the social level of those who lived there, or perhaps on their social aspirations. The house-proud ladies of Lewisham Road in Slaithwaite lived on Brassknob Row, and not too far away there was a Beefsteak Row, whose residents were said to be charged higher prices at the local doctor's. Hawthorn Terrace in Crosland was known as Piano Street: this was another dig at the aspirations of families living there, and in sharp contrast to Bluemilk Row, Fattycake Row, Rhubarb Row, Broth Row and Potato Row. These surely refer to the low-cost diet of the inhabitants. Fattycakes in particular were very 'working class', made with flour and dripping. Nippins Row in Hopton is another derogatory name; a reference to the nippins or waste yarn in spinning. The stone in these houses was said to have come from a burnt-out mill. Tenpetty Row was a reference to the ten petties or outside privies, whilst Readymoney Row indicated that the tenants did not need to hide from the rent collector.

It was not just terrace houses that had nicknames. They were given also to narrow lanes and alleys, single dwellings, pieces of waste land, woods, working men's clubs and even villages themselves. Jigby for Jackson Bridge and Shat for Skelmanthorpe have never been explained, and I linked them until recently with Doggus, the nickname for Norristhorpe near Liversedge. Now I believe that this is simply the dialect pronunciation of Doghouse, and that it was formerly where one of the local gentry families kept their hounds. There is a lease, written in 1725, that records the sale of the 'messuage called Doghouse in Liversedge' to Sir John Armytage of Kirklees. Perhaps the explanations of other apparently intractable names lie hidden in the records.

A few names identify former local characters or 'worthies', some of them otherwise long forgotten. Snuffy Ginnel in Golcar is one of several ginnels or alleys that connect Handel Street and Church Street. I was told that 'Snuffy' was a blacksmith named Baxter at the beginning of the 1900s, a man who made domestic utensils, agricultural tools and all kinds of iron implements. Fussey's in Almondbury, a footpath that leads off Northgate, was where Fred Fussey kept the wagons he used for his haulage business. Nobody seems to know who Snotty Billy was, but his name became the unofficial title of the Spring Grove Pleasure Grounds, between Mirfield and Upper Heaton. TP Woods in Gledholt commemorated Colonel Thomas Pearson Crosland (1815–68), who lived near by at Gledholt Hall, and was one of the original Improvement Commissioners for Huddersfield.

The delightful name Sheet o' Pins formerly applied to a block of houses in Golcar that have now been demolished. The buildings were located on the hillside between Rock Fold and Knowle Road; they were five storeys high viewed from the lower side and two storeys from the top. The three lower storeys were built against the rock face, in a space where stone had been dug out of the steep slope. The lowest of these, known as an 'underneath house', was a separate dwelling entered from Rock Fold. A flight of steps gave access to the two above it. Seen from below the five rows of windows gave the facade the appearance of an old-fashioned sheet of pins.

Many of the names are colourful, and part of a dying dialect tradition. Giddle Gaddle in Rastrick is a footpath that takes its name from a form of local stile called a giddle gaddle, and Tallycrap in Thurlstone is the alternative name for High Bank. It refers to the shreds of skin that were left after pig fat had been rendered into lard. Stories have grown up around some of the names that may or may not be true. Near Meltham, for example, are the Three 'awpny houses, where the name alludes to one and a half old pence. It might just be that it once cost that to get there on the bus, as some say, but I prefer the explanation that Meltham band, having played carols there one Christmas, were offered a penny at one of the houses and a halfpenny at the other. Goose Muck Hall near Carlecoates was a small farm house opposite the much more prosperous Saville Gate House. Many similar 'hall' names also highlight the difference in living standards between the poor and the well-off, and some of them have become official. Examples include Laverock Hall and Molewarp Hall, the first referring to the skylark and the second to the mole. We are told by the author of a piece on Cannon Hall near Barnsley that it was known locally as Roast Beef Hall because Sir Walter Spencer-Stanhope who lived there 'was renowned ... for his hospitality'. That may be a charitable interpretation.

There is a certain ambivalence towards such names, for what is colourful to the outsider may be embarrassing to those directly concerned. An estate agent who recently tried to sell a weaver's cottage named Greystones obviously thought that its nickname Pound of Pepper was a selling point, whereas the residents of Highlands Lane in Halifax were anxious to lose their association with Nangnail Lane. This derives from the dialect word for a corn or in-growing toenail, but its figurative use for a rascal may explain how the nickname developed. Newspapers commonly record such names. A recent article that had to do with an incident in Holmfirth said that it took place 'in the Rose and Crown, commonly known as the Nook'. Such references emphasise how widespread the tradition is and the interest and value these local nicknames still have.

11

Streets

There is probably more awareness now about street naming than at any time in our history, for we are constantly being invited in our local newspapers to suggest names for new streets and housing developments, 'preference being given to names with local links'. This style of naming is not new, although it has certainly become more commonplace in relatively recent times, one result of an ever-increasing demand for housing.

The creation of new towns such as Milton Keynes involved planners in designing the street names as carefully as the grid plan itself, with decisions about which should be 'boulevards' and which should be 'gates', 'streets' and 'places'. In the rectangular town plan it was the tree-lined streets running east to west that were named Boulevard and the shorter, intersecting streets that were called Gate.[1] These were the decisions of planners, however, or of people connected with local government, whereas now we are all being invited to take part in the naming process.

We are unlikely to respond to this challenge with much enthusiasm, if David McKie has judged the nation correctly. He thinks the British have been unimaginative in naming their streets, content in the past with Industrial Street in the workaday nineteenth century and the equally formulaic (his word) Acacia Avenue for the modern, leafier suburbs.[2] He is envious of French street names such as Avenue du Professeur André Lemierre, and Rue du Docteur Jacquemaire-Clemenceau, which honour individuals with their full name and title, unlike the British who are quite satisfied with Mandela Street. He concedes that in some cities the names are even more prosaic than our own, particularly in New York, with its 42nd Street and Fifth Avenue, but pleads for greater integration with Europe, so that Bradford might dare to have a Boulevard Alderman Stafford Heginbotham.

In fact this arbitrary naming of new streets is hardly typical of the way in which many of our oldest and most familiar names evolved. In London, for example, we have Half Moon Street, named from an inn; Chancery Lane which reminds us of the office of Master of the Rolls of Chancery, apparently set up there in 1290; and Threadneedle Street, with a debated origin, but possibly a corruption of 'three needles', the sign of the city's needle-makers.[3] In York, Whip-ma Whop-ma Gate is often said to be where the whipping post and pillory once stood, but the spelling Whitnourwhatnourgate (1506), makes that seem unlikely.[4] Grape Lane is a sort of medieval Lovers Lane, having replaced the fourteenth-century 'Grapecuntlane'. We should, of course, be careful in our interpretation of such names, for it is easy to read too much into them. Adrian Room made this point, saying that Grapecuntlane may not have referred to over-amorous advances, but to feeling one's way in the darkness of an unlit alley. He also suggested, however, that Bradford's Hustlergate was a place frequented by hustlers or pickpockets, although a more likely explanation is that it commemorates a member of the locally well-known Hustler family. They came from Silsden, in Airedale, and their name probably derived from a northern form of 'ostler'.[5]

Adrian Room's main aim was to capture our interest in the subject, but he sought also to provide a work of reference for those readers who wanted to explore the names of their own locality. Immediately after the title page he quoted a couple of sentences from Warwick Deeping, lines which invite us to share the author's delight in the 'pleasant sounding, richly English and romantic' names of an English town. He then went on to say in his introduction that the history of a town is 'to a greater or lesser degree encapsulated in its street names', and stressed the important role of local knowledge in this subject. He drew attention also to the vulnerability of street names compared with names of other classes, particularly those in towns of continuing growth. There is no doubt that such encouragement is needed, for many towns are still waiting for their names to be taken seriously.

My own town of Huddersfield is a case in point, for its street names were dismissed in a few lines by Professor Smith in his volumes on West Riding Place-Names. He described the town as one of modern growth, with 'few street names of any antiquity' and even those 'not recorded at all early'. In fact, he listed just sixteen names, and offered barely any evidence or comment in support of them. Included in even this small number were some which, sadly, do not even belong to Huddersfield, and the impression we are left with is that there can be little worth saying about the street names of this modern industrial town.

For my part, I think that the transition from village to modern town is a fascinating subject, for the place-names can be shown to reflect the different stages of growth and urbanisation. In such cases we should perhaps talk of 'town-centre' names, rather than just street names, and include the names of fields, inns, dwelling houses and public amenities, all the names in fact within the modern town boundaries. It is only by widening the scope in this way that we can tell the full story. The impermanence of many town-centre names is of course the result of growth, as buildings are replaced, and fields and footpaths give way to houses, streets and roads. One great advantage in a study of this kind, where we are dealing with relatively recent events, is that we are seldom obliged to speculate about what a name might mean, and can even hope to find the origins and changes adequately documented. That is not always possible where more ancient names are concerned.[6]

It is true that Huddersfield, like many other northern textile towns, was little more than a village before the late 1700s, consisting of one main street, a market-place, and a couple of short side streets called Row and Northbar. There were several named houses on the surrounding greens, but only a handful of names until the town's dramatic expansion during the Industrial Revolution. In fact Huddersfield's modern names reflect both those periods of its history, and, even though they cannot be compared with the names of more ancient boroughs, they still have a fascinating story to tell. Part of that story has to do with the use of the words 'gate' and 'street', the first of which is characteristic of many northern towns from early in their history, whereas the second occurred much later, and brought with it a degree of sophistication.

The Gates

The use of 'gate' as a word for street is regional because it derives from the Scandinavian 'gata', and passed into local dialects in those parts of Britain where Scandinavian influence was strong. It is therefore different in origin from 'gate' in the sense of 'opening', which has an Old English origin, but the modern spellings mean that the two can easily be confused. Among the sixteen Huddersfield street names listed by Smith were no fewer than five with 'gate' as a suffix, but he offered no evidence for these and clearly thought they required no explanation. We are therefore asked to infer that Huddersfield, in common with many other northern towns, has a core of street names that go back to when the Scandinavian word was in general use, at least back into the late middle ages. Kirkgate in particular would seem to have been named when kirk rather than church was also usual, certainly no later than Elizabeth's reign. The others are less distinctive: Northgate and Westgate predictably refer to streets leading in those directions; Watergate runs down towards the river; and Castlegate invites us to believe that it once lead to or from an ancient fortress, perhaps the castle on neighbouring Castle Hill. As a group these names seem to point to a comparison between the history of Huddersfield, and neighbours such as Leeds, Wakefield and Bradford, all with similar names.

We would be wrong to make that comparison. If we take Kirkgate as an example, the difference is that its use, in the three cities mentioned above, is supported by documentary evidence going back to 1275 in Wakefield and 1320 in Leeds. In Huddersfield, on the other hand, there is no record of the name until about 1800, in either documents or maps, and the same is true of the other Huddersfield 'gates' quoted. In fact, Huddersfield at that time belonged almost exclusively to one family, the Ramsdens of Byram and Longley Halls, and their estate maps make it clear that all these names were arbitrarily chosen, probably in an attempt to put Huddersfield's status on a par with that of its neighbours. Indeed the documentation reflects the indecision about which names to use, and which streets to give them to. Significantly, an article in the local newspaper, in 1878, referred to a date around the turn of the century 'when the streets were named' – exactly when Kirkgate became Huddersfield's main street, and Westgate its extension to the west.

Huddersfield, like other small places in west Yorkshire, was always referred to as a 'town' in old records, never as a village, but the truth is that it had only one major street, even in the 1700s. This ran downhill from west to east, and it was referred to as the 'town gate' in the early court rolls. In some local villages Town Gate has survived as a place-name, but that did not happen in Huddersfield. By 1657 the inhabitants were being ordered 'to well and sufficiently repair the town street', and this use of 'street' is evidence of the growing pressure on regional vocabulary. It was part of a process that saw words such as town, greave, garth, kirk and water replaced by their standard English equivalents, village, steward, yard, church and river.

A 'cawsey' or paved way ran down Huddersfield's town street, and there was also a stream there, called the 'Towne Ditch'. As late as 1740 people were forbidden from throwing rubbish into this open sewer or, indeed, 'any other thing which is any annoyance to the Street of the town'. This stream was probably to one side of the thoroughfare rather than in the middle, for a widow, in 1690, was told that she must not divert it but 'permitt ... the water that runns under the Brigg Stone before Thomas Beaumont dore, to pass through the ancient course'. Such 'bridge stones' can still be seen in towns such as Settle, where the pace of change has been much slower in the last couple of hundred years.

There were many individually named houses in the town in the sixteenth and seventeenth centuries, some of them on the line of the town street. These included Chamber, Causey, Fold, Smithy Hill and Well, whilst others, situated on parts of the undeveloped green areas, were Backside, Broad Tenter, Crofthead, Outcote and Shore Head. The meanings in almost all these cases are quite clear, but their earliest history is less obvious, mainly because important documents have not survived. However, they went through similar processes of change after 1671, when the town received a market charter and began to develop commercially. In fact only two of those names have survived, and many seem to have disappeared when areas were set aside for market use, soon after 1671. In just a few cases, where the place-names came to be applied to groups of dwellings, this helped them to survive, but they were finally swept away during the town's dramatic expansion in the nineteenth century.

The Fields and Greens

It is interesting also to see how areas away from the main street developed. A map of 1716 has fields to the north and south of the Town Street, and 'greens' or unimproved land to the south, east and west.

The two areas at the ends of the street were known in the sixteenth century as the Over Green and the Nether Green, and there is an enclosure document of 1571 which lists parcels of land there that had just been taken into cultivation by tenants. For example, Edward Hirst had 'one acre by estimacion inclosed from the over gren of huddersfield', and Robert Woodhead a 'third parte of an acre ... from the neither grene'. These two areas of 'waste' were linked to the south, beyond some ancient enclosures, by the Back Green, and seven roods of this were given to John Bothomley 'at a place called prestroid banke', close to where Priestroyd Mills now stand. It was in these three areas that the growing town eventually expanded, and as one illustration of that we can look in more detail at the history of the Over or Upper Green.

Most of Huddersfield's early place-names had 'town' as the first element, for example Town Brook, Town Lane and Townend, and, by the seventeenth century, there was a house at the upper end of the Town Gate called Townhead. However, this name fell out of use as more and more houses were built near by, so that from the early 1700s this western end of the street came to be known as Top of Town, colloquially Top o' Town. Interestingly the name has remained in popular use, although it has no official status, and despite the fact that it is now part of a much bigger built-up area. Because the buildings there were not confined by the street or the fields, the Top of Town eventually developed into a cluster of narrow lanes and alleys, and it is actually called 'the Maze' on an undated map of about 1780. On the same map are two major groups of houses described as Midwood Row and Marshall Row, both named after tenants.

Beyond the ever-growing Top of Town there was still a large area of green to the west, and this was where John Hirst had his house as early as 1524, possibly on an encroachment. The enclosure of 1571 refers to a later John Hirst 'of the Greene', but it was more usual to describe the family as 'of Greenhead' and they remained there for something like 150 years, increasing the amount of land they held, and acquiring gentry status. After they had departed, successive owners were able to preserve Greenhead as an estate, despite the pressures from expansion in that part of Huddersfield, and it was finally laid out as the major park in the town after 1884, when the Corporation purchased it from Sir John Ramsden, the lord of the manor.

Nineteenth-Century Huddersfield

The landlords of Huddersfield were undoubtedly responsible for much of the town's development, establishing the market there in 1671, and the canal and cloth hall in the later 1700s. All these initiatives are commemorated in street-names such as Cloth Hall Street, Dock Street, Quay Street and Market Walk. Their aspirations for the town are reflected also in several of the names given to new streets in the 1800s, not just the 'gates' already referred to. These include Chancery Lane, Threadneedle Street and Half Moon Street, all apparently based on London models, whilst Upper and Lower Headrow are likely to have been inspired by The Headrow in Leeds. There were, even so, several strong local influences on name-giving, and nineteenth-century directories list scores of Yards, Buildings, Courts and Folds, most of them commemorating local families or public houses. Not all these were transitory in nature, and recent town-centre improvements have ensured the survival of Battye's Buildings, Hawksby Court and Goldthorpe's Yard, to name but a few.

Typical of these is Hammond's Yard at the bottom of King Street, which has just been saved from demolition, and incorporated in a new shopping development called Kingsgate (2002). It owes its present name to a grocer and tea merchant called Joseph Hammond. The property was still in the family's hands in 1982, when I spoke to Miss Dixon, a direct descendant. Her copy of the family tree showed that Joseph had married the daughter of a surgeon called William Wilks, who started up a dispensary in Huddersfield in the early 1800s, before the town had a hospital. In fact what we now call Hammond's Yard was known as Wilk's Yard in the nineteenth century, and the title deeds to the property reveal that it dates from 1807, when part 'of a croft called Bone Croft [was] staked and marked out to be made use of for erecting a dwelling house and other buildings thereupon'.

Also part of that more recent history are streets such as Castlegate, Shambles, Temple Close and Venn Street. I have chosen to look at their history in some detail because they too illustrate the importance of nineteenth-century sources. For the first three I am heavily indebted to the well-written reminiscences of Huddersfield men in the 1800s, published in the local newspapers. John Hanson, for example, destroyed any illusions we might have had about the antiquity of Castlegate, when he wrote about Samuel Mosley, the town constable around 1800:

> He had a large dog which rejoiced in the name of Towser. After a while, on the 'Love my dog, love me' principle, the dog's master was commonly called Towser also. He had no lock-up in which to put prisoners, so one was built at that part of the town called Low Green and ... called Towser Castle. When the streets were named, Castlegate received its name from Towser Castle which stood there.

Another informant described Castlegate, or Low Green, as one of the most respectable parts of the town, and he too commented on the prison or Towser which stood there, describing it as a two-storey, stone building with six 'dismal cells' on each floor. From the same source we learn that today's Temple Close, which owes its name to an earlier Temple Street, was where a celebrated quack named 'Doctor' Solomon once had his practice. He made his living by selling a nostrum which he called 'Solomon's Balm of Gilead' and his house, which faced towards West-gate, was known locally as Solomon's Temple. Such explanations would normally be treated with great caution, but the names in these cases would have been coined in the writers' lifetimes, and I am reluctant to dismiss them out of hand. At the very least the stories tell us what the local inhabitants understood by these names.

Certainly John Hanson's reminiscences about the Shambles ring true. This ancient name, recalling the Shambles of York, has been used in Huddersfield from 1723, and probably dates back to the meat market established after 1671. An estate rental refers to the New Shambles in 1771 so, by the time John Hanson was a boy, around 1800, this building already had a history. His reminiscence is worth quoting in full, for it throws light not just on the Shambles, but on King Street and the Bone Croft mentioned above; even on a much earlier history, possibly going back to a time when the initial settlement was surrounded by forest. He was mistaken, however, if he believed the name Bone Croft had any connection with the nearby slaughter house. Late medieval deeds for the town suggest that it was land worked by tenants as part of their 'boon' labour for the lord of the manor.

> The old Shambles and slaughter house stood where now King Street joins New Street. I well remember standing when a boy on a butcher's cratch

and looking out of the grated window of the slaughter house into the fields below, where the late Shambles afterwards stood. There behind the building was a large pool of blood and refuse which had run from the slaughter house ... the fields were called the Bone Crofts.

After the Shambles had been removed (which must be about 1807), cellars were dug for the buildings which now stand on the right as one looks down King Street. In the course of their operations the excavators laid bare a number of very large tree roots and some trunks of trees. These still remained perfectly sound and were as black as ebony. The cabinet-makers bought them for use in their work.

Huddersfield Vicarage

The name Venn Street commemorates the Rev. Henry Venn, who took up his post as Vicar of Huddersfield in 1759. The vicarage then occupied a prominent position on the south side of the Town Street, below the church and facing the Corn Market. A terrier of 1684 describes it as set back from the street, flanked by gardens, a barn, stables and 'a piece of ground in the Street ... about three yards in breadth ... for a Dunghill'. To the rear was a croft of glebe land. There are many more items of interest in the document, but this extract serves to convey a picture of Huddersfield as a rural village at that time. A later vicarage, recorded in 1795, was built of brick, a rare material in the modern town centre, but one favoured by the Ramsdens for important municipal buildings in the late 1700s. No doubt they were familiar with it as a building material in Leeds and Wakefield, and imagined that it was more civilised than stone. The vicarage still had extensive gardens to the rear and a courtyard to the front, but now there was a public house called the Rose and Crown on the glebe land to the east, with stables and other out-buildings. An eight-acre piece of waste land in the hamlet of Marsh, annexed to the vicarage in lieu of all small tithes, would later be the site of Glebe Street.

When the Rev. Bateman arrived in Huddersfield, in 1840, he con-sidered the vicarage to be 'a very old building, in the worst part of the town ... hemmed in by tall chimneys and wretched buildings'. There was still a garden but nothing would grow in it, and it was not long before he moved to 'a handsome Gothic vicarage ... just outside the town'. We are given this information in his *Clerical Reminiscences* (1882), but the decisions which led to his former home being demolished, and then replaced by Venn Street, are to be found in a letter of 31 July 1849. This was written by Alexander Hathorne, the Ramsdens' local agent, and it was accompanied by a map. The vicarage was still there in 1849, but occupied as a warehouse, and two inns on the glebe land, the Fleece and the Rose and Crown, were both 'very much out of repair. The letter paints a detailed picture of the decline in that part of Huddersfield, and outlines a plan to make major improvements.

According to Mr Hathorne, this part of the town 'was as ill-contrived, unhealthy and disreputable as it is possible to conceive', and he proposed opening out a street 'right through the centre' of the old glebe land, 'extending from King Street to Kirkgate, and thence along the projected new street called Byram Street'. The latter was to run along the bottom side of the church, and the name was no doubt intended to commem-orate the link between Huddersfield and Byram Hall near Castleford, where the Ramsdens had their main home. In the end, however, it was decided to name the new street Lord Street and the Byram Street name was shelved, until the old Swan Yard on the top side of the church was demolished. The expressed aim was to purchase the glebe land from the vicar, knock down a number of buildings, including the vicarage, and increase the rents paid to the estate. When this was finally done the new street was called Venn Street, in honour of the town's best-loved vicar.

These are just a few of Huddersfield's town centre names, but they help to illustrate the physical development of the town over the cen-turies, and some of the personalities involved. It may be only two hundred years since the major changes began, but in that period the rural village of Huddersfield has been transformed into an energetic university town of more than 100,000 people. One final quote from John Hanson, writing in his old age about developments along the Back Green in the early 1800s, helps to convey the impact these changes had on those who lived through them:

> I will now move to Ramsden Street. On the south side, from the Wool
> Pack down to Clegg Lane, now Commercial Street, there was not a house,
> neither was there one in Clegg Lane. On the north side, all the way from
> the top corner where the watchmaker's shop now is to the Ship Inn near

the Shorehead, there was not a single house. I have gathered mushrooms in the field where Ramsden Street Chapel now stands.

12

Ships and Fabrics

Very little has been written about the names of ships. Recently, however, Malcolm Jones of Sheffield University published an article in which he analysed the names of 344 ships assembled by Edward III in 1338 for an expedition to France. The names are likely to be fairly typical of English ships in general, as they came from seventy-six different ports.[1] That was not his only source: he also considered names from an article on vessel types by O. Arngart; an unpublished paper by Margaret Aston; and some shorter lists of ships, both before and after 1338. His evidence overall covered the period from the 1200s to 1588, and his main conclusions were that popular saints were the biggest influence on early ships' names. He thought, however, that the smaller number of non-religious names might be of particular value, since they can make a significant contribution to our knowledge and understanding of the vocabulary of the English language.

Examples of important non-religious names include the *Lopside*, a ship's name of 1291. The earliest entry for the word 'lopsided' in the OED is 1711, and it is defined as descriptive of a ship that is unevenly balanced. The ship's name predates that by more than four hundred years. The *Slodogge*, of Heacham in Norfolk (1347), is an equally valuable lexical item. It is a version of 'sleuth-dog', a term not otherwise recorded before the 1770s. Also of interest were a number of names from elliptical phrases, such as *Smotheweder*, *Godyer*, *Portejoye* and *Welfare*. *Smotheweder*, for instance, should probably be interpreted as 'may the ship have calm weather'. To east coast fishermen a 'smooth' is still a wave that does not break. *Welfare* could be taken literally, but it might alternatively be a form of 'farewell', although few of us consciously use that word now to mean 'may you travel safely'.

As a contribution to the growing interest in this neglected area of name-studies I propose to look at the names of ships that occur in the records of the port of Hull, initially for the period 1391–1490. It should be said at the outset that these ships came from many ports, not just from Hull. There were clearly important links with towns all down the east coast, from Leith and Dysart in Scotland to Yarmouth, Brightlingsea and Dover in the south. One or two ships came from as far west as Plymouth and Dartmouth, and many more from the Low Countries and Danzig in the Baltic. Less frequent were visitors from France, although occasional ships came into Hull from Calais, Rouen, Brittany and even Spain.

East Coast Vessels

Before we consider the names given to ships in Hull records, it is worth saying something briefly about the wide variety of vessel types on Yorkshire's east coast. From the interior came the boats that plied up and down the Ouse and its tributaries, and there were one or two vessels specially designed for inshore fishing and coastal trade. Others were intended for longer and more dangerous voyages: the seamen and fishermen of the east coast were familiar not only with the continental ports already referred to, but with routes to Bordeaux, Russia and Iceland. As the ships listed in the customs accounts are described simply as 'navis', we learn little about them, not even their tonnage or size. Some records give the type of ship but no other details: 'hoys', for example, are referred to frequently, from as early as 1395, but all we are told is that they came mostly from East Anglia; in the sixteenth century they are sometimes linked with 'hulks', and both needed pilots to enter Hull harbour. We know that hulks were transport ships, and that the word was not then pejorative, but the records tell us nothing more. 'Flyboats' were merchant ships of Dutch design, but they are referred to only very occasionally in Yorkshire in the seventeenth century. Fortunately, there are some records which allow us to piece together a few details of the more characteristic local vessels.

One type of small boat was the 'catch'. In 1477, William Carter of York used a 'cache' to transport his corn.[2] In 1505, a rich Scarborough merchant left his 'shippe called the *Martyn*' to his sons John and Henry, and 'j quarter of [his] cache callyd the *Marye*' to John.[3] This catch is likely to have been used along the coast, but most other references link such vessels to river trade. It was agreed in York, for example, in 1572, that catches should not use the staithes there 'except they have twoo good fendars of wood'.[4] They were operated by 'catchmen' and carried cargoes far inland, along rivers like the Aire and Calder. In 1578, one catchman carried 'two webbes of leade in his catche to Burrow brygge', that is Boroughbridge on the River Ure.[5] These boats were made in yards along the River Ouse: John le schipwrith was working in York in 1308,[6] and a bequest in a York will of 1558 set on one side sixty 'of the best bords ... for the building of a catche'.[7]

The 'pink' was another boat used on the rivers, although an early entry in the Trinity House records of Hull establishes that some were sea-going. In 1575, John Adams was fined ten shillings for refusing to pay duties 'on a voyage from Hamburgh in Christopher Wormeley's pink'. Perhaps the most interesting references are in the inventories of John and Willam Wiseman, two Selby shipwrights. These were valued in 1678 and 1680 and the items listed offer us a partial picture of a boatyard. They include 'one pincke now upon the stocks, ready builded', valued at £250, and 'one 32 parte of Sam. Hodgson pinke', valued at £12. There were also working tools, such as 'quart saws, axes, adges, wombles, iron craws', together with 'props and wedges, ring boults and sett boults, a plaite of iron to sett before the fire, 2 pigg playtes, 102½ tunns of timber, made plancke, 3000 trenalds, dager screwes, several mouldes', etc.[8]

Also used on the Ouse were 'crayers' and 'keylls', and both types of vessel were mentioned in a letter to the Duke of Suffolk from the Mayor of York in 1544. The two crayers were of thirty-six tons and each had a crew of six: they were 'hable to go to the see', whereas the ten keels, it was claimed, could only 'convay merchaundyses from Hull to York'.[9] It was also said that the water level was often too low for the crayers to pass between Hull and York, although they too were made on the river. In 1599 William Robinson claimed that he was owed wages from Mr Railstone 'for going to rig and fetch down a new crayer from Selby'.[10] The earliest evidence I have for this word is the name of a Dutch ship. In 1471 the *Crayer* of Delft was in the port of Hull with a mixed cargo, and a master called Jacob Johnson. The earliest direct reference I have to 'a kele' is at Cawood in 1484.[11]

The keels were flat-bottomed vessels, and 'keelmen' are referred to frequently in the records, some from as far inland as Fishlake. An eighteenth-century description of Thorne Moors informs us that turf was dug there in the summer by labourers and then conveyed 'on board keels and other small vessels ... to York, Selby, Leeds, Wakefield, Hull, Gainsborough, Lincoln, etc.' [12] One of the major problems for boatmen on the rivers, from the fifteenth century at least, was the fishgarths, which hindered 'keyllys and other vessels daily passyng up and doune the water of Owse'.[13] It had been claimed in York that they were not sea-going ships, but they certainly carried coal from Newcastle, as did the crayers, for there are references to this in the records of Hull's Trinity House. In 1602 Cuthbert Wardell claimed wages from Thomas Barughe, 'having trafficked all summer in a keel with coals'.[14] The trade accounts for Bridlington in 1642–43 contain references to keels from York, Hull and Patrington, with cargoes of wheat, beans and malt.[15]

Also referred to in the Bridlington records was the 'buss', a fishing boat that had its origins in the Netherlands, at least as early as the 1400s. In 1670 a Dutch man of war was sighted in the bay, acting 'as convoy to 300 busses ... fishing within sight of Flambro' Head'. A ship in the port of Hull in 1461 had the name *Blakbusse*: its home port was Dordrecht and it was carrying cloth and lead.[16] The *Golden Buss* of Hamburg had a similar cargo in 1653.[17] The English herring buss of those years was recently described as a deep-sea boat of some forty tons burthen, three-masted and square-sailed, with blunt bows and the raised stern of the Elizabethan period. From it developed the so-called 'farmin or farm boats' that later operated from ports such as Staithes, Runswick and Scarborough.[18] 'Farmin' is said to have developed from the phrase 'five-man', a term met with earlier in connection with the 'coble', possibly the Yorkshire coast's most distinctive craft. Cobles were designed to beach stern first, and a monastic rental of about 1540 records an annual rent of twelve pence, paid by Henry Webster of Sandsend, for a close 'where the Cobles put in'.[19]

Some of the earliest references to this type of boat are in Latin, as 'cobella' (1414), and it is described by P. Frank and others as an inshore fishing vessel, carrying three to five men.[20] The Conyers family of Whitby owned cobles, and Gregory Conyers described one of them in 1540 as his 'holl boit fyve man coble'. The following year his uncle James bequeathed one of his 'five men boittes' to Thomas Lancaster. Curiously the same words were used in a Scarborough will of 1505 to describe a 'cog' or 'cock'. This is usually said to be a very small boat, either carried on board a larger ship or towed behind it. Half the 'five mannys koke' was bequeathed by Peter Shilbotell to his wife and son Alexander, and half to his sons John and Henry. This seems to imply something rather more important than a cock boat.

Some of the documents already quoted have made it clear that individuals could own half or quarter shares in a vessel, and that river boats in particular might be even further subdivided. The inventory of Robert Haxby of Selby, a master mariner, shows that in 1678 he possessed 'the one sixteenth part of Joseph Hall keele', valued at £5. John Todd, another Selby mariner, made his will in 1683 and left to his son 'all that sixteenth parte of the keell knowen by the name *Caire-for-all* ... and the sixteenth parte of the cogg boate'.[21] We have already seen that the relatively small pink could eventually be divided and subdivided into thirty-two parts.

Ships of Hull, 1391–1401

From the late thirteenth century there existed national customs duties, and a system to administer them. As a result there are fragmentary accounts for Hull from 1304, but these unfortunately tell us little about the ships themselves. In fact, we have only a partial picture of the port's total maritime trade, since such duties did not fall on ships trading between English ports, and the only vessels recorded were those leaving Hull. Some details are given of the cargoes and the names of the masters, but the ships were mostly aliens and there are no names in the accounts until 1391–92.[22] In fact the only Hull ship that I have found named from the earlier period is the *Trinity*, which was 'sent well provisioned from Hull to Scotland on the king's business' in 1322.[23]

From 1391 the picture is very different, and we have almost one hundred different names, many of them repeated several times. They occur in two main periods, 1391 to 1401 and 1453 to 1490. Although many of these ships are from Hull and neighbouring ports, almost half are from overseas. In the first period of ten years there are about thirty different names, and most of them have religious associations. In addition to Trinity and Maudelin (Magdalena), there are the two archangels, Gabriel and Michael, and no fewer than thirteen names of saints, several of them directly from the Bible. The male names are

Bartholomew, Christopher, Clement, Cuthbert, George, James, John, Laurence, Leonard and Peter. Female saints represented are Ellen, Katherine and Mary. This emphasis on religious names is scarcely surprising; sailors are likely to have seen them as some sort of protection against the hazards they faced at sea. Nevertheless, in one respect the list is surprising, for most of the names chosen contrast with what we know about them as baptismal names. With the exception of John and Peter, the male names listed were rare in England in 1379; one or two, such as Leonard and Christopher, had fallen almost completely out of fashion. Even Mary was not common, and the earliest example I have of Maudelin is 1510.

There are several names in the group that are of particular interest. The *Seyntmariebote*, from Barton upon Humber, and the *Seynt Marie Shipp* from Nottingham are distinctive because they employ the word 'saint', and also because the generics 'boat' and 'ship' appear to be part of the names. They are not the only ones of this type. Also from Barton is the *Swan Ship*, a name that is etymologically transparent but difficult to interpret. It might just be that the name-giver was seeking to compare the ship with the bird, because of its graceful appearance on the water, but the swan as a symbol was associated with St Hugh of Lincoln, and it was used as a heraldic device by Edward III and others.

A small group of names have 'knight' as a second element. Possibly of English origin are the *Marie Knyght*, *Seintjohnsknight* and *Godsknight*, but two other *Maryknights* were certainly not English: one was from 'Camfer', or Veere, in Holland, and one from 'Gonesbergh', possibly Königsberg in the Baltic. Later there was a *Jerom Knyght* from the Dutch port of Noordwijk (1463), and the impression is that these names may have a continental rather than a British origin. They are in either case difficult to interpret, for 'knight' had a range of meanings in the Germanic languages. The prevailing senses, however, were 'servant', 'soldier' and 'youth'.

In fact many of the ships sailing out of Hull in 1391–1401 were from France, the Low Countries and the Baltic. In some cases the names appear to have been English, and some of the masters were probably Englishmen, including John Lacye, the master of the *Trinity* of Danzig, John Longe of the *Katharine* of Bayonne and, possibly, Robert Utlaw of the *James*, also of Danzig. These three ships had names already met with in Hull, and there are others from these foreign ports that we are familiar with, that is *Maudelin, Christopher* and *Saint Mary*. More obviously foreign, if only because their names have no transparent meaning to an English speaker, are *Godbyrade, Goldenbergh, Pasdagh* and *Shenkwin*.

The home port of the *Garderote Van Gose* was probably Goes in Holland, and the ship is likely to have been named in honour of St Gertrude of Nivelles. Her cult was strongly established in the Low Countries in the middle ages and she was thought of especially as protective of travellers. The first example I have noted of Gertrude as a christian name in England is in 1567, and the early spellings confirm how unusual it was. They include Gartricke, Garterit and Gartrew. There was a ship from Veere in 1463 named *Gertrude*.

Ships of Hull, 1453–90

Many of the names from 1391–1401 are found in this period also, and the majority of new names, both English and foreign, continued to have religious associations. They include the Hull ship *Alhalow* (1460), the *Goddesgrace* of Dysart (1453), and the equivalent *Gracedew* of Newcastle (1473). From Veere there was the *Holigost*, and from Arnemuiden the *Gost*. *Jacob* was a popular name for foreign ships, and it is recorded frequently between 1453 and 1471, from ports in the Baltic, all along the Channel coast, and as far west as St-Pol-de-Leon in Brittany. There seems to have been no Hull ship of that name until 1597. A very rare name was the *Lazarus* of Zierickzee (1471), the only example I have noted. It may have been unpopular in England because the word was used there to describe lepers and beggars.

As in the 1390s a large proportion of the names chosen for ships were those of saints, many of them again not popular as baptismal names. They are Anne, Antony, Barbara, David, Gregory and Valentine. There were others, however, that were popular, such as Julian, Thomas, Margaret and Nicholas. Among the new and less-familiar foreign names were Bastian, Brigida and Vincent, and several that we might have expected to be British, such as Andrew, Columba and Edmond. More obvious regional favourites are the *Hilda* of Hull (1472), probably inspired by St Hilda of Whitby Abbey, and the *Botalff* of Boston in

Lincolnshire, a clear reference to St Botulf. The place-name Boston actually means 'Botulf's stone'.

Perhaps the most important new name in this category was the *Jesus* (1489), a Hull ship. Jesus has enjoyed some popularity in Spain and Portugal as a baptismal name, but was always avoided in England. Its use in this case further emphasises how different the customs were that related to the naming of ships. It was also known on the Continent; in 1528 a ship from Danzig called *Jhesus* cast anchor in the Humber, confident that it would be secure. It was captured there by French pirates, however, and then sold to several Whitby men, along with the cargo. The case was brought to the king's attention at the court of Star Chamber, and the documents are of particular interest. The ship's rigging is itemised meticulously, as are the merchandise and individual pieces of tackle. On board, for example, were a pump, three compasses and sand glasses for measuring the time. In the cargo there were 'sprewes skynnes', that is leather from Prussia.[24]

If the name *Bonaventur* of Hull (1489) was inspired by St Bonaventure, it had a certain topicality, for he was canonised only in 1482. There is apparently no evidence of an early cult for this thirteenth-century Franciscan cleric, but his name was well enough known in England by the 1500s to be used by as a christian name. It is recorded first in Lancashire and Nottinghamshire: Bonaventure Walkeden, for example, was baptised in Rochdale in 1582. Alternatively the ship's name may just have meant 'good fortune', and the break with Rome certainly had no influence on its popularity in England. Later examples in Hull include *York Bonaventure* (1600), *John Bonaventure* (1602) and *Thomas Bonad-venture* (1614). On 27 August 1647, the master of the *Hopewell* successfully claimed damages from the master of the *Bonadventure*, after a collision in the port of Hull that sank his ship's boat.[25] An attractive name that appears to have something in common with Bonaventure and Hopewell is *Cumweltohous* (1466).

A few examples of compound names have already been noted. Malcolm Jones was of the opinion that these often identified individual owners or ports of origin, especially where popular ships' names like Mary were concerned. So we have the *Marie Durras* from Calais (1464), the *Mari Albryght* from Danzig (1489), the *Mary Donston* from London (1465) and the Mary *Busshell* from York (1491).[26] The *Marykirkland*

(1465), later called the *Marie* of Kirkland, was probably therefore from Kirkland on the River Leven in Fife. The *Mary Flower* of Hull (1464) is an intriguing name. If it is not a surname reference it might possibly be the 'Virgin's flower', like the marigold. Such an interpretation might have implications for the better-known *Mayflower*, since 'May' is known later as a pet form of Mary. There were ships called the *Mayflower* in Hull from at least 1598, rather earlier than the evidence for 'mayflower' as a plant name. The *Mary Gale* of Dartmouth (1465) might refer to 'gale' as a plant but seems more likely to be a surname. The *Mairie Rose* was in the port of Hull in 1583.

Among the small number of non-religious names are several that appear to have straightforward etymologies, such as the *Brown Cross*, the *Mone* or Moon, the *Bere* or Bear, and the *Roos* or Rose. The *Serfe* may be from *cerf*, the French word for 'stag', and the *Bono* from the Latin, short possibly for 'pro bono'. The *Huse* seems likely to be from the German word for 'hare', and later there were two Hull ships with similar names, that is the *Haire* (1605) and the *Little Haire* (1604). The interpretations of the *Cowe*, the *Showte*, the *Potteshed* and the *Gyrsse* (grass?) pose problems, but the *Spetill* is short for 'hospital' and possibly refers to one of the great medieval hospitals, founded by a religious body.

Several names from this period are worth considering in more detail. The first two, *Catyntroghe* (1453) and *Rotheship* (1437),[27] may both belong to that group of names already discussed, where a generic was part of the name. Additional examples in the period 1453–1490 are *Antonykeele* (1466), *Blakboote* (1465) and simply *Barque* (1483). Certainly the word 'trough' was occasionally used in early records as a generic term for a boat, for an undated Elizabethan document refers to fishermen who would 'hazard 20 or 40 myles into the seas in a small troughe', or coble.[28] The *Catyntroghe* may therefore have been a 'trough' called 'Catyn', perhaps a diminutive of Katherine. The surname Catin can have this origin. *Rotheship* brings to mind Malcolm Jones's problem with the name *Rodecog*, which was recorded eleven times in 1338 and once in 1326. He mentioned also *Rodship* (1294), surely the same name as Rotheship, but with 'th' for 'd', as in north-country dialect generally. Rod-cogs and rod-ships are likely therefore to be boats that did not venture out of the 'roads' round any particular port.

The final name for consideration is *Tulpyn* (1461), a ship from the port of Dunkirk. This appears to be the Dutch spelling of 'tulip', a flower said to have been introduced into Europe from Turkey in the sixteenth century. The earliest reference to the word in the OED is *c.* 1554, and the English botanist Lyte first referred to it in 1578. Gerard called it a 'strange and forrein floure' in 1597, and also commented on its etymology, saying, 'After it hath been some few dayes floured, the points and brims of the floure turn backward, like a Dalmatian or Turkish Cap, called Tulipan, Tolepan, Turban, and Turfan, whereof it tooke his name'.[29] In other words it was named after the turban, which it was thought to resemble. If the ship's name means 'tulip' it takes the word's history back almost one hundred years.

The Names of Fabrics

The names of different fabrics or materials often derive from the names of the places where they were first made, like the Lincoln green worn by Robin Hood. Other green garments were made in Kendal, and the dye used for that is said to be from a plant known from the sixteenth century as 'dyer's greenweed'. However, clothiers from Kendal were selling their cloths at northern markets long before that, at least from the 1300s, and the material was popular for making jackets.[30] These were valuable enough to be handed down from one generation to the next and they are frequently referred to in wills. For example Thomas Wrote of Pontefract left his 'togam de Kendale' to a friend in 1438, and Brian Oates of Halifax left his 'Kendall jackett' to John Firth in 1529.

Two English villages that are thought to have given their names to woollen fabrics are Kersey in Suffolk and Worstead in Norfolk. Kerseys were coarse narrow cloths, sometimes called 'northern dozens', and the spelling varied considerably from the 1300s. In 1535 'white narowe karcy' was contrasted with 'brode cloth', and a list of stolen goods in 1684 included 'one wastcoate cloth, beinge 5 quarters of carsey and trimminge for it'. Because of its workaday qualities kersey came to be associated with whatever was plain or straightforward, and Shakespeare used the word in that sense.

Worsted was also a woollen fabric, but the yarn was spun from long-staple wool and the name carried more prestige. Whereas most kerseys were black, white or drab, worsted could also be red, green and blue, particularly in the 1300s and 1400s, when it was typically used for bed clothes. Later it served to line hoods, and garments such as hose, doublets and 'kirtles' (that is gowns) were made from it. The earliest local reference that I have noted is for the year 1310, when the ship of a man called Nankyn of Herderwik sailed from the port of Hull with a cargo that included 'sayes of Wortstede'. 'Say' was a fine-textured and colourful cloth, defined later as a delicate serge, and the term 'of Wortstede' here has the force of an adjective. The spelling is close to that of the original place-name, which had 'worth', that is enclosure, as its first element.[31]

Of course many materials were from other countries, and 'oversea' was formerly an adjective that had the sense of 'manufactured abroad'. There is mention of an 'oversee coverynge of a bedde' in 1544, and of 'an over-sea hanging of wrought stuffe' in 1636. A 'carpet of overse worke', mentioned in 1562, may have been a carpet in the modern sense, or a table cover, but in either case it reminds us that such materials often had to be imported. They were woven in one piece, of richly coloured wools, and had a deep pile; they featured regularly in the inventories of gentlemen. Turkey, not Persia, seems to have been the usual source, and the goods of Thomas, Lord Wharton, in 1568, listed twenty-six carpets, including '7 litell turkey carpetts' and 'one longe turkey carpet'. Among the remaining eighteen were '3 olde kentish carpets'. There is no mention of Turkey carpets in the inventory of Alderman Webster of Doncaster (1674), but in the garret over his shop there was 'a Kitterminster Covering for the table'. We are more familiar now with carpets that take their name from Wilton in Wiltshire or Axminster in Devon, but it was Kidderminster in the seventeenth century that was renowned for the quality of its two-ply carpets.

There were many other exotic materials from overseas. Damask, which took its name from Damascus, was a richly-coloured silk fabric, popular as bed hangings. Lord Wharton had one old tester or bed canopy made of 'black velvet, black satten and yellow damaske'; rich vestments for a church in York included nine yards of 'flowryd damesse to make the whytt coppys apon' (that is copes).[32] Words we no longer use are 'baudkin' and 'sarsenet', but both referred to rich materials and both feature regularly in records of the Tudor period. The first of these was a form of 'baldachin', and it is said to derive from Bagdad where the stuff was made. Something of its attraction is apparent in a description in 1490 of a 'vestyment of cloith of gold of bawdkyne, the ground reid and grene with lions of gold'. The canopies over altars or thrones, either suspended from the roof or on columns, were originally called balda-chins because they were made from this material. Sarsenet is actually a diminutive of the word 'saracen', and I have found it referred to as 'Indian sersnit' (1675). The curtains at Bretton Hall near Wakefield were made of 'chaungeable sarcenet' in 1542, a description that captures the material's silky sheen.

Not all the imported materials came from so far afield, and many linen cloths were imported from France and the Low Countries. An account by Henry Best of what was available in east Yorkshire, in the 1640s, tells us a great deal about the different qualities these possessed, their prices, and the articles of clothing they were used for:

> There is holland from ij*s.* an ell, to vj*s.* viij*d.* an ell, for holland is most commonly sold by the ell, wheareof one sorte is called slezy-holland. It is sayde to bee spunne by the nunnes in the Lowe Countryes, brought over by our merchants, and solde to our linnen drapers, att whose shopps our country-pedlars furnish themselves. It is a strong cloath and much used for men's bands, gentlewomen's handkerchiefs, and crosse-cloathes, and halfe shirts etc. One may buy course lawne for iiij*s.* vj*d.* a yard, and the finest for vj*s.* and vj*s.* viij*d.* a yard. It is much used for fine necke-kerchers, and fine shadowes and dressinges. Cambricke is aboute viij*s* the yard and much used for womens ruffes. Cambricke-lawne, which is the finest of them all and most used for gentlewomen and Ladyes ruffes, is x*s.* a yard or thereaboutes. Cocke-webbe-lawne or tiffeny is the sheirest and cheapest lawne of all, and may bee bought for 10 groates and iiij*s.* a yard. It is used of gentlewomen for handkerchers for the necke, and is worne over another holland handkercher.[33]

Cambrick derived from the Flemish form of Cambrai near Lille, and lawn took its name from Laon in France. It was the district around Dordrecht that gave its name to holland as a material and this Low Countries provincial name came eventually to describe the whole king-dom. Best's slezy-holland was a thin, insubstantial material which eventually gave us the much more pejorative word sleazy. Its origin is uncertain but one theory is that it was originally imitation holland from 'Silesia'. Duffel, so familiar during the Second World War, and among students afterwards, was a coarse woollen cloth from a place near Antwerp. A warm cloak mentioned by Wordsworth in the poem *Alice Fell* was of 'duffil gray'. Dornex, once a common word for curtains and bed canopies, was a sort of damask made at Doornick, the Flemish form of Tournai. Lord Wharton's pair of 'hanginges of Arrase lined' derived their name from Arras in France, and the shalloons that John Windle stole 'of the tenters' at Keighley in 1739 owed their name to Chalons sur Marne. This French place-name had already given us the surname Challoner, that is a coverlet weaver, and 'Chalons of Guildford' had been purchased at Winchester Fair for the king's use in 1252.

It is easy now to forget that clothes were formerly made to last, being thought of as a major asset by our ancestors, who guarded them jealously and then bequeathed them to the next generation. Something of this emerges in the delightful will of Rachel Thornhill (1770), who was the housekeeper to Christopher Green at Green House, a hamlet near Holmfirth. She had moved there from Derbyshire as a young woman, and had herself been given 'all the cloaths late of Mrs Mary Green' by her master, a significant gift when we consider that his sister and several sisters-in-law were all close neighbours. In her will Rachel returned these clothes to the family, leaving them to the elder daughter of Benjamin Green, a younger brother of her employer.

Of greater interest, however, are Rachel's own clothes, for she singled out no fewer than sixteen items from her wardrobe, almost all of which were left to nieces. She never married, but the list dispels any idea we might have of Rachel as a rather dowdy old spinster. It included seven gowns, made of materials such as striped cotton and silk, some of them extremely colourful – blue, green and yellow. No doubt she had a gown fit for each occasion, for one was white, another of black crepe, and a third 'dark coloured' and 'printed'. There were also three cloaks, two of them scarlet and the other made of satin, not to mention three petticoats, one of which was 'blue quilted'. That almost completes the list, but not quite, for Rachel left her 'best staies' to her sister and her 'worst staies' to Sarah, the daughter of Robert Thornhill. Her final bequest was a 'new lawn handkerchief', which was passed down to Benjamin's daughter Mary, along with the blue silk gown and petticoat. The only money bequest was £2, which went to her deceased sister's son, Joseph.[34]

All the fabrics mentioned so far were once familiar to our ancestors, and for centuries they could be purchased across the counter or, for those who lived in outlying country districts, from the many pedlars who carried their packs around the country, keeping their customers in touch with the wider world. In the north of England, if not elsewhere, these salesmen were called 'Scotchmen', and we discover something about their activities from the depositions of two men brought before the magistrates in west Yorkshire in 1682:

> John Smith saith that he was borne in Dumfres and he came into England the foore-ende of May last and sells hollan and scotchcloath, cambrick, callecoe and blew linne and that he came from Almondbury to Kirkheaton and there was taken up by the watch and hath used this pedding traide for five yeares last paste in England and that he byes the commodityes, except the scotchcloath, of Mr Hardwick and Mr Hey of Leeds.

> Thomas Baite saith that he was borne in Carlile and after went into Scotland to live with his parents and he sells hollan, scotchcloath, lawne, muslins, callecoe etc.

Calico or Calicut cloth was a cheap, imported cotton cloth, named after Calicut, formerly the chief port of south India. It was coarser than muslin, which had originally been made in the town of Mosul in ancient Mesopotamia. Like other names of material these are in themselves milestones in the history of textile manufacture across the world, and their transition from specific adjectives to generics highlights the way in which successful products were copied by competitors. As these names passed into English some of them became so familiar, and so closely linked to the behaviour of certain kinds of people, that they acquired pejorative meanings that had nothing at all to do with cloth. All these aspects of the subject figure in the history of the word fustian, which will now be looked at in more detail.

Fustian

Chaucer's 'verray parfit gentil knight' was a seasoned campaigner who had fought through Christendom and against the heathen, so we are not surprised to read that his attire was somewhat travel-stained, at least his short doublet, which was made of fustian and spotted with rust from the coat of mail that he wore over it. Fustian was then a coarse material, and the doublet would have been made of cotton and flax, so it is puzzling initially to find that the same word was used adjectivally in the sixteenth century, to describe bombastic language – Robert Greene's 'fustian eloquence'. In fact there is a close parallel, for 'bombast' was cotton wool or wadding, used to pad garments, so fustian in this sense may have been the unnecessary padding that is so attractive to the long-winded.

Fustian now is a thick, twilled cotton cloth, and only the word's etymology links it with Fostat or Fustat, the suburb of Cairo where it was first made. However, its semantic development is no stranger than that of the copycat fabrics that were later produced around the Mediterranean. In *The Romance of Words*, Ernest Weekley wrote of 'fustian-anapes', a kind of fustian made in Naples, and I have found this mentioned several times in early documents. It is recognisable as 'reid fusshene Naples' in Durham in 1558, but less obvious in Calverley in 1498, when Sir Robert Wambersley wore a 'blake gown lined with fustyan in abills'. It is the loss of the initial 'n' in this case that masks the link with Naples. Actually such changes were not uncommon in the language, and our word 'apron' developed in much the same way from Middle English 'napron'.

The history of the type of fustian that was formerly made in Genoa is much better documented. In Richmond, in 1572, seven yards of 'geanes fustian', that is Genoese fustian, were valued at four shillings, a reference that does not immediately identify this material as the modern 'jeans'. However, only one small spelling change was needed for that connection to become clear and, in 1616, 'jeanes' was selling in one north Yorkshire parish at one shilling a yard. Incidentally three yards of 'myllan', listed in the same invoice, may refer to a similar material made in Milan, or to hand-made lace from that city. It is obvious that 'jeans' was by then on its way to becoming a noun rather than an adjective, and that the 'Genoese' connection was being lost. Just when that happened is not certain but, in 1751, a witness in a quarter sessions trial talked about the theft of 'seven pieces of fustian commonly called jeans'.

Of course, jeans was still some way from having the meaning that it now has. According to a recent advertising feature, the first Levi jeans were brown and made from tenting canvas, a product put on the market

by a young Bavarian immigrant to America in the 1850s. He had started
in business selling canvas wagon covers and tents to the gold prospectors,
but soon saw the need for tougher, more hard-wearing working clothes.
The garment that he eventually offered for sale was a waist-high overall,
and it was apparently an immediate success, although still not what we
understand now by jeans. The immigrant's name was Levi Strauss.

Levi was not yet satisfied with his product, and experimented until
he was able to produce the trousers or levis that are still so popular.
These were made from a tougher fabric than canvas and dyed indigo
blue. Other improvements soon followed, including the copper, rust-
proof rivets, added at the points of strain, and the double-arc stitching
on the back pockets, put there it is said because it reminded Levi of an
eagle's wings. The leather label was an indication of the durability of
the trousers. Ironically this new material was also derived from a place-
name: it was a kind of serge that came from France or, more precisely,
'de Nîmes', that is denim.

In what I am sure was an accidental interpretation of the word's
etymology, the writer of the advertisement claimed that Genoese sailors
really liked these blue denims and it was through their trade with
America that 'Genoese' was shortened to jeans. His escape clause was
in the words 'and legend has it'.

13

Plants

Many plant names have close links with personal names, especially those that have been brought into this country relatively recently from more exotic places. In some the link is apparent, even if the individual commemorated is not: the Douglas Fir, for example, is named after the Scottish botanical explorer David Douglas (1798–1834), and the Banksian Rose honours Lady Dorothy Banks. Her husband, Sir Joseph Banks, accompanied Captain Cook on his expedition round the world, and later became the President of the Royal Society. He was responsible also for the genus of Australian shrubs known as Banksia. Other plant names linked with British botanists include Forsythia, after William Forsyth (1737–1804), and Buddleia, the so-called Butterfly Bush. The inspiration here was the Reverend Adam Buddle, who died in 1715.

Many more names are linked directly with foreign botanists. From France we have Claude Aubriet (1665–1742), the great botanical artist who gave us Aubrietia, and Pierre Magnol (1638–1715), a professor at Montpellier University, whose name is commemorated in the genus Magnolia. Montbretia was a Latin name given in honour of the botanist who accompanied Napoleon's Egyptian expedition in 1798. The names of German botanists lie behind the Latin names Fuchsia and Weigalia, and Andreas Dahl was the Swedish botanist remembered in the genus Dahlia. Other well-known garden favourites with similar links are Begonia, Camelia, Freesia and Wistaria. The botanists' Latin name Lobelia dates from the early 1700s, but was given in honour of a great Flemish botanist, Mathias de l'Obel (1538–1616).

There are also scores of names, particularly those of flowers, that are based on popular first names. Among the most obvious are Black-Eyed Susan, Creeping Jenny, Ragged Robin and Sweet William, although such names do not always belong exclusively to one plant. Two sixteenth-century names are Jack-by-the-Hedge and Jack-Go-to-Bed-at-Noon, the latter a flower that shuts at midday. The names of saints are commemorated in St John's Wort, St Barnaby's Thistle and St George's Mushroom, and any number of plants refer to the Virgin Mary. Lady's Bedstraw, for example, owes its name to the legend that it was one of the plants in the bedstraw on which the Virgin lay, blossoming in honour of the child Jesus. Bracken is said to have lost its flowers because it did not welcome the child. Obvious biblical names include Aaron's Rod. Jacob's Ladder, Adam's Needle and Solomon's Seal, and in these cases the inspiration is often in the shape of the flower or the leaves. In Jacob's Ladder, for example, the ladder-like arrangement of the leaves recalled the ladder of Jacob in Genesis. Timothy Grass, on the other hand, was so named about 1720 after Timothy Hanson, the American farmer who introduced the plant to Carolina.

In other cases it is a place-name that is remembered in the plant name. London Pride, Canterbury Bells, Cornish Moneywort and Bath Asparagus are all of English origin, and other parts of the British Isles are named in Scotch Thistle, Irish Moss and Welsh Poppy. From much further afield are Currant, originally 'raisins de Corinthe', from Greece, and Damson, which owes its name to Damascus in Syria. The Virginia Creeper was introduced from America in 1629. Also announcing their foreign origins are vegetables such as Brussels Sprouts, the Savoy and the Swede, the last-named brought here from Sweden in 1781. The Brazil nut and the Seville orange belong here too, although the latter is said to be a native of China and not of Spain. Pine trees from Monterey and Norfolk Island are among many tree names linked directly with foreign places.

Perhaps the most interesting of these borrowed tree names is the Spruce. In the seventeenth century John Evelyn, the author of the influential book *Sylva* (1664), said that the best fir trees were 'of Prussia, which we call Spruce'. In fact, Spruce or Pruce referred to Prussia, and the word has a long history in the English language. From the early fifteenth century, for example, 'spruce' or 'pruce' coffers or chests featured regularly in wills and inventories. They are likely to have been made of spruce pine, for there is evidence in Hull shipping accounts of 'pruse delys', that is deals brought over from Danzig in the mid 1400s.[1] Some circumstantial evidence for the trade dates back even earlier. More explicitly, about 1640, an East Riding farmer wrote of 'deales which are bought and solde immediately after they bee brought over, whiles the shippe ... is yett in the haven'. Some were 'sold to the joyners for makinge of tables, chests, or sealinge worke'.[2] The word 'deal' actually derives from a Low German word. Somewhat ironically, spruce imported from Scandinavia was later called Norway Spruce.

Some of our more traditional plant names have fascinating etymologies. The daisy was 'dayeseye' in the fifteenth century, because its small yellow sun is hidden overnight by the enfolding petals. The Pink is not so named because of its colour, but from the resemblance the open flowers have to the 'pinks' in Elizabethan clothes, that is the ornamental cuts that revealed brightly-coloured backing. The colour has been said to derive from the flower. Dandelions are from the French *dent de lion* or lion's tooth, possibly descriptive of the jagged edge of the leaves. Its alternative name pissabed again compares directly with the French *pissenlit* and the plant actually has diuretic powers. We might think of the bluebell as one of our oldest and most straightforward names, but the woodland flower, or English hyacinth, was known as the harebell until the late eighteenth century. Shakespeare called it 'the azur'd harebell'. The present harebell has vernacular names that suggest a connection with the hare as a magic animal.[3]

The magic and medicinal qualities of plants were of fundamental importance in our ancestors' lives. When the Rev. Ismay was writing about the coppice woods in Mirfield, in 1755, he said they 'produce such a number of medicinal plants that one of them has got the denomination of the Garden of Eden'.[4] Gerard wrote in 1597 of the 'harmelesse treasure of herbes, trees, and plants, as the earth ... offereth unto our most necessary uses'.[5] He found 'vertues' in most plants, saying of Stitchwort, for instance, that people were 'wont to drinke it in wine with the pouder of acornes, against the paine in the side, stitches, and such like'. The virtues of plants are referred to frequently by Henry Best, the very practical East Riding farmer mentioned earlier. Blindness in sheep was treated by the application of 'grownd-Ivy leaves', chewed first in the shepherd's mouth. The time to mow was 'soe soone as the pennie grasse beginne to welke and seeme dry'. The following is one of the remedies entered into his memorandum book about 1630:

> To lay to a young child's navel to cure the worms. Wormwood, rue, bull's gall, and hog's grease all fried together and laid to the child's navel and anoint their stomach with the same.

Early Place-Names

Names of plants figure prominently in our early place-names, helping us first of all to imagine which trees, shrubs and grasses were familiar to our ancestors, and then which crops were commonly grown. Hundreds of place-names from the Old English period incorporate plant elements, particularly those referring to trees, shrubs and waste land. The list includes ash (Ashford), oak (Oakhurst), elm (Elmham) and thorn (Thornton); fruit trees such as the apple (Appleby), plum (Plumstead) and pear (Pyrford). Also in common use were broom (Brompton), rush (Rushbrooke), reed (Redgrave), nettle (Nettleton) and dock (Docking). The list is almost endless, but it is in some ways disappointing, for we seldom have additional evidence, in those cases, to throw light on the role of the plants concerned. In the Middle English period, however, we can hope to find out much more about the meaning and significance of plants as name elements, and I have chosen to illustrate this point with the words broom, bracken, hollin and whin.

Broom

Broom is neither a tree nor a shrub, but it has several characteristics which led Rackham to call it an 'undershrub', one of a distinctive category of plants found commonly on heath land.[6] Like gorse, heaths and ling, it is permanently low-growing and has a relatively short life span, usually about thirty years; it does not easily withstand severe frost or drought, but is nevertheless a common enough sight on unimproved land.

The place-name evidence suggests that it may formerly have been even more prolific and widespread than it is now, for the element is found over a wide area in numerous compounds, normally as the specific. It is disguised to a certain extent in many of the oldest names, such as Bramham and Branthwaite, Bromley and Brompton, but in most later minor names it can be easily identified, for instance Broom Field and Broom Close. One or two such names can be misleading. The East Riding Broomfleet, for example, was recorded in the very early twelfth century as Brungareflet, and is judged to derive from a personal name that has not survived.

The etymology poses no significant problems and most editors are content to interpret the word at face value. John Field, for example, quoted numerous compounds with generics such as bank, butts, close, field and hill, and said of all of them that they were 'land on which broom grew'.[7] Of course that must almost always have been the case, and it is accurate as far as it goes. Local records, however, suggest or define a number of more specific interpretations, and these increase our understanding of the element and emphasise the important role that broom once had.

Names such as Broom Bank or Broom Hill seem likely to refer to the presence of broom on uncultivated land, whereas in Broom Royd or Broom Ridding, where the generic points to land that has been cleared, the broom may have been removed, or survive on the fringes of the clearance. In those circumstances it is not surprising to find that the Elizabethan husbandman was exhorted by Tusser to cut back the broom in January, for it might otherwise have become a nuisance in spring.[8] Broom hooks and broom scythes feature in early inventories. It is most unlikely, however, that the farmer was being encouraged to eradicate broom completely, for it was far too useful to our ancestors for that.

The plant was employed, for example, in certain remedies, and William Ramsden of Longley Hall made a salve for his dogs by mixing it with urine: about 1580 he wrote in his commonplace book 'for curinge the maungye boyle lant and browme together and washe him sore therewith'. 'Lant' was the local word for human urine. Perhaps more importantly the wood made good kindling, and the advice given to Robert Kaye, the heir of the Woodsome estate, was to 'kyd thy brome', that is to say he was to cut it into faggots for the house fire, in much the same way that he used gorse and the roots of any newly stubbed bushes and shrubs. That was about 1570.[9]

Nor should we forget that bundles of broom were fixed to a wooden handle and used for sweeping. These were called brooms or besoms, and the practice was directly referred to in a quarter sessions case in 1671. The witness claimed to have seen 'John Hanson of Lightcliffe in a broome close ... getting beesoms'. In the same case John Thorpp was said to have been 'windowing bareley in a broomefield', possibly the same enclosure.[10] Strictly speaking these were phrases describing the enclosure's function, and not place-names, but it is easy to see how the place-names Broom Close or Broom Field could have developed in such circumstances. No doubt a certain amount of broom was tolerated in a croft or close near to the house for precisely that purpose.

Bracken

Those English place-names which have 'bracken' as an element are concentrated in the counties of the former Danelaw, which suggests that the word is Scandinavian in origin (*brakni) rather than Old English (*braecen).[11] It is particularly frequent in Yorkshire, and Professor Smith listed over forty places in the county which have 'bracken' as the specific element. Brackenhill or Bracken Hill(s) occurs no less than sixteen times, and there are at least three Bracken Halls, one each in Baildon, Silsden and Huddersfield.[12]

The earliest place-name evidence takes the use of the word back more than one thousand years, but the only sure inference we can draw from those examples is that the plant was very familiar to the first generations of Scandinavian settlers. In fact, the word passed into the everyday language, and some of the names are first recorded soon after the Norman Conquest, combined with specifically Old English words such as 'ley' and 'burgh'. Many more were almost certainly coined much later, during the Middle and early Modern English periods. The fact that 'bracken' remained in the language as a creative element means, therefore, that we can expect its use to reflect the role that the plant once played in a variety of rural practices, some of them long forgotten. Indeed there is clear evidence that it once served our ancestors as fuel, as a roofing material, as bedding for livestock, and as a source of potash.

The value it had within the community is obvious from the by-laws which regulated exactly how and when it might be harvested. In Wakefield, for example, it was ordered in 1664 that 'no person ... burne any brakens in the Outwood before Lammas' (1 August),[13] whereas in Lund, in 1734, the ban on cutting extended until Michaelmas (29 September).[14] Evidently the bracken was protected in those parishes during the growing season. The Lund by-law goes much further than that, for it clearly sought, in a number of practical ways, to control the amount of bracken that could be used. It was ordered that 'none be cutt down with scythes, but sickles only', and that bracken should not be made into 'Heaps or

Cocks, but brought away on their [the tenants'] Backs'. Although it is not made clear what the bracken was being used for, there is an interesting section in the by-law that states exactly where and by whom one section of bracken might be cut: 'the brackons which grow in the piece of common lying in the moor be only for the use of the poor that have none belonging to their houses'. The inference is that the better-off tenants had their rights allowed for in deeds and leases.

Other records can be more explicit. An indictment at the quarter sessions, in 1675, states that 'Mary Armytage of Meltham, beeing burneing brackons upon Meltham Common, was desperately assaulted by John Pogson of Thickhollins'. That is all we learn about the offence, which may have been a random act of violence rather than on-the-spot punishment for a by-law infringement. It is likely, though, that Mary had been intending to burn the bracken to produce a lye from the ashes, for that was used by housewives, both as a detergent and in soap-making. Celia Fiennes commented in 1698 on the fact that country folk rolled the ashes into the shape of balls, which were then used for washing, and it was also normal practice to produce soap by mixing the lye with tallow, usually mutton fat. In fact, the number of incidental references to the burning of bracken in eighteenth-century records seems likely to bear testimony to the greater commercial importance of soap making.

In 1715, for example, two labourers in Yeadon appeared before the magistrates, and were required to explain why they had 'been cutting and mowing of brackens upon the commons in Guiseley'. They stated that they 'sold the ashes thereof to John Garnett the younger of Idle and received twenty shillings and sixpence for the same', a sum which suggests that considerable amounts of bracken were involved. More specifically the labourers claimed to be partners, saying they 'did joyn in burning bracken to ashes for the soape makers', so it may be that John Garnett was producing soap commercially. One of the accused labourers, Joseph Jennings, gave his age as seventy-four, which might imply that bracken cutting on such a scale was a privilege enjoyed by the 'poor', offering them a livelihood which would minimise the claims on the poor rate.[15] In north-west England bracken ash was being exported in huge quantities in this century.[16] In south Yorkshire, as late as 1791, one thousand acres of rocky ground in Stannington were defined as a place 'where the poor burn fearne and raise £120 by the ashes'. No doubt many of the late, minor place-names, especially those on the commons, identify the areas once set aside for these activities.

Hollin

There is a distinct regional flavour to many of the tree names used in Yorkshire. Among those frequently mentioned are the birk, eller, hollin, owler and whicken. Their equivalents in English are birch, elder, holly, alder and mountain ash. As both specifics and generics these regional words are preserved in literally hundreds of minor place-names, and that frequency is evidence of the vital role that such trees had in folklore and the local economy. 'Eller powylles' or poles, for example, were used to make a 'stey' or ladder in 1530; 'owler' was the wood used for 'a paire of cart leggs' (1678), and for troughs taking water to the brewhouse (1640). The protective power of the whicken is alluded to in a deposition of 1674, when an alleged witch said 'they tye soe much whighen about him I cannot come to my purpose'.[17]

The most prominent of all these elements is 'hollin', commonly found as a specific in conjunction with greave, hall, hill, hirst and wood. As a generic it is preceded by broad, thick, green and various township names. It occurs most commonly, however, just on its own, as Hollins or Hollings and these testify to the value of holly as fodder for animals. Indeed, there is evidence that it was used for beasts of the chase in the forest laws of Canute, and as winter feed for cattle from the 1200s.

Most of these early references simply mention branches of holly cut illegally from the lord's trees, but, in 1316, Adam del Grene paid 4s. 6d. 'to have six beasts feeding on the hollins in the Holnefrith for the Winter'.[18] In the records of Fountains Abbey there are important leases in the early 1500s which provide further information. In 1518, tenants at Pott were given permission to fell 'hollynge bowes ande othre brushewode at seasonable tyme of the yere ... for pastour of cattell'. These cut branches were referred to as 'broge' or 'brusynge'. Some holdings had stands of holly on the premises, and one at Winsley, in 1526, was 'markyde and abownded', that is surrounded by a fence.[19] Such stands came to be known as 'parcels of hollynge' or 'hollins', and they became a customary part of the leased property. In the Sheffield area they were called 'hags'.[20] This must often be the sense of the word in many compound place-names.

We know from a seventeenth-century source that great numbers of holly trees were being planted and, even today, the landscape in certain districts carries evidence of the practice. These are sometimes seen as separate clumps of trees close to farms, but they can also be the dominant tree in the hedgerows, as at Hollingreave in Fulstone. Where a tenant's lease gave him grazing rights in certain stinted pastures, locally called 'beastgates', the rights could include access to holly trees. In Saddleworth, in 1654, John Radcliffe's land carried with it 'four beastgates and the hollins to the said four beastgates belonging'.[21] In Lepton, there are still hollies along part of the lane that once gave access to the open arable fields, even though elsewhere it is bordered by dry stone walls. In 1323 this division of the field was called Kirkland, but the 'hollinge called Kirklingeholling' seems to have referred specifically to this group of trees in 1600.[22]

Other seventeenth-century deeds build up the picture, showing that tenants had rights of access to the hollins, either with their animals or so that they might lop off branches and carry them away.[23] These rights became a 'commodity' that could be passed on from one person to another. In 1621, for example, there is a bequest in the will of John Sunderland of all his 'hollings and ... bruise of hollings in Langfield'. It appears to have been a paragraph in a late seventeenth-century diary that once more brought the practice to our attention:

> In the south west of Yorkshire, at and about Bradfield, and in Derbyshire, they feed all their sheep in the winter with holly leaves and bark, which they eat more greedily than any grass. To every farm there is so many holly trees; and the more there is the farm is dearer; but care is taken to plant great numbers of them in all farms thereabouts. And all these holly trees are smooth leaved and not prockly. As soon as the sheep sees the sheppard come with an ax in his hand they all follow him to the first tree he comes at, and stands all in a round about the tree, expecting impatiently the fall of a bough, which, when it is falln, as many as can eats thereof ...[24]

This observation was made in 1697, but by the mid 1700s there were other more satisfactory sources of winter fodder, and the hollins gradually ceased to be so important. Now, we are dependent on minor place-names and surviving features of the landscape to remind us of this forgotten practice.

Whin

Whin, and its adjective whinny, are popular minor place-name elements in the northern counties, typically linked with the generics bank, brow, close, field and hill. Equally common is Whinns, just on its own. Whin was formerly the regional word for gorse or furze and this is the meaning given in works on place-names, unaccompanied by any comment on the value of the plant, particularly to the hill farmer. In Cumbria, for example, 'whin dalts', or doles, were assigned to individual holdings, in much the same way as turf, moss and bracken. Not everybody had access to the plant in that way, but in some manors tenants were allowed to collect whins on the common, and this practice probably lies behind some of the place-names. For example, in 1624, Thomas Waite of Acomb near York was indicted 'for allowing his son to take a burden of whins from Skew Whinns'. No fewer than ten tenants were accused of similar offences, including Christopher Milner who had cut three burdens and tried to sell them.[25]

The earliest indication I have found that this plant was considered to be a valuable resource is in the early 1500s, when manorial by-laws sought to prevent tenants from taking 'any fuell called whynnes' from common land in neighbouring townships. A tithe case of 1556 had to do with practices from this period, and one witness remembered that 'the Parson had whinnes and thornes opon Whitwell More ... so many as servid his kitchyn'.[26] In this instance whins were clearly being used as fuel, possibly to heat an oven. A quarter sessions case in 1620 hints at the quantities used as fuel. It was claimed that John Pease maliciously 'sett on fire most part of the firres or whinnes growing on a pasture of Leonard Cleasbie's within the Lordshipp of Cleasbie ... to the number of 200 waine loades or thereaboutes'. This man had previously granted a lease of the land to two neighbours, but 'reserved the whinnes ... for his house use, having occasion yearlie to use 30 waine loades'.[27] A document of 1703 refers to 'whinheaps adjoining the houses' as a potential fire hazard.

By-laws involving whins appear to have increased in the 1600s, possibly because enclosure was limiting the quantities available, and manors

had to husband their resources. It is not always clear what lay behind
the various orders, but one or two draw our attention to additional
ways in which the plant was of value. Hedges made of whins are referred
to in the 1600s, and some of these are likely to have been temporary
structures, made from severed branches. Angus Winchester, writing
about the northern uplands, described the plant as an 'important ...
fencing material in the making of dry hedges'.[28] In other cases the
growing whins may have formed a hedge, as they still do in parts of
Ireland and Wales. They were certainly grown close to the house. In
1672, when Anthony Young was accused at the quarter sessions of
stealing a shirt, it was claimed that he had taken it off 'the whinns ...
where it was laid out to dry'. A similar case in 1740 had to do with 'two
capps and one handkerchief ... hanging upon some whinns', near a
house in Sheffield.

Whins were also used as animal fodder. A diarist in 1805 noted that
'the young shoots of whins ... are excellent fotherage for fattening
horses', a piece of information he had from his brother.[29] In fact, this
was a well-established custom and it had been commented over one
hundred years earlier by Abraham de la Pryme:

> about Hallifax side the necessity of the winter has caused them to find out
> a strange new meat for their goods [that is quick goods or cattle] ... they
> took green whinz, chopt them a little, put them in a trough and stampt
> them a little to bruise all their pricles and then gave them to their beasts.[30]

> 4 May 1698

The decline of such practices, even of the word itself, has been remarkable. In the *English Dialect Dictionary* there are references to whin-kids,
used as faggots or for thatching, whin-dykes or hedges, and whin-stones,
broad flat stones on which whins were bruised for cattle fodder. In
Lancashire the yellow blossoms were used as a dye. The word, scarcely
used at all now, was still in general dialect use in many parts of the
British Isles into the twentieth century.

A Spring Wood Glossary

Many of our minor place-names were not the result of a conscious naming process but had their origins in the everyday vocabulary. Used initially to describe work locations or practices, they developed into names over a period of time. I have chosen to illustrate how this could happen by placing the words 'spring woods' in a vocabulary that was once familiar to those involved in wood management, but has been lost or become more specialised as the function of the English woodlands has changed. The following glossary has been compiled from wood leases, court rolls, estate and iron forge accounts and a variety of other records. Many of the words I have listed emerged as significant place-name elements in the post-medieval period, for example bark, greave, hagg, holt, laund, plain, rein, shrogg and stub. Of less importance, but responsible nevertheless for some local names were brogg, coal, cock-glade, collier, copy, fleak, pit, standall and waver. 'Timber' itself was the principal element in Timberwood Grange, the name of a Roche Abbey estate that was devoted to wood management. The name was 'lost' at the Dissolution, but has been restored quite recently for a building development on the site of the grange farm.

Avoid: To make void; to remove or clear: 'avoyde the seyd woodes offe the grownde within ... thre yeres' (1549).

Bark (sb): The bark of the oak tree, used in the tanning process: 'the barke worth 12*d.* a tre' (1568); 'barke unpilled' (1622); 'bark chopt and unchopt' (1681). Associated words are: **bark bill** (1799), **barkehouse** (1395), **barke chamber** (1699), **bark sack** (1699), **barke skeps** (1660), **bark stack** (1657).

Bark (v): To treat a skin with bark: 'no glover, pouchemaker, sadeler, ne shomaker of this citie wyrk no shep skynnes barked ...' (1500); 'lether not fullie barkit' (1540).

Barker: The northern word for tanner: 'William Cook, barker' (1379); 'that no barker by [buy] any heir of his nebor to sell' (1538).

Blackbark: A specialist term for an oak at a certain number of years' growth: 'blackbarkes now standing and groweing' (1672); 'blackbarkes or polls' (1690); 'reserving ... eight black barks in every acre' (1720).

Border: A boundary or hedge of a wood, but assessed independently: 'within the bordres of the said two greafes' (1527).

Brog (sb): Brushwood used as animal fodder: 'brogge for the cattle' (1524); 'kepyng suche catell with hay, oke and hollyn broge' (1526).

Brog (v): To browse on trees: 'cattell to brogg the same woodes' (1646).

Bruse (v): A northern form of 'browse': 'small brashe ... for ther cattell to bruse on' (1616).

Brusyng (sb): The noun from **bruse**: 'fellynge of hollynge bowes and other brushewode ... callide brusynge, for pastour of cattell' (1518).

Brush (v): To lop off small branches: 'from hedgis and treys brush all nedefull spriggs' (c. 1570); 'felled and brushed' (1795).

Brushwood: The cut branches and twigs: 'cordwood, rammel and brush-wood' (1766).

Chatt (sb): The seed of various trees: 'Ackornes and Sycamore chatts' (1650).

Chop (v): Part of the processing of bark: 'to pill and chop the bark' (1763).

Chopwood: Wood prepared for use in a kiln: 'paid ... for getting chopwood into the kill' (1658); 'a gang of horses ... to bring chopwood to the mill' (1709).

Cleanse: To clear the ground after trees had been felled and stubbed: 'libertye to stube upe and clense certayn growndes ... to ther more advantage and profet' (1520).

Coal (sb): Charcoal: 'a horsse to carrye the sayd colle ... to the smethe' (1567).

Coal (v): To convert wood to charcoal: 'the woddes ... shall be coled or sold' (1457); 'to cut downe, cole and carye away ... woodes in the several springes' (1595).

Cockglade: An open space in the wood, where nets were set up to catch woodcocks: 'cokglades in the seyd woodes' (1549); 'a wodcock nett knytted by Thomas Peckett sonne ... who hanges my cockgloads' (1617).

Collier: A charcoal burner: 'certain colyers dwellinge in Ampleford had a close called Collyer Carr in ther possession' (1586).

Copy: A coppice or spring: 'my sprynges and my copies to kept and saved' (1499); 'woodes, springes, copies' (1573).

Cord (sb): A measure of wood prepared for the collier: 'thre lode of wood, and to every lode three corde and everye corde must be 8 foulte [sic] longe, four foulte brode and four foulte hye' (1572–75).

Cord (v): To cut and stack the wood according to the local custom: 'liberty ... to take away, coarde and coale the sayde woode' (1675); 'to rank and cord the cordwood' (1763).

Cordwood: Wood for fuel, cut to certain dimensions and stacked: 'a bundle of cordwood' (1661); 'the cordwood or charcoal' (1766).

Defence: The word from which 'fence' developed: 'which said ... spryngewodd they shall repeyre with honest heidges and defenses' (1565).

Dish (v): To cut in an unworkmanlike way, leaving the stoven with a hollow: 'rounded off ... the stoven not dished ... but in such manner as no water will stand ... upon the stoven (1763).

Dozen: A measure of charcoal: 'the dusson ys 12 seme or 12 quarter alle one mesuer so that 3 colyeres wyll burne 12 score dousson colle in the yere, wyche 240 dousson wyll burne 288 blome of irene, that ys, to a blome, of colle 10 quarter or seme' (1568).

Fall (sb): A division of a wood set out to be felled: 'such ... usuall hagges and falles as have beene yearlie accustomed to bee felled' (1534); 'setting out one fall of Lepton Great Wood' (1796). Also called a **panel** (1710).

Fall (v): To fell: 'to falle the underwood and ockes and saplynges' (1568).

Fence row: A hedge containing timber trees: 'hedge boot out of the trees in the fence rows' (1763).

Fence time: The period during which the springs were fenced to prevent animals from browsing: 'to keep the sprynges during the fense tyme'

(1520). Grazing in the wood was not allowed 'for the space of four years after the fall' (1746).

Fleak: A hurdle, made of wattle work or a wooden frame with bars. Recorded from the fourteenth century. In wood management it served as a temporary gate: 'sett two stoopes ... and keepe theire a yate or fleicke during the time that the corne is leadinge' (1678).

Garsell: Brushwood, used for hedging: 'great timber and garsyll' (1396); 'not to fell any wood except garsell for making hedges' (1507).

Greave: A copse or small wood: 'two greafes of wodde, that oon called Holerhede ... and that other Frere Parke' (1527).

Groove: The ring marked on a tree to show where it should be felled: 'before ye pill ... the grofe I trowe shall show the workman's skill' (*c.* 1570); 'felled below the ringing of the bark' (1766).

Hagg (sb): A division of a wood set aside for felling: 'de portione sua cuiusdam 'hagg' de Grenehamerton' (1410); 'a copye and hagge of the said woddes and spryngies in fagottes after the old mesure' (1524); 'a wood ... in which are 18 coppices called haggs, viz. 1 of the age of 18 years another of the age of 17 years and so in succession' (*c.* 1540).

Hagg (sb): A stand of trees all of one kind, particularly hollies: 'one hage of hollen ... letten ... for 5s. a yeare' (1574); 'a hagg of hollin in the wood banke' (1637).

Hagg (v): To fell a hagg: '5 years within which to sell, hagge, leade and convey away ... 3 parcells of wood' (1555).

Hainbote: The older word for hedgebote: 'haybote' (1251); 'haynebote' (1442); 'heynbote for making of the egges [hedges]' (1555).

Hedgebote: A bote was a liberty given to a tenant to take wood for a specific purpose, e.g. ax-, cart-, fire-, harrow-, house-, plough-, wain-, etc. 'hege botte' (1313); 'hedgboote to be taken in the underwoods only' (1652).

Hilling (sb): Sods, bracken etc., used to cover a charcoal stack: 'turves and hillinges to cover his charcole pittes' (1527); 'sufficiente ... hillinge for the collinge of the woodes' (1595).

Holt: A small wood or group of trees: 'one holte of yonge okes' (1555); 'a small holt of wood' (1763); 'a clump or holt of trees' (1775).

Kid, Kidwood (sb): A faggot or bundle of twigs, gorse etc., suitable for kindling: 'Item servientibus portant kyds apud Dunsley' (1395); 'I will that my suster Anne have halfe a thousand kiddes yerlie for her fier' (1548); 'kydwod for thy howsse' (*c.* 1570).

Laund (sb): An obsolete word for an open space in a wood (compare the modern 'lawn'): 'in reparacione muri circa lawnd iij*d.*' (*c.* 1450); 'greate covertes of underwood and tymber and large laundes' (1570).

Lead: To move by cart: 'gapps to be left for leadeing or carrying away of wood, bark or charcoale' (1690).

Lop: To cut off branches, twigs etc. It was linked with 'to top', if the top of the tree was included in the arrangement: 'to loppe alle ockes and saplynges ... and for the loppyng thereof shalle have a ½*d.*' (1568).

Lording: A specialist term for an oak at a certain number of years growth: 'all the lordins now standing and groweing' (1672); 'the lordings in the wood and hedgrows' (1727).

Peark (v): To perch or stack bark, possibly on frames: 'pearke the barke for drying therof in the pasture grounds lying neare the wood' (1672).

Pill: To strip the bark from a tree: 'noe inhabitant ... shall pill any barke of any oake, ash, hollinge or elder' (1564); 'workemen were pilling the woods' (1682).

Pitstead: A level area on which to stack and burn charcoal: 'pit steads for coaling' (1795).

Plain: An open tract of land in the wood: 'nor any playnes ... within the seyd woodes' (1549); 'a right of way ... over the West Wood plaine' (1571); 'paring and stubing a plain 10s. 6*d.*' (1751).

Pole: A tree in the coppice cycle that has reached certain dimensions: 'thirtie such polles or dooble wavers' (1675); 'polls now already marked, ringed and sett oute for standing for future growth' (1719).

Polling tree: Apparently a tree reserved for timber: 'ther be growinge aboute ... the seyd tenementes ... in hedgis ... lx polling okes, aishes and elmes of lx and lxxx yeres growthe ... reservid for tymber' (1544).

Punch wood: Wood suitable for making 'puncheons' or pit props: 'get punch wood for the use of the coale pits' (1637).

Radlings: Long, slender poles: '300 radlings' (1710).

Ramell: It has a general meaning of 'rubbish', but in wood management it referred to what was left over when the tanners and charcoal burners had used what they wanted; usually branches, but sometimes small trees: 'Habeant ramillum ad claudendas sepes circa terram' (*c.* 1270); 'bushes, thornes and other ramell ... for fuel' (1549); 'Hessell, Birch and such like ramill' (1711).

Rein: A thin strip of land, although the precise meaning varies from one district to another. In West Yorkshire it referred to short but steeply wooded slopes leading down to a stream: 'all the wodes within the birke stubyng except a reyne in the north syde' (1519); 'one little reyne of spring wood of small value' (1611).

Reparell (v): An obsolete word meaning to repair: 'to make and reparell all the heges ... aboute the woddes for sawing [saving] of the spryng' (1457); 'the fence, wall and gates ... shalbe cast downe and broken and ... at no tyme repareld' (1499).

Ring about: To mark a tree with a ring as a sign to the woodcutter, sometimes with paint: 'marked and ringed about for standing' (1690); 'unpilled wavers, marked, ringed and sett oute for standinge ... by the pillers' (1719); 'rung about with red paint' (1766).

Rive: To sever or split wood into laths or spars: 'long revyn burdes' (1457); 'riveinge old rootes ... into cords' (1636); 'Richard Dyson, lathriver' (1754). It was done 'with mell and wedge' (*c.* 1570).

Seam: A measure of various commodities. Used of charcoal that was conveyed by pack horses in 'banisters', i.e. wickerwork baskets: 'wych banesteres ys a quarter of colle and the quarter is a seame and the seme ys 8 busshell' (1568).

Set forth: To mark out an area: 'sutche meares and markes as ys appointed and set furthe' (1590).

Shrogg: Brush or brushwood: 'two men came out of a little shroge or wood' (1697); 'some wood in the shroggs' (1763).

Spire: A sapling or young timber tree: 'hesshpires' (1389); 'lx spierres de quercu' (1421); 'sex quercos ... voc. saplinge spieres' (1526).

Spring (sb): A coppice wood: 'le Spryng bosci' (1421); 'unto the tyme that the sprenge be resonabely waxen' (1425).

Spring (sb): A fall of the wood: 'the last fall or springe of the same' (1684).

Spring (v): To prepare for the next growth in the coppice cycle: 'to cut downe, coale and springe' (1466); 'the future springing and growth of the woods' (1766).

Spring (v): To fell a spring wood within the cycle: 'cannot be measured untill they shalbe sprung' (1684); 'before the pilling or springing' (1719); 'to pill, bark, springfel, cut, peark and stack' (1762).

Square, *see* **work.**

Standall: A standard; a tree left in a coppice to grow into a timber tree: 'two hagges ... in which are noe standalls nor any other trees' (1608); 'standalls and wavers' (1797).

Stander: An alternative form of **standall:** 'always reserved ... so manye standers and wavers' (1595).

Stove, *see* **stoven.** To cut a tree close to the ground: 'from one gappe ... unto one oak tree heretofore stoved' (1606).

Stoven: The stump of a tree from which young shoots spring: 'to fence all trees, stoven and undergrowth' (1524); 'all the springe woodes, underwoods and stovens now growinge' (1672).

Stoving: A branch or twig lopped from a tree: 'plashings, shreddings and stovings of trees' (1563).

Stub: To take the stump of a tree out by the roots: 'licence to stube upe and clense certayn growndes' (1520); 'Stephen Allen was betwixt his blow and the root of the tree that he was then stubbing, and by that meanes ... sore cut into the head' (1674).

Timber: Trees of a girth suitable for beams, planks and major building projects; it contrasts with wood, i.e. smaller branches, and underwood: 'at their own cost, except great timber' (1536).

Turf, turves: In a woodland context these were sods, used to cover the charcoal stacks: 'to have sufficiently turves ... to cover his charcole pittes' (1527); 'sufficient turfe and hillinge for the collinge' (1595).

Underwood: Contrasted with timber. These were the trees that were coppiced, i.e. cut to near ground level in order to produce a new crop of poles: 'brush off and fell all the underwood low by the earth' (1763).

Wave (v): To leave with sufficient wavers after felling, a practice governed first by custom and then by law: 'leve them abilly waived after the custom of the contree' (1527); 'shall wayfe the said C acres ... accordynge to the king his statute' (1549).

Waver: A young oak left standing for future growth into a timber tree: 'sufficiaunt wayvers' (1462); 'so many standers and wavers as hathe bene usuallye reserved' (1595); 'powles and wavers' (1763).

Wayleave: Permission to make and use a way across a person's ground: 'wayeleave for servantes, workemen ... to get coales' (1579); 'waye leave in and through all the ground' (1659); 'way and leive for carrying off the said trees, bark, etc.' (1763).

Weaver: An alternative spelling of waver: 'agreed that weyvers shall be left in the two sprynges' (1549); 'presented for felling and carrying away a weaver' (1645).

White coal: Ashes resulting from burning the ramell: 'white coal arising from the said woods' (1720).

White wood: 'white wood, as firrs, ash, elm' (1763).

Wood measure: The acre was reckoned by the long hundred, i.e. 120: 'one hundrethe acres of woods at sex score the hundrethe' (1549); 'above sixteene acres of wood measure' (1690).

Wood monger: A dealer in wood: 'William Roberts, wood munger' (1795).

Work (v): Part of the sawyer's job as he cut the timber that he had felled into planks: 'making of saw pitts and working of the said trees' (1717); 'liberty to ... square, work up and saw into planks' (1762).

Workmanlike: In line with established standards of woodmanship: 'to be weyvered workmonlyke' (1496); 'in an orderly and workmanlike manner, according to the best and most approved method' (1766).

APPENDIX 2

Ruddle and Copperas

The Ruddle Industry

The mineral called Ruddle or Raddle is obtained ... near Doncaster. A shaft is sunk of about twenty-three feet in depth, and five in diameter, which passes through strata of limestone and gritstone, and immediately under this last the ruddle is embedded universally in clay which is three feet thick above and below the vein. It lies nearly horizontal and is generally about 9 inches in thickness. The miner in working sits down and uses a short sharp axe similar to that of the lead miner. He excavates to a distance of about four yards from the centre of the shaft; but as the clay cannot be easily supported, as soon as he has reached this distance, a new shaft is sunk near to the other. The ruddle is carried to a mill, where it is ground to a powder; then mixed with water and ground afresh and afterwards let off into a reservoir where the raddle subsides, and the water is evaporated. It is afterwards cut into small squares, packed up in casks and sent to Hull and London.

G. Walker, *The Costume of Yorkshire* (1814).

The Manufacture of Copperas

What follows is an extract from a paper read before the Geological Section of the British Association at Bradford, September 1873. A similar, but less detailed account of the process was published in the *Northern Star*, vol. 1, October 1817, pp. 248–49. There it is called 'green copperas'.

The roof of the Halifax Bed contains nodules of iron pyrites, the so-called 'bullions' which are worked for the manufacture of sulphuric acid or sulphate of iron, at Denholme, Huddersfield and some other places along the line of the outcrop. Of late years the manufacture of sulphuric acid has been almost entirely given up, [but] the manufacture of sulphate of iron or copperas is still carried on. The pyrites, when freed from the matrix, is laid in a large bed, about four feet deep. The ground is previously prepared, by having drains laid through it in different directions, all converging to the same point. The rain which falls upon the bed of pyrites sinks slowly through the mass, and is carried away by the drains to a large tank. From this tank the liquid is led into a leaden evaporating pan, where it is greatly reduced in bulk. A quantity of waste iron wire, or other refuse iron, is then added. When the acid has taken up all the iron which it can the liquid is run into coolers, and forked sticks are put into it, around which large masses of crystals (from ten to twenty pounds weight) form. After crystallization has ceased, the spent liquor is returned to the evaporating pan. The sulphate of iron is principally used for the dyeing of black or dark brown.

J. Brigg, *The Industrial Geology of Bradford* (Leeds, 1874).

A Use of Copperas (1690)

The Copperas water: Take faire water two quarts and put it into a clean skellet and put thereto of green copperas half a pound and of salt one handfull, and of ordinary honey one spoonfull and a branch or two of rosemary boil all these together till one half of the water be consumed and a little before you take it from the fire put to it the quantity of a dove's egg of allom, when it is cold put it in a glass bottle close stopt for use when you are to dress any sore first wash it clean with this water and if the wound be deep, inject it with a serringe, this water of it self will cure any reasonable sore or wound, but the green oyntment being applied after it is wash'd will heal any old ulcer or fistula whatsoever if you can but come to the bottom. When the green oyntment is applied its not to be ventur'd longer on the fire or before the fire then half melted for it will turn red and lose its vertue of healing. Anoint the sore with a feather and if there be a hole make a tent of fire tow dipt in the oyntment and keep out cold or wind. This oyntment and water keeps long enough.

Wakefield Registry of Deeds, West Yorkshire Archive Service, C/86.

Notes

Notes to Introduction

1. I am grateful to Paul Jeffries for these examples from his own family history.

Notes to Chapter 1: Source Detective

1. Kirklees Archives, West Yorkshire Archive Service, Beaumont of Whitley, DD/WBE/I/1.
2. Sheepscar Library, Leeds, West Yorkshire Archive Service, Dartmouth, DT 289.
3. Bradford Archives, West Yorkshire Archive Service, Horton MSS, E 108/4.
4. In June 1806 a London lawyer wrote to the Earl of Dartmouth about 'the St John's Rents', saying that they were paid by several owners of estates in different parts of the West Riding and that 'the advantage these people have is that they are Toll free wherever they go – both Market and Fair, Mill and Malt'.
5. The collection was fully catalogued in 1999 by Emmeline Garnett of Wray, near Lancaster.
6. Copies of the *Kansas Deeds* were given to the West Yorkshire Archive Service, the Kenneth Spencer Library and the New England Historic Genealogical Society.
7. J. Stead (ed.), *The Diary of a Quack Doctor* (Huddersfield, 2002).
8. This was published as a special issue of the journal *Old West Riding*, vol. 7, no. 2 (1987).
9. For a fuller account of the 'Three Greenhorns', see G. Redmonds, *The Heirs of Woodsome* (Huddersfield, 1982).
10. *Emigrants from England, 1773–1776*, reprinted from *The New England Historic and Genealogical Register*, vols 62, 63, 64, 65 (Boston, 1913).
11. P. Finney (ed.), *Nathaniel Smith: A Stranger in a Strange Land* (New Brunswick, 2000).
12. There are also numerous academic books and articles which have the Yorkshire settlement as their theme and these are listed in a bibliography, prepared by Renée de Gannes and published by the Tantramar Heritage

Trust in March 2000. Among the many local and family histories published are H. Trueman, *The Chignecto Isthmus and its First Settlers* (Toronto, 1902) and R. G. Bowser, *A Genealogical Review of the Bowser Family* (New Brunswick, 1981).

Notes to Chapter 2: The Surname Revolution

1. J. Titford, *Succeeding in Family History* (Newbury, 2001), p. 12.
2. J. Titford, *Searching for Surnames* (Newbury, 2002), pp. 84, 181–86.
3. Private communication.
4. G. Redmonds, *Surnames and Genealogy: A New Approach* (Boston, 1997), pp. 217, 238.
5. Ibid., p. 164.
6. J. C. Atkinson (ed.), *Quarter Sessions Records*, 9 North Riding Record Society (1892), p. 236.
7. K. Holt (ed.), *The Parish Register of Beverley St Mary, 1561–1638*, Yorkshire Archaeological Society, Parish Register Series, 165 (2002), p. 16.
8. R. F. Hunnisett, *Sussex Coroners' Inquests, 1558–1603* (PRO, 1996), p. 68.
9. S. J. Doliante, *Maryland and Virginia Colonials: Genealogies of Some Colonial Families* (1991).
10. Most of the information in this section has been gleaned from the following articles: M. A. Jobling, 'In the Name of the Father: Surnames and Genetics', *Trends in Genetics*, 17 (2001), pp. 353–57; B. Sykes and C. Irven, 'Surnames and the Y-Chromosome', *American Journal of Human Genetics*, 66 (2000), pp. 1417–19; T. Roderick, 'The Y-Chromosome in Genealogical Research', *National Genealogical Society Quarterly*, 88 (2000), pp. 122–43.
11. G. Redmonds, 'All in the Genes', *Ancestors*, 6 (2002), pp. 17–20.

Notes to Chapter 3: Surname Excursions

1. These statistics and the accompanying distribution maps are on the CD-Rom *The British Nineteenth-Century Surname Atlas*, published by Stephen Archer (2003).
2. G. Redmonds, *Bradford and District*, Yorkshire Surnames Series, part 1 (Huddersfield, 1990).
3. G. D. Lumb (ed.), *Testamenta Leodiensia, 1553 to 1561*, Thoresby Society, 27 (1930), p. 53.
4. J. Raine (ed.), *Testamenta Eboracensia*, iii, Surtees Society, 45 (1865), p. 80.
5. The Southwark names are those from the poll tax returns of Surrey in part 2 of C. C. Fenwick (ed.), *The Poll Taxes of 1377, 1379 and 1381* (Oxford, 1998).

6. Yorkshire Archaeological Society, Claremont, Leeds, West Yorkshire Archive Service, Wakefield Court Rolls, MD 225.

7. 'Lay Subsidy of the Wapentakes of Agbrigg and Morley, 1545', *Thoresby Society*, 11 (1904).

8. A. Weikel (ed.), *The Court Rolls of the Manor of Wakefield, 1583–85*, Yorkshire Archaeological Society, Wakefield Court Rolls Series, 4 (1984).

9. L. Robinson (ed.), *The Court Rolls of the Manor of Wakefield, 1651–52*, Yorkshire Archaeological Society, Wakefield Court Rolls Series, 8 (1990).

10. A. Weikel (ed.), *The Court Rolls of the Manor of Wakefield, 1537–40*, Yorkshire Archaeological Society, Wakefield Court Rolls Series, 9 (1993).

11. R. W. Hoyle (ed.), *Early Tudor Craven: Subsidies and Assessments, 1510–47*, Yorkshire Archaeological Society Record Series, 145 (1987).

12. I am grateful to Gerald Fox for this information.

13. See, for example, G. Redmonds, *Slaithwaite Places and Place-Names* (Huddersfield, 1988).

14. I am grateful to Mrs Hazel Topham of Marsden for this information.

15. G. Redmonds, *Huddersfield and District*, Yorkshire Surnames Series, part 2 (Huddersfield, 1992).

16. B. Cottle, *Names* (London, 1983), p. 126.

17. David Postles recognised this dilemma. See, for example, *The Surnames of Devon* (Oxford, 1995), p. 8.

18. There is a full and annotated account of this name in G. Redmonds, *The Making of Huddersfield* (Barnsley, 2003), pp. 165–68.

19. Wakefield Court Rolls, MD 225.

20. S. Archer, *The British Nineteenth-Century Surname Atlas* (2003). This is a CD-Rom which displays distribution maps of surnames and first names, based on data in the 1881 census.

Notes to Chapter 4: The Local History of Place-Names

1. A full explanation appears in A. H. Smith, *The Place-Names of the West Riding of Yorkshire*, part 7 (Cambridge, 1962), p. 114, entitled 'Notes on Arrangement'.

2. G. Redmonds, *The Making of Huddersfield* (Barnsley, 2003), pp. 149–54.

3. As yet there is no satisfactory history of the separate medieval divisions of Quarmby, that is Golcar, Lindley, Scammonden, Longwood and parts of Crosland. Indeed the editors of *West Yorkshire: An Archaeological Survey to AD 1500* (1981), of which the second volume is a township gazetteer, were clearly confused by the arrangement.

4. The lease of 1743 was brought to my attention by David Shore.

5. G. Redmonds, *Huddersfield and District*, Yorkshire Surnames Series, part 2 (Huddersfield, 1992).

6. From a tithe dispute, Borthwick Institute of Historical Research, St. Anthony's Hall, York, CP. F. 60.

7. W. Brown (ed.), *Yorkshire Deeds*, Yorkshire Archaeological Society Record Series, 39 (1909), p. 58.

Notes to Chapter 5: Minor Place-Names

1. G. Redmonds, *Holmfirth: Place-Names and Settlement* (Huddersfield, 1994).

2. The earliest independent reference to Cow Gill in Bordley is 1457, so it is just possible that it was named after the family. If that were true 'Colgill' would be even more difficult to identify since there is nothing in the other Cow Gills to suggest that they were the source of the surname.

3. W. P. Baildon (ed.), *Wakefield Court Rolls, 1274–97*, Yorkshire Archaeological Society Record Series, 29 (1901), p. 97.

4. Redmonds, *Holmfirth*.

5. Calderdale Archives, West Yorkshire Archive Service, Armytage MSS, KM 431.

6. Wakefield Registry of Deeds, West Yorkshire Archive Service, Quarter Sessions Order Books, QS10/2/248.

7. Ibid., Indictment Books, QS4/4/147.

8. There is more on this subject in G. Redmonds, 'Steaners and Wears', *Old West Riding*, vol. 1, no. 1 (1981), pp. 25–29.

9. *Huddersfield Daily Examiner*, 18 January 1999.

10. H. S. Darbyshire and G. D. Lumb, *The History of Methley*, Thoresby Society, 35 (1934), p. 195.

11. G. Redmonds, 'Spring Woods, 1500–1800', *Old West Riding*, vol. 3, no. 1 (1983), pp. 4–9. Since this article was written additional material has come to light and some of this is referred to in the glossary in Appendix 1.

12. Some of these names are from my private collection but others are drawn from the following sources: J. Field, *English Field Names: A Dictionary* (second impression, 1982); J. Miles, *The House Names Book* (London, 1982); S. Beckensall, *Northumberland Field Names* (Newcastle upon Tyne, n.d.); L. Dunkling and G. Wright, *A Dictionary of Pub Names* (London, 1987).

13. O. Padel, *A Popular Dictionary of Cornish Place-Names* (Penzance, 1988).

14. K. Cameron, *English Place-Names* (London, 1961), p. 210; Field, *English Field Names*, p. 149.

15. For a fuller account of this connection, see G. Redmonds, 'Clitheroe Wood and Farm, Almondbury', *Lancashire Local Historian*, 13 (1998).

Notes to Chapter 6: Field Names

1. G. Redmonds (ed.), *Yorkshire Deeds in Kansas* (Huddersfield, 2000), p. 50.
2. J. S. Purvis (ed.), *Select XVI Century Causes in Tithe*, Yorkshire Archaeological Society Record Series, 114 (1949), p. 50.
3. Dealt with more fully in G. Redmonds, 'Barkisland Enclosures', *Old West Riding*, vol. 2, no. 1, pp. 34- 35.
4. This manorial survey is kept in the Dartmouths' estate office in Slaithwaite.
5. Corporation of London Records Office, R.C.E. Rental 6.16.
6. A collock was a bucket or pail, found alongside 'kit' and 'piggin' in inventories, so probably made of wood.
7. W. Brown (ed.), *Yorkshire Deeds*, Yorkshire Archaeological Society Record Series, 50 (1914), p. 175.
8. Kirklees Archives, West Yorkshire Archive Service, Beaumont of Whitley, DD/WBD/IV/194.
9. From the account book of Joseph Green-Armytage, still in the family's hands.
10. M. A. Faull and S. A. Moorhouse (eds), *West Yorkshire: An Archaeological Survey to AD 1500*, 1 (Wakefield, 1981), pp. 41–44.
11. J. W. Morkill, 'The Manor and Park of Roundhay', *Thoresby Society*, 2 (1891), pp. 214–48.
12. Corporation of London Records Office, R.C.E. Rental 6.16.

Notes to Chapter 7: First Names

1. W. Coster, *Baptism and Spiritual Kinship in Early Modern England* (Aldershot 2002).
2. C. W. Bardsley, *Curiosities of Puritan Nomenclature* (1880; reprinted 1996), pp. 162–63.
3. G. D. Lumb (ed.), *Testamenta Leodiensia, 1539–1553*, Thoresby Society, 19 (1913), p. 47.
4. P. Hanks and F. Hodges, *A Dictionary of First Names* (Oxford, 1990).
5. E. G. Withycombe, *The Oxford Dictionary of English Christian Names* (3rd edn, 1977).
6. J. J. Kneen, *The Personal Names of the Isle of Man* (Oxford, 1937). The author did not say whether he thought Christian was a male name.
7. Jenkin was used to distinguish a younger John from an older John as late as the sixteenth century.
8. S. J. Whittle (ed.), *The Court Rolls of Yeadon, 1361–1476* (Draughton, 1984). The transcript also includes early rentals, charters and associated material.

9. I say apparently because some of these may refer to just one man.

10. It must be suspected that he is the Adinet del Forest taxed in 1379 and possibly the Adinett Wodward of 1370.

11. He is probably the Adinet Norcroft referred to in 1445.

12. The surname Adnett/Adnitt also developed from Adinet, but it is a Leicestershire and Northamptonshire name.

13. S. Archer, *The British Nineteenth-Century Surname Atlas* (2003). See Chapter 3, n. 20.

14. *Index of Wills in the York Registry, 1514–1553*, Yorkshire Archaeological Society Record Series, 11 (1891).

15. In earlier centuries the records point to 'Reynold' as the vernacular pronunciation.

16. Archer, *The British Surname Atlas*.

17. Torben Kisbye, 'The Ossianic Names: A Contribution to the History of Celtic Personal Names in Scandinavia', *Nomina*, 9 (1985), pp. 93–102.

Notes to Chapter 8: Inns and Public Houses

1. H. S. Darbyshire and G. D. Lumb, *The History of Methley*, Thoresby Society, 35 (1934), pp. 158, 182, 190.

2. J. C. Atkinson (ed.), *Quarter Sessions Records*, 2, North Riding Record Society (1884), p. 31.

3. J. H. Turner (ed.), *The Diaries of the Rev. Oliver Heywood, B.A. 1630–1702*, i (1882), p. 359.

4. A 'flash' was a pool or marshy place and there were local variants such as 'flush' and 'flosh'. In Hunsworth, in 1623, a by-law required Edward Copley to 'make his dike alonge his hedge ... and lett in the water forthe of the floshe upon the top of the hill'.

5. G. Redmonds, 'Bowling, Pressure on the Greens', *Old West Riding*, vol. 1, no. 1, p. 16.

6. Yorkshire Archaeological Society, Claremont, Leeds, West Yorkshire Archive Service, MD 63/D21.

7. Wakefield Registry of Deeds, West Yorkshire Archive Service, Quarter Sessions Rolls, QS1/67/2.

8. Kirklees Archives, West Yorkshire Archive Service, Beaumont of Whitley, WBE/1/5.

9. For a fuller account of the inn see G. Redmonds, *The Making of Huddersfield* (Barnsley, 2003), pp. 168–71.

10. O. Rackham, *Trees and Woodland in the British Landscape* (1976; revised 1990), and *The History of the Countryside* (1986).

11. T. Langdale, *A Topographical Dictionary of Yorkshire* (Northallerton, 1822).

12. Redmonds, *Huddersfield* (2003), pp. 72–74.

13. W. Brown (ed.), *Yorkshire Star Chamber Proceedings*, Yorkshire Archaeological Society Record Series, 41 (1909), p. 168.

14. W. Rollinson, *The Cumbrian Dictionary of Dialect, Tradition and Folklore* (Otley, 1997).

15. Turner (ed.), *The Rev. Oliver Heywood, 1630–1702*, iii (1883), p. 91.

Notes to Chapter 9: Animals

1. It is remarkable how closely the names of animals parallel the by-names or surnames found in medieval records. We might expect to find individuals named directly after birds and animals, e.g. Cockerel, Sparrow, Fox and Hare, but in just one section of the poll tax for the West Riding of Yorkshire (1379) I came across the following surnames, all of which have also been found as animal names: Topping, Pert, Nutte, Brand, Blyth, Leming, Gryme and Tydy.

2. J. Raine (ed.), *Testamenta Eboracensia*, i, Surtees Society, 4 (1836), p. 107.

3. Ibid., p. 189.

4. J. Raine (ed.), *Testamenta Eboracensia*, iii, Surtees Society, 45 (1865), p. 15.

5. Raine, *Testamenta Eboracensia*, i, p. 39.

6. Ibid., p. 189.

7. J. Raine (ed.), *Testamenta Eboracensia*, ii, Surtees Society, 30 (1855).

8. Ibid., p. 160.

9. J. Raine (ed.), *Testamenta Eboracensia*, iv, Surtees Society, 53 (1869), p. 114.

10. Ibid., p. 215.

11. Ibid., p. 289.

12. Raine, *Testamenta Eboracensia*, i, p. 39.

13. Raine, *Testamenta Eboracensia*, iv, p. 114.

14. E. K. Berry, *Swaledale Wills and Inventories, 1522–1600*, Yorkshire Archaeological Society Record Series, 152 (1998), pp. 102–3.

15. J. Raine (ed.), *Richmondshire Wills*, Surtees Society, 26 (1853), p. 154.

16. J. W. Clay, 'The Clifford Family', *Yorkshire Archaeological Journal*, 18 (1905), p. 390.

17. North Yorkshire Record Office, Memorandum Book of Richard Cholmeley, 1602–23, NY44.

18. Raine, *Richmondshire Wills*, p. 70.

19. Raine, *Testamenta Eboracensia*, ii, Surtees Society, 30.

20. J. Raine (ed.), *The Ripon Chapter Acts, 1452–1506*, Surtees Society, 64 (1875), p. 372.

21. C. Jackson and S. Margerison (eds), *Yorkshire Diaries*, Surtees Society, 77 (1886), p. 61.
22. H. Thwaite (ed.), *Abstracts of Abbotside Wills, 1552–1688*, Yorkshire Archaeological Society Record Series, 130 (1968), p. 98.
23. Memorandum Book of Richard Cholmeley, 1602–23, NY44.
24. C. Jackson (ed.), *Yorkshire Diaries*, Surtees Society, 65 (1875).
25. Jackson and Margerison (eds), *Yorkshire Diaries*, 77, p. 61.
26. P. Edwards, *The Horse Trade of Tudor and Stuart England* (Cambridge, 1988), pp. 149–52.
27. W. Robertshaw, 'Adwalton Horse Fair', *Transactions of the Yorkshire Dialect Society*, 60.
28. A 'racke' or ratch was a white mark or streak on a horse's face.
29. G. D. Lumb (ed.), *Testamenta Leodiensa, 1553–1561*, Thoresby Society, 27 (1930), p. 216.
30. Ibid., p. 80.
31. Borthwick Institute, York, vol. 25b 1537.
32. Lumb, *Testamenta Leodiensia*, Thoresby Society, 27, p. 194.
33. Ibid., p. 316.
34. F. Collins (ed.), *Bishop Stubbs' Genealogical History*, Yorkshire Archaeological Society Record Series, 55 (1915), p. 292.
35. M. Robinson (ed.), *The Concise Scots Dictionary* (Aberdeen, 1985).
36. S. Beckensall, *Northumberland Field Names* (Newcastle upon Tyne, n.d.).
37. *Miscellanea*, Thoresby Society, 9 (1899), p. 273.
38. G. D. Lumb (ed.), *Testamenta Leodiensia, 1539–1553*, Thoresby Society, 19 (1913), p. 168.
39. *Miscellanea*, Thoresby Society, 4 (1893), p. 165.
40. W. Brown (ed.), 'Proceedings in 1912', *Yorkshire Archaeological Journal*, 22 (1913), p. 230.
41. J. C. Atkinson (ed.), *Quarter Sessions Records*, 2, North Riding Record Society (1884), p. 11.
42. Kirklees Archives, West Yorkshire Archive Service, Ramsden, DD/RA/f/4b.
43. Lumb, *Testamenta Leodiensia*, Thoresby Society, 19, p. 221.
44. Lumb, *Testamenta Leodiensia*, Thoresby Society, 27, p. 194.
45. Lumb, *Testamenta Leodiensia*, Thoresby Society, 19, p. 96.
46. Kirklees Archives, West Yorkshire Archive Service, Ramsden, DD/RA/f/4b.
47. F. Collins (ed.), *Selby Wills*, Yorkshire Archaeological Society Record Series, 47 (1912), p. 20.
48. Raine, *Ripon Chapter Acts*, Surtees Society, 64, p. 75.
49. J. S. Purvis 'A Note on Sixteenth-Century Farming in Yorkshire', *Yorkshire Archaeological Journal*, 36 (1947), p. 438.

50. Lumb, *Testamenta Leodiensia*, Thoresby Society, 27, p. 146.

51. Collins, *Selby Wills*, p. 158.

52. Brown, *Yorkshire Archaeological Journal*, 22, pp. 203–4.

53. Lumb, *Testamenta Leodiensia*, Thoresby Society, 19, p. 184.

54. *Miscellanea*, Thoresby Society, 9 (1899), p. 176.

55. G. D. Lumb (ed.), *The Parish Registers of Barwick in Elmet, 1653–1812* (1908).

56. J. W. Clay (ed.), *Testamenta Eboracensia* vi, Surtees Society, 106 (1902), p. 306.

57. Berry, *Swaledale Wills*, pp. 198, 358.

58. Farming Book of William Sykes, in my possession.

59. Berry, *Swaledale Wills*, pp. 281 (Flooreld), 137 (Gawrelt), 252 (Raggalt), 281 (Taggelde).

60. Berry, *Swaledale Wills*, p. 310.

61. J. S. Purvis, *Yorkshire Archaeological Journal*, 36, p. 451.

62. Lumb, *Testamenta Leodiensia*, Thoresby Society, 27, p. 194. There are also numerous references to 'gorded' or 'garded' cows, e.g. 'a garded qwhie calf' (1541), Surtees Society, 104, p. 36, which may mean 'striped'. This word was used also for material, e.g. 'one gownc garded with velvett' (1558), Thoresby, 27, p. 150. The variations in spelling complicate the identification of these words.

63. This group of names has some obvious parallels in the vocabulary of everyday English, e.g. brindled, dappled, speckled and spangled. The names may therefore throw some light on the early history of such adjectives, for their etymologies in the OED appear to leave some questions unanswered. I am particularly grateful to Peter McClure for the help he has given me with this category of names.

64. Wakefield Registry of Deeds, West Yorkshire Archive Service, C 86.

65. S. Shaw and K. Green, *Scarlet and Green* (Huddersfield, 1995). T. Dufton, *Hunters' Songs*, Holme Valley Beagles Hunt (Holmfirth, 1948).

66. Shaw and Green, *Scarlet and Green*, p. 31.

67. Ibid., p. 12.

Notes to Chapter 10: Unofficial Place-Names

1. J. Smail (ed.), *Woollen Manufacturing in Yorkshire*, Yorkshire Archaeological Society Record Series, 155 (2001).

2. See Appendix 2.

3. For the meaning of 'wafer' or waver see Appendix 1.

4. Kirklees Archives, West Yorkshire Archive Service, Thornhill Papers, T/R/a/33. This reference was brought to my attention by David Shore.

5. Bradford Archives, West Yorkshire Archive Service, Spencer/Stanhope Papers.

6. P. C. D. Brears (ed.), *Yorkshire Probate Inventories, 1542–1689*, Yorkshire Archaeological Society Record Series, 134 (1972), p. 137.

7. W. R. Childs (ed.), *The Customs Accounts of Hull, 1453–1490*, Yorkshire Archaeological Society Record Series, 144 (1986), p. 48.

8. Letter from Mrs M. Haywood, 9 November 1983.

9. The Doncaster references were given to me by George Owen of Warmsworth.

10. E. R. Pyke, *Human Documents of the Industrial Revolution in Britain* (sixth impression, London, 1978), pp. 238–40.

11. B. Clarke, *History of Lockwood and North Crosland* (Huddersfield, 1980), p. 132.

12. Information from Mary Parry of Doncaster.

13. J. Seymour, *Forgotten Household Crafts* (London, 1987), pp. 96–97.

14. Wakefield Registry of Deeds, West Yorkshire Archive Service, D35/162.

15. Wakefield Registry of Deeds, West Yorkshire Archive Service, West Riding Quarter Sessions, QS1/128/7.

16. L. Caffyn, *Workers' Housing in West Yorkshire, 1750–1920* (London, 1986), p. 45.

Notes to Chapter 11: Streets

1. A. Room, *The Street Names of England* (Stamford, 1992). This pioneer study looks at the different words used for streets, e.g. avenue, road, close, and then discusses the different types of name in a dozen or so chapters. It also contains advice on the study of street names and has a number of appendixes, including lists of the major streets of London and Manchester.

2. David McKie, *Guardian* article, October 1996.

3. For a more general account of the city's place-names read J. Field, *Place-Names of Greater London* (London, 1980).

4. A. Raine (ed.), *York Civic Records*, iii, Yorkshire Archaeological Society Record Series, 106 (1942), p. 20.

5. G. Redmonds, *Bradford and District*, Yorkshire Surnames Series, part 1 (Huddersfield, 1990).

6. The full story of Huddersfield's older street names is told in G. Redmonds, *Old Huddersfield, 1500–1800* (Huddersfield, 1981).

Notes to Chapter 12: Ships and Fabrics

1. M. Jones, 'The Names Given to Ships in Fourteenth- and Fifteenth-Century England', *Nomina*, 23 (2000), pp. 23–36.
2. A. Raine (ed.), *York Civic Records*, i, Yorkshire Archaeological Society Record Series, 98 (1939), p. 16.
3. J. Raine (ed.), *Testamenta Eboracensia*, iv, Surtees Society, 53 (1869), p. 236.
4. A. Raine (ed.), *York Civic Records*, vii, Yorkshire Archaeological Society Record Series, 115 (1950), p. 48.
5. J. Raine (ed.), *The Fabric Rolls of York Minster*, Surtees Society, 35 (1859).
6. *Register of the Freemen of York, 1272–1558*, Surtees Society, 96 (1897).
7. *The Genealogical History of Bishop William Stubbs*, Yorkshire Archaeological Society Record Series, 55 (1915), p. 223.
8. F. Collins (ed.), *Selby Wills*, Yorkshire Archaeological Society Record Series, 47 (1912), p. 195.
9. A. Raine (ed.), *York Civic Records* iv, Yorkshire Archaeological Society Record Series, 108 (1945), p. 99
10. F. W. Brookes (ed.), *Miscellanea*, Yorkshire Archaeological Society Record Series, 116 (1951), p. 14.
11. Raine, *York Civic Records*, i, p. 89.
12. C. V. Collier (ed.), 'Stovin's Manuscript', *Transactions of the East Riding Antiquarian Society*, 12 (1905), p. 36.
13. Raine, *York Civic Records*, iv, p. 32.
14. Brookes, *Miscellanea*, p. 16.
15. J. S. Purvis (ed.), *Bridlington Charters, Court Rolls and Papers XVIth-XIXth Century* (1926), p. 179.
16. W. R. Childs (ed.), *The Customs Accounts of Hull, 1453–1490*, Yorkshire Archaeological Society Record Series, 144 (1986), p. 34.
17. F. W. Brookes (ed.), *First Order Book of the Hull Trinity House, 1632–65*, Yorkshire Archaeological Society Record Series, 105 (1942), p. 116.
18. P. Frank, *Yorkshire Fisherfolk* (Chichester, 2002), p. 67.
19. J. S. Purvis (ed.), 'A Selection of Monastic Rentals and Dissolution Papers', *Miscellanea*, Yorkshire Archaeological Society Record Series, 80 (1931), p. 109.
20. P. Heath, 'North Sea Fishing in the Fifteenth Century: The Scarborough Fleet', *Northern History*, 3 (1968), pp. 53–69.
21. Collins, *Selby Wills*, p. 171.
22. J. Lister (ed.), *The Early Yorkshire Woollen Trade*, Yorkshire Archaeological Society Record Series, 64 (1924).
23. R. Horrox (ed.), *Selected Rentals and Accounts of Medieval Hull, 1293–1528*, Yorkshire Archaeological Society Record Series, 141 (1983), p. 53.

24. E. Peacock (ed.), 'Star Chamber Complaint against Humber Pirates', *York-shire Archaeological and Topographical Journal*, 2 (1873), pp. 246–51.

25. Brookes, *Trinity House*, p. 82.

26. A. Raine, *York Civic Records*, ii, Yorkshire Archaeological Society Record Series, 103 (1941), p. 64.

27. Heath, *North Sea Fishing*, p. 58.

28. Frank, *Yorkshire Fisherfolk*, p. 57.

29. M. Woodward (ed.), *Gerard's Herbal* (from the edition of 1636, London, 1985), p. 31.

30. Lister, *The Early Yorkshire Woollen Trade*, p. 39.

31. Ibid. p. 5. The other references in this section are taken mostly from wills, although the felony referred to in 1684 was from the West Riding Quarter Sessions, QS1/23/8.

32. C. C. Webb (ed.), *Churchwardens' Accounts of St Michael, Spurriergate, York, 1518–1548*, 1 (1997) p. 94.

33. D. Woodward (ed.), *The Farming and Memorandum Books of Henry Best of Elmswell, 1642* (British Academy, 1984), p. 111. The book has a fine glossary and linguistic commentary by Peter McClure.

34. This will is in the private collection of Mr J. Green-Armytage.

Notes to Chapter 13: Plants

1. W. R. Childs (ed.), *The Customs Accounts of Hull, 1453–1490*, Yorkshire Archaeological Society Record Series, 144 (1986), pp. 5, 58–60.

2. D. Woodward (ed.), *The Farming and Memorandum Books of Henry Best of Elmswell, 1642* (London, 1984), pp. 116–17.

3. For much of the information in this section I am indebted to G. Grigson, *A Dictionary of English Plant Names* (London, 1974).

4. Wakefield Registry of Deeds, West Yorkshire Archive Service, D/I 192.

5. M. Woodward (ed.), *Gerard's Herball* (from the edition of 1636, London, 1985), p. 4.

6. O. Rackham, *The History of the Countryside* (London, 1986; reprinted 1993), p. 283.

7. J. Field, *English Field-Names: A Dictionary* (London, 1982), p. 31.

8. T. Tusser, *Five Hundred Points of Good Husbandry* (Oxford, 1984), p. 71.

9. The Kaye Commonplace Book, microfilm copy, Huddersfield Library.

10. 'Windowing' was a relatively common form locally of 'winnowing': Wake-field Registry of Deeds, West Yorkshire Archive Service, Quarter Sessions Rolls, QS1/11/1.

11. The asterisk here means that the words are not found recorded independently.

12. A. H. Smith (ed.), *The Place-Names of the West Riding of Yorkshire*, 1–8 (1961–62).

13. C. M. Fraser and K. Emsley (eds), *The Court Rolls of the Manor of Wakefield, 1664–65*, Yorkshire Archaeological Society, Wakefield Court Rolls Series, 5 (1986), p. 169.

14. C. T. Clay (ed.), *Yorkshire Deeds*, Yorkshire Archaeological Society Record Series, 69 (1926), p. 100.

15. Quarter Sessions Rolls, QS1/54/9.

16. A. J. L. Winchester, *The Harvest of the Hills: Rural Life in Northern England and the Scottish Borders, 1400–1700* (Edinburgh, 2000), pp. 133–36. This account discusses the by-laws that regulated the management of bracken in upland communities, first evidenced in 1526. It also introduces us to the specialised vocabulary that had to do with the areas of common set aside for its exploitation, and the different ways in which it might be harvested.

17. J Raine (ed.), *Depositions from York Castle*, Surtees Society, 40 (1860).

18. J. Lister (ed.), *Court Rolls of the Manor of Wakefield*, 1313–16 and 1286, Yorkshire Archaeological Society Record Series, 57 (1917), p. 101.

19. D. J. H. Michelmore (ed.), *The Fountains Abbey Lease Book*, Yorkshire Archaeological Society Record Series (1981), pp. 147, 187.

20. J. Hunter (ed.), *The Hallamshire Glossary* (London, 1829; facsimile edition, 1983), p. 47.

21. A. J. Petford, 'For Their Sheepe in the Winter Season', *Saddleworth Historical Journal* (1982).

22. Kirklees Archives, West Yorkshire Archive Service, Beaumont of Whitley Papers, DD/WBD/IV.

23. W. Brown (ed.), *Yorkshire Deeds*, Yorkshire Archaeological Society Record Series, 50 (1914), p. 138.

24. *The Diary of Abraham de la Pryme*, Surtees Society, 54 (1869), p. 165.

25. H. Richardson (ed.), *Court Rolls of the Manor of Acomb*, 1 Yorkshire Archaeological Society Record Series, 131 (1969), pp. 140, 145.

26. J. S. Purvis (ed.), *Select XVI Century Causes in Tithe*, Yorkshire Archaeological Society Record Series, 114 (1949), p. 93.

27. J. C. Atkinson (ed.), *Quarter Sessions Records*, 2 North Riding Record Society (1884), p. 227.

28. Winchester, *Harvest of the Hills*, p. 138.

29. P. Romney (ed.), *The Diary of Charles Fothergill*, Yorkshire Archaeological Society Record Series, 142 (1984).

30. *De la Pryme*, Surtees Society, 54.

Select Bibliography

Archer, S., *The British Nineteenth-Century Surname Atlas* (2003), CD-ROM.

Childs, W. R. (ed.), *The Customs Accounts of Hull, 1453–1490*, Yorkshire Archaeological Society Record Series, 144 (1986).

Cameron, K., *English Place-Names* (London, 1961, 4th edn, 1988).

Coster, W., *Baptism and Spiritual Kinship in Early Modern England* (Aldershot, 2002).

Cox, B., *English Inn and Tavern Names* (Nottingham, 1994).

Dunkling, L. and Gosling, W., *Everyman's Dictionary of First Names* (London, 1984).

Dunkling, L. and Wright, G., *A Dictionary of Pub Names* (London, 1987).

Farmer, D. H., *The Oxford Dictionary of Saints* (3rd edn, Oxford, 1992).

Fellows Jensen, G., *Scandinavian Settlement Names in Yorkshire* (Copenhagen, 1972).

Field, J., *English Field Names: A Dictionary* (second impression, London, 1982).

Gelling, M., *Sign-Posts to the Past: Place-Names and the History of England* (2nd edn, London, 1988).

Grigson, G., *A Dictionary of English Plant Names* (London, 1974).

Hanks, P. and Hodges, F., *A Dictionary of First Names* (Oxford, 1990).

Hey, D., *Family Names and Family History* (London, 2000).

Jobling, M. A., 'In the Name of the Father: Surnames and Genetics', *Trends in Genetics*, 17 (2001).

Jones, M., 'The Names Given to Ships in Fourteenth- and Fifteenth-Century England', *Nomina*, 23 (2000).

McKinley, R. A., *A History of British Surnames* (London, 1990).

Rackham, O., *The History of the Countryside* (London, 1986; reprinted 1993).

Reaney, P. H. and Wilson, R. M., *A Dictionary of English Surnames* (Oxford, 1997).

Redmonds, G., *Christian Names in Local and Family History*, National Archives (2004).

Redmonds, G., *Surnames and Genealogy: A New Approach* (Boston, 1997; reprinted by the Federation of Family History Societies, 2003).

Room, A., *The Street Names of England* (Stamford, 1992).

Smith, A. H., *The Place-Names of the West Riding of Yorkshire*, 8 vols (1961–62).

Smith-Bannister, S., *Names and Naming Patterns in England, 1538–1700* (Oxford, 1997).

Sykes, B. and Irven, C., 'Surnames and the Y-Chromosome', *American Journal of Human Genetics*, 66 (2000).

Titford, J., *Searching for Surnames* (Newbury, 2002).

Wagner, Sir Anthony, *English Genealogy* (Oxford, 1960).

Withycombe, E. G., *The Oxford Dictionary of English Christian Names* (3rd edn, Oxford, 1977).

Index

The surnames in this index are identified by a following (s), and the place-names by county, except for the counties themselves, countries and other major places. Other categories of name are listed in alphabetical order under the appropriate heading.